Stein,
Bishop,
&
Rich

Stein, Bishop, & Rich

Lyrics of Love, War, & Place

Margaret Dickie

The
University of
North Carolina Press
Chapel Hill &
London

© 1997
The University of
North Carolina Press
All rights reserved
Manufactured in the
United States of America
The paper in this book
meets the guidelines for
permanence and
durability of the
Committee on
Production Guidelines
for Book Longevity
of the Council on
Library Resources.

Library of Congress Cataloging-in-Publication Data

Dickie, Margaret, 1935–

Stein, Bishop, and Rich: lyrics of love, war, and place /
Margaret Dickie.

p.   cm.

Includes bibliographical references (p.   ) and index.

ISBN 0-8078-2308-2 (alk. paper).—

ISBN 0-8078-4622-8 (pbk.: alk. paper)

1. American poetry—Women authors—History and criticism.
2. Women and literature—United States—History—20th
century. 3. Lesbians' writings, American—History and
criticism. 4. American poetry—20th century—History and
criticism. 5. Stein, Gertrude, 1874–1946—Criticism and
interpretation. 6. Bishop, Elizabeth, 1911–1979—Criticism and
interpretation. 7. Rich, Adrienne Cecile, 1929–   —Criticism
and interpretation. 8. Love poetry, American—History and
criticism. 9. War poetry, American—History and criticism.
10. Place (Philosophy) in literature. I. Title.

PS151.D53   1997

811'.5099206643—dc20   96-9615

CIP

01 00 99 98 97   5 4 3 2 1

CONTENTS

ACKNOWLEDGMENTS

A chance remark by James Merrill turned me in the direction of this book. On a visit to the University of Georgia for a reading in 1989, he asked me what I was teaching, and, when I told him Marianne Moore, he suggested that her chief importance was making Elizabeth Bishop possible. I looked into Bishop, found little of Moore there, but was drawn to the secrecy of the poetry, its bafflements, and the restraints of its artifice. I set out to read her manuscripts at Vassar College Library, trying to ferret out what I felt she had layered in the elaborate forms of her writing. Eventually, I came to see that the questions she posed were also there in the work of Gertrude Stein and later, in a quite different form, in Adrienne Rich's poetry as well. So my attention turned in their direction and, like Bishop's own "proliferal style," this study grew.

In the course of this work, I have accrued substantial debts first to Merrill, then to the staff of Vassar College Library, and certainly to Helen S. Lanier who has provided the generous terms of my appointment at the University of Georgia. I should also mention two incomparable colleagues, Anne Williams and Douglas Anderson, whose conversations have improved this book and my understanding of literature. I have also been especially helped by the wit of another colleague, Tricia Lootens, in discussions of these poets. Three exceptionally talented graduate students have provided plenty of questions and even some answers—my graduate assistant Leigh-Anne Urbanowicz Marcellin who also proofread the manuscript, Sylvia Henneberg, and Marisa Pagnattaro. I am grateful, too, to the scrupulous commentaries of the University of North Carolina Press's two anonymous readers. The birth of my grandson Samuel Colt in New Canaan, Connecticut, made trips to nearby Vassar College Library all the more pleasant and frequent, and I am glad to acknowledge his importance as I worked on this project.

ABBREVIATIONS OF WORKS CITED
IN THE TEXT AND NOTES

ELIZABETH BISHOP:

B	*Life World Library: Brazil*
CP	*The Complete Poems, 1927–1979*
CPr	*The Collected Prose*
OA	*One Art*

ADRIENNE RICH:

ADW	*An Atlas of the Difficult World: Poems, 1988–1991*
BBP	*Blood, Bread, and Poetry: Selected Prose, 1979–1985*
CEP	*Collected Early Poems, 1950–1970*
FofD	*The Fact of a Doorframe: Poems Selected and New, 1950–1984*
OLSS	*On Lies, Secrets, and Silence: Selected Prose, 1966–1978*
TP	*Time's Power: Poems, 1985–1988*
WIFT	*What Is Found There: Notebooks on Poetry and Politics*
YNYL	*Your Native Land, Your Life: Poems*

GERTRUDE STEIN:

BTV	*Bee Time Vine and Other Pieces, 1913–1927*
FQED	*Fernhurst, Q.E.D., and Other Early Writings*
GH	*The Geographical History of America, or the Relation of Human Nature to the Human Mind*
GofM	*The Gender of Modernism: A Critical Anthology*, edited by Bonnie Kime Scott
GP	*Geography and Plays*
LA	*Lectures in America*
N	*Narration: Four Lectures by Gertrude Stein*
PF	*Paris France*
R	*Reflection on the Atomic Bomb*
SR	*A Stein Reader*
SW	*Selected Writings of Gertrude Stein*
UK	*Useful Knowledge* (1988 ed.)
WIHS	*Wars I Have Seen*
YGS	*The Yale Gertrude Stein*

Stein,
Bishop,
&
Rich

"A Sonnet" that Gertrude Stein embeds in "Patriarchal Poetry" appears to be a parody of the conventional love sonnet:

> To the wife of my bosom
> All happiness from everything
> And her husband.
> May he be good and considerate
> Gay and cheerful and restful. (*YGS*, 124)

But, because the language here is reminiscent of Stein's celebration of her lover in "Lifting Belly," its aim seems more ambivalent, less clearly parodic. Ambivalence marks Elizabeth Bishop's "Sonnet," which opens with the acknowledgment that the speaker is "Caught—the bubble / in the spirit-level, / a creature divided" (*CP*, 192), although it closes emphatically with the image of the "rainbow-bird" "flying wherever / it feels like, gay!" (192). When Adrienne Rich addresses her lover in "Love Poem," she is more forthright, claiming that "to write for you / a pretty sonnet / would be untrue" (*TP*, 7).

These poets' use of the sonnet form, however problematic, suggests their uneasy claim on its tradition. Stein heads her sonnet with the phrase repeated throughout "Patriarchal Poetry," as if she intended to mimic and deflate that poetry:

> Patriarchal Poetry.
> SONNET (*YGS*, 124)

But when she writes of the wife "Whose transcendent virtues / Are those to be most admired / Loved and adored," she is addressing this wife as she did Alice B. Toklas, and thus she seems to be attempting to find a place for herself in the tradition of patriarchal poetry.

Rich, too, denying herself "the pretty sonnet," names it and thus declares its importance. It could be argued that the pretty sonnet has been untrue to most lovers for a very long time, and so we might wonder, why make an issue of it in the plain style of this poem, so unsuitable to the artifice, not to say prettiness, of the sonnet? Yet Rich may have her reasons. She has written, if not sonnets, love poems that call up the tradition of the sonnet sequence. Here she draws attention to that earlier work and to the fact that she has moved on to a point that will not elicit such a poem. Still, she seems to want to keep in mind the "pretty sonnet" as a form not adequate, an opportunity deliberately forsworn, in the important pursuit of truth in this love. However, even within that free range outside the sonnet's formal conventions and limitations, she keeps the possibility of the form hovering over this poem because in the end she refers to the "something more" that these lovers must face which is death. And from death the sonnet has rescued many lovers and—without her refusal—might even, she seems to suggest, have saved them. But she will not have it.

The turns and counterturns toward and away from the sonnet in this poem trace an uneasiness with its form and conventional subject that Rich shares with Bishop and Stein, who each wrote at least one such poem with that name. Although, like Rich, neither Bishop nor Stein adheres to the formal requirements of the sonnet, each appropriates its name in order to change it, turn it, try it, keep it, as Rich does.

That their love poems are addressed to women does not distinguish them from traditional love poems, and, in one of their turns toward the sonnet, they clearly acknowledge their rightful place in that tradition. But that they themselves are women, speaking their love, does make a difference in their works. It imposed on them a censorship, both self-generated and external, as they confronted immediately a literary vacuum as well as the legal and social sanctions against their love. Thus their love poems, expressions of their private feelings, are intimately informed by an awareness of the public reception they would elicit. These three women poets, so different in every way, have in common this knowledge that their love lyrics would be read not just as poetry but as polemic.

This awareness varied with each writer, infiltrating the rest of her work—heightening the hermeticism of Stein's poetry, the stylistic elaboration of Bishop's, and the complexity and uncertainty of Rich's. It turned them toward the intricacies of artifice as they worked, in Rich's terms, to "stay true // even in poems" to their own affectionate and erotic experience (*TP*, 7). But, curiously, this same awareness also opened their work to public subjects and to subjects that are unusually similar, given the differences of their interests, their generations, and their moods. Stein, Bishop, and Rich all wrote about love, war, and place. These subjects are not unconnected—their poems of love are often situated in wartime, if they are situated at all, and their poems of place detail the unease they felt about their physical location as well as the location of their physical life. In both cases, they lived in lands not native to themselves.

This book explores the poetry of these three women working at different points in the twentieth century, who experimented with forms that would allow them to write and succeeded in creating poems that have become part of the public testimony of their times. As white, well-educated women—two of them Jewish, two of them exiles—these poets were privileged members of their society; but, as lesbians, they could also feel themselves to be outsiders, and their poetry reveals how little their privilege protected them from censorship, how severe even the literary restraints their desire imposed. Their story is different from one that could be told through a different selection of women poets—for example, Laura Riding, Muriel Rukeyser, and Denise Levertov who consistently used the lyric voice to comment directly on political issues, or Anne Spencer, Gwendolyn Brooks, and Audre Lorde whose lyric poetry adds race to political commentary. But together, Stein, Bishop, and Rich focus important issues of secrecy and openness, marginality and dominance, poetry and politics, artifice and truth, that are relevant to other twentieth-century women writers.

Read together, they suggest, first, a continuity of interests in twentieth-century lesbian poetry. Love, war, and place are topics neither new to the twentieth century nor to women poets; but, in returning to them again and again, Stein, Bishop, and Rich suggest the importance of their interconnection. As the secrecy of their love poems intersects with the openness of their poems of war and place, it reveals the intimacy of the two—the private and the public, the marginal and the dominant, poetry and politics. These poets' interest in public and political issues—all the more remarkable because they had such an uneasy relationship with the public—develops within their commitment to artistic experimentation, their politics and their poetry cross-fertilizing.

Read together, these poets also suggest the continuity of the lesbian poet's need to confront a culturally encouraged silence. Because they all came to public utterance from a deep need for secrecy about their erotic attachments, they wrote under a censorship that heightened their artifice. In this, their poetry differs from that of Muriel Rukeyser, for example, who made an early frontal attack on such censorship, or a poet such as H.D., who succumbed entirely to it; Stein, Bishop, and Rich tried a third strategy. Neither attacking nor succumbing, they simply circumvented the censors by pushing language and form to the extreme as Stein experimented with nonreferentiality, Bishop with elaborate artifice, and Rich with common language. In the clash between the will to speak and the need to remain silent, the desire to tell the truth and the need to dissimulate, lies their art. In twentieth-century America where nothing seems to be forbidden expression, these poets, like many women poets, lived, as

Rich has claimed in another context, "under house arrest" (*WIFT*, 19).[1] They are, as I shall argue, central to the poetry of their periods, and yet they were forced to write in code, to use elaborate and archaic forms, to search restlessly even for a common language in which to express themselves. Thus, the examples of their careers draw attention to the complicated ways in which art can be nurtured by being restrained, poetry can and does respond to political interference.

Yet, I want to claim that their public voice grew out of their most private subject, their love and erotic desire for women, expanding its range to subjects that may have a particular resonance for women but are not solely women's concerns, subjects such as war, place, class, and race, for example. That these three poets were lesbians is crucial to their creative development, and I shall argue that this identity is important to their achievement within the dominant culture of their generations. In this, I disagree with recent critics of lesbian love poetry who have emphasized the marginal nature of their poetry and abstracted their love poetry from the context of their other works.[2] For example, Liz Yorke makes an important case for a "lesbian strategy of survival" that will "subvert, contest, or displace conventional heterosexist poetic discourses" (208–9). But, if their aim were to subvert, contest, or displace poetic conventions, they succeeded so completely that their work has become, if not conventional, at least incontestable. In arguing this position, I shall set their love poetry in the context of their other poems, maintaining that the strategy of these three poets was not simply to survive as sexual beings (however important that may have been), but to survive as social, political, and literary beings, creating poems that would connect their lives with the larger life around them. Gertrude Stein once claimed, "I lived my life with emotion and with things happening but I was creating in my writing by simply looking" (*LA*, 191).

Theirs could be a simple story of repression, suppression, and political intrusion into the private. It may be that, but it is also a triumph of art over politics, of language over a culturally encouraged silence, of concern with the world over retreat into secrecy. Or, rather, the achievement of their poetry suggests the awareness of restrictive politics in their art, the presence too of silence in their language, of privacy in their worldliness. Their creative impulses were charged, in different ways, by being thwarted, and, as a result, they developed a range of poetic strategies from the most radically experimental to the strictly formal that would not only acknowledge and express their full sexual beings, but also allow them to engage public issues.

Beyond the subversive impulse with which they are often credited and despite their position as outsiders, these poets became the dominant voices of their respective generations.[3] For example, when Stein wrote "Patriarchal Poetry," she was claiming, as we shall see, to write patriarchal poetry herself. Bishop won many of the most prestigious poetry prizes available to her generation. She wrote a eulogy for the most publicly acclaimed poet of her day, expressing her affection for him but also pointing out his limitations. However much she owed to Robert Lowell, she also knew—and he acknowledged—that he had an equal debt to her. She addressed him as an equal, as one who shared with her the task of writing down the times in which they lived. Rich's writing has been central to the women's movement for two decades, and, as such, she has made American poetry central to that movement in her time. These poets can hardly be considered marginal figures in their culture. As poets, they have assumed a major role in the cultural work of their age.

Because together their works span almost the entire century, these poets may reveal some of the different stages of lesbian poetry as it burgeoned in the twentieth century. And sharing the same preoccupations, they may illuminate each other's work. For example, read with Stein and Bishop, Rich's love poems may appear more eccentric than they might otherwise seem, or, conversely, Stein's interest in geography appears less bizarre as it is placed against similar interests in Bishop and Rich. Bishop's interest in war becomes an obvious subject as she is placed with Stein and Rich. Each one of these poets is a major figure and thus unique. Together, they demonstrate the force of twentieth-century lesbian poetry.

That these poets are lesbians is central to this study, because I believe that their desire to write love poems fueled their poetic experimentation. I realize that, in naming these poets lesbians, I elide the varieties of lesbian sexuality that the "sex wars" of 1980s feminism have made known. Also I am using a term—lesbian desire—that is not uncontested in the extensive discussions of lesbian psychoanalytic theorists. And, in identifying these poets as dominant voices in their culture, I may be denying ranges of their marginality that are important to lesbian literary critics who want to claim them in a different history. Finally, in acknowledging a lesbian lyric, I may seem to harbor essentialist notions or to hold to the idea that there is some platonic model of gender and genre. I do not.

I want to write about the poetry; an inquiry into the variety of the lesbian sexualities of these poets and the psychoanalytic understanding of their desire must form another study. I shall argue that their poems reveal different models of lesbian erotic relationships, but I make no claim for the possibilities of their lived experiences. That these three poets are women is significant not because they represent all women, but rather because they write about their experiences as particular women—specifically about the food they cooked and ate, about their visits to the lesbian brothels of Marrakesh, about conflicted relationships with their fathers. These are experiences that are individually and perhaps essentially different—different from each other and different from the experiences of men—and they have shaped a poetry that reveals the variety of that difference.[4]

The development from Stein to Rich appears to be one of continuing public attention. Rich occupies a place of public prominence and serious recognition that is much more expansive than Stein's position in her society. But Rich, too, has drawn her share of attacks even from the feminist community she has done so much to create. Bishop lived a more reclusive life than either Stein or Rich, and yet, surprisingly, she advanced the seriousness with which women poets have had to be regarded. But public attention has not always meant public acclaim for these poets as Rich's career so clearly indicates, and the culture's accommodation of her genius has not been without an impetus to silence or negate her voice.

I have to admit at the outset that these three poets do not form a self-evident group. Among them, Rich may seem most out of place, both because her political positions are overtly expressed in her poetry and because she has acknowledged other predecessors. She admits that she came to read and appreciate Bishop only late in her career and after she began to see her as part of a lesbian tradition (*BBP*, 125), and she seldom mentions Stein. Moreover, because Rich herself has politicized her poetry so thoroughly, it is harder to read it in the context of the work of Stein and Bishop who did not take on the political roles that Rich has assumed, although Stein, at least, considered herself a public personage of some consequence. Stein and Bishop, who appear more dedicated to artifice and less committed to political change, may not have been either; but where Rich, as a poet, felt she needed to speak out, they felt, in different ways, that they needed to guard what they said. Yet Rich's work is connected to that of Stein and Bishop by her commitment to write the truth of an existence that everywhere was trapped in lies, to both speak and keep secrets.

Some will argue that Marianne Moore would be a more suitable predecessor for Bishop than Stein, and that H.D. would be more appropriate for Rich. Clearly, there are obvious connections between these modernists and these younger poets. Bishop was Moore's protégée, learned from her, disagreed with her, and yet maintained a long and enduring friendship with her. Although there are many traces of Moore's influence in Bishop, the two poets are fundamentally unlike. Moore is a private person and a private poet who liked to reveal neither herself nor her hand. Bishop, however reserved, appears to be more secretive than private both as a person and a poet. The difference between privacy and secrecy is subtle but important, as Sissela Bok has pointed out: privacy is the condition of being protected from unwanted access by others, whereas secrecy must be considered intentional concealment.[5] As a poet, Bishop played with concealment, not just to keep secret her lesbianism and her alcoholism, but because it allowed her to hide—behind masks and in complicated structures—a range of emotions and sympathies she did not want to acknowledge fully. It permitted her to erect elaborate texts for subtexts that were as elaborate. At the same time, the plain style even of her complicated forms provided such a placid surface that it did not elicit the critical curiosity that Moore's, layered with curious quotations, inspired, and so it kept Bishop's secrets well hidden. In this, Bishop resembles Stein.

But what could Bishop's secrecy have to do with Rich's openness, her coming out? Bishop or perhaps her friends erected a wall of silence around her lesbianism. She herself had none of Rich's sympathy for the sisterhood, objecting when she was considered even one of the best "women" poets, and refusing to be included in anthologies of women poets. If she ever did take part in political events, Bishop always seemed just to happen upon them—the revolution in Brazil, the student revolutions in San Francisco in the 1960s, for example. But it is Rich herself who has dispelled this conventional idea of Bishop, praising her poems about multiracial Brazil, about the poor and the tenant, and claiming, "What I value is her attempt to acknowledge other outsiders, lives marginal in ways that hers is not, long before the Civil Rights movement made such awareness temporarily fashionable for some white writers" (*BBP*, 131). Although, in her comments on Bishop's poetry, Rich fails to notice her poems of intimate relationships, she values her for her conscious effort "to explore marginality, power and powerlessness, often in poetry of great beauty and sensuousness" (135). It is Rich's own subject. Moreover, like Rich, Bishop writes in what Harold Bloom identifies as a tradition marked by "firm rhetorical control, overt moral authority, and sometimes by fairly strict economy of means" (1). If Bishop owes some of her moral fervor to Moore as well as to the grandparents she writes about, she reinterprets it as she passes it on to Rich, adding to Moore's unswerving uprightness a sympathy for the backslider, the outsider, the other, that was useful to Rich.[6]

As an experimental writer, Stein would appear to have little in common with either Bishop, who wrote often in highly traditional form, or with Rich, whose dream of a common language has many parts but none that so self-consciously excludes the common reader as Stein's. Stein shares with Bishop a need to code her erotic experience, and her experimental writing performed the same service that Bishop's extremely elaborate forms often accomplished. Rich, too, has acknowledged her need for coded expression as a protection not only from the public censor but also from herself. Describing an unsatisfactory meeting she had with Robert Duncan in 1960, Rich claimed that he talked without stopping (the "monologue" of "a gifted talker" started up "when the person doesn't know what to say"). It was at that time that he was just beginning to write openly gay poetry, and she concludes: "Like Gertrude Stein, I'm sure he needed the veil of language, and of a highly discursive personality, that could at times be switched off but that also could be used as protection. I too was using my poetic language as protection in those years, as a woman, angry, feeling herself evil, other" (*WIFT*, 167).

This idea of language working as protection, not just in Stein's experimental style but in the traditional and the common styles of poetic language that Bishop and Rich chose, connects these poets and remains a central need even now in lesbian writing. It was not enough that each of them wanted to express herself and her experience; she also wanted or needed to hide that expression from too intrusive eyes. And the hiding and secrecy were part of the pleasure of the expression, part of the pains they took in their poetry. Thus, these poets learned to write in code, to create texts with powerful subtexts, even to create the illusion of a common language. In some sense, what they were doing was not different from what all poets do; they simply heightened the pressure on poetic language which is always coded, always multivalent, always illusory in its ambition toward the common.

Their strategies were multiple and subtle. However, Catharine Stimpson points to one such strategy in Stein, noting the "plain and simple style" of her autobiographies where "her plainness and simplicity are masterstrokes in covering up and covering over her lesbianism. For her immediacies and limpidities promise that her language is a transparent window onto reality, even onto the reality that fact and fiction can blur into each other. She is direct. . . . How could she lie? Deliberately, egregiously, meanly deceive?" ("Stein and the Lesbian Lie," 161). Although Stimpson credits Stein with a more "sophisticated engagement with the naive" (162) in her experimental poetry, she also claims that Stein's more radical poetic texts create a "ritualistic theater," aiming to "strengthen the community of liars, to remind them that the lie is a lie, and to give the liars enough rest and relaxation to go on to further feats of linguistic inventiveness" (163). In this way, Stein's "lies" are a kind of truth.

Much of what Stimpson says about Stein here could apply to Rich and Bishop as well. Bishop's plain and simple style as well as her contrasting use of highly elaborate forms such as the double sonnet or the sestina were used to concentrate attention at the surface of the text while underneath an even more elaborate story was being explored or confessed. Although in interviews and commentaries Bishop always acknowledged—with a specificity of which we might be slightly suspicious—the direct and simple source of her poetry in particular personal experiences, she also insisted on the mystery of these sources. "Varick Street," that strange poem of betrayal and intimacy, grew out of her life on that street of factories, she claimed; it was a "dream poem" and "all of it, except a few fixed-up words toward the end, was in my head" when she woke up, she told U. T. and Joseph Summers. (*OA*, 308). Or, again, she maintained, "'At the Fish-houses' came to me in a dream" (308). Sometimes she felt that form itself offered her a subject, such as the dramatic monologue which allowed her to "say all kinds of things you couldn't in a lyric" (Schwartz and Estess, 298). Or the sestina's rhyme scheme could cast up a poem. Poems that could come in dreams or arise out of particular forms would appear to be creations outside of Bishop's conscious control, simple and direct expressions like Stein's "transparent window onto reality"; but they were also, like Stein's again, a "sophisticated engagement with the naive."

In linking the public and the private in their poetry, Stein, Bishop, and Rich responded to a common need to find not just a protective language that would express their erotic desire without revealing it openly, but also their place in a world that they felt in varying ways did not acknowledge their presence. Central to this public role is the consideration of how a lesbian poet can be true to herself in language addressed to a world that has denied her. In refusing the pretty sonnet and abandoning a form she herself has found useful, Rich sets up a dilemma that has come increasingly to haunt her career: how to lay down the truth in language that lies— language that lies between lover and beloved, between poet and reader, and language that lies because of the inescapable distance between these figures as between the poet and her own experience. Rich's "even in poems" is a quick acknowledgment of that dilemma, a hastily stated awareness that she has both exploited the way language "lies" for her own purposes and attempted to confront the "lie."

Her denunciation of lying in her 1975 essay, "Women and Honor: Some

Notes on Lying," and her poem, "Cartographies of Silence," indicates her early resistance to one particular way that language lies or has been made to lie. Women, in Rich's view, have been encouraged to lie, forgiven for lying with their bodies, forced to lie for survival in the heterosexual world. Merely victims of the system, perhaps driven mad by it, women are still largely innocent even when the habit becomes a dangerous form of emotional repression; as Rich notes, "Women's love for women has been represented almost entirely through silence and lies. The institution of heterosexuality has forced the lesbian to dissemble, or be labeled a pervert, a criminal, a sick or dangerous woman, etc., etc. The lesbian, then, has often been forced to lie, like the prostitute or the married woman" (*OLSS*, 190).

The passive constructions in Rich's prose reflect her political understanding of women as victims two decades ago when she delivered these remarks at Hartwick College. They do not address the problem of the poet she has become who must break out of the victim's role into the silence she acknowledges and to move beyond the subterfuges that Stimpson has identified in Gertrude Stein's *The Autobiography of Alice B. Toklas* as "the lesbian lie." Stimpson explains of Stein:

> In a complex act of deception, confession, and assertion, a misunderstood, under-published author is giving the public what she calculates it can take. Her gift demands that she handle a sub-genre we insufficiently understand: the lesbian lie. This lie insists that no lesbians lie abed here. To imagine erotics is to fall victim to cognitive errotics [*sic*]. The author respects, indeed shares, a reader's sense of decorum. At its finest, such decorum construes all sexuality as private and then begs private things to stay private. At its worst, such decorum is repression's etiquette. ("Stein and the Lesbian Lie," 152–53)

Stimpson addresses here Stein's problematic autobiographical writing; but she has extended her comments to Rich, writing elsewhere, "Language lies. Language invents. Poetry lies. Poetry invents. Rich accepts that 'truth'" ("Rich and Lesbian/Feminist Poetry," 265). Working to find the poetic form and language in which to be true, Stein and Bishop have relied on the "lesbian lie." It allowed Stein to modulate subversion into entertainment that, Stimpson argues, follows and refines a homosexual method of seeking acceptance in modern heterosexual culture ("Stein and the Lesbian Lie," 153); its gifts for Stein have been "a courageous, jaunty, often outrageous style" (163). No less has the "lesbian lie" served Bishop, whose "instinctive, modest, life-long impersonations of an ordinary woman," in James Merrill's memorable phrase, had their source in that lie and their outlet in poetry that is, in Merrill's terms, "wryly radiant, more touching, more unaffectedly intelligent than any written in our lifetime" (259, 262).

By comparison to Stein's outrageous and Bishop's wryly radiant style, Rich's plain style is not an accommodation to but rather a sustained engagement with the "lesbian lie." She will have it out on her own terms, even if those terms call into question the artifice she requires to write at all. Her plain style is connected, as Helen Vendler has noted, to the long history in American culture of Protestant dissent with its tradition of political and religious reform. It favors, to use Rich's words, accountability and communal responsibility, over the ornament and embellishment of poetry (369). It is hard to lie in the plain style, and yet, as Rich's love poem suggests, it is hard to stay true even in poems or, she might have written, especially in poems where the temptations of language are so seductive.

Traditionally, the plain style has incorporated a kind of moral rectitude that, as Rich carries it into the last decades of the twentieth century and into wider and wider ranges of experience, she has found increasingly difficult to register. The imaginative and emotional—and certainly, political—pressures to speak her love have strained Rich's plain style, as the legal and social codes that governed both Stein's mannered style and Bishop's reticence have not entirely relaxed in Rich's time. For Stein, "dissimulation is a tax that homosexuals pay in order to go on being members of a society that would abhor their honesty" ("Stein and the Lesbian Lie," 161), according to Stimpson, and though the women's movement has improved such circumstances, it has not completely freed Rich from the same tax. She also has had to dissimulate, and, even in coming out, she has had to devote herself to combating the necessity of dissimulating. The legal restraints have not been lifted, and there still remains a powerful public censure of lesbians and gays that has forced Rich to divide her energies in order to fight.

Certainly, Rich's poetry and her political involvement have been important to women's writing today. Read with Stein and Bishop on a continuum from hermetic to common language, from unpublished to popular poet, from closeted to out lesbian, from dissimulation to direct statement, from coded to more openly expressed eroticism, Rich's efforts to allow the lesbian in her to drive her imagination appear to have succeeded in bringing public attention to this lyric voice, encouraging the celebration of sameness *and* difference. But long before Rich's achievements, other poets—preeminently Stein and Bishop—were engaged in similar imaginative efforts, working to expand the woman's lyric voice to include their experience as lesbian women. Although the political pressures on Stein and Bishop were quite different from those on Rich and they responded to them in different ways, these two poets started the creative work that Rich was to continue. Examining the poetry of these three women as a continuing experiment in representing lesbian experience, I shall suggest that they are more alike than the continuum above might suggest, sharing a similar search for language and a common testing of poetic resources. There are, for example, hermetic moments and coded expressions in Rich's poetry as there are a common language and an openness in Stein's.

Here, I shall look at three subjects: love, war, and place. They may seem arbitrary choices, and yet they come from the poets themselves, who, despite their differences, have been riveted to these same subjects. Their love poetry is, I shall argue, the source of their creativity. Beyond that, war, as a subject, was a gift of the violent century in which they lived. Its disruptions as well as their own dislocations brought them to a consideration of their place in the world. Stein and Bishop were exiles, and Rich was a restless wanderer in the regions of the United States; Stein and Rich were Jews; they were all women and lesbians exploring "the politics of location." Place is a woman's subject according to Judy Grahn, who writes that the nature of place or location is "female, that is, the word derived from the female body, from *placenta*, the place where the child is joined to the mother" (43).

If Rich's achievements in her public role, as she moved from women's issues and from gay rights activism to broader social and political issues, have been amply studied, Bishop's similar interests are only now beginning to be noticed, as, for example, critics take an interest in women's war poetry.[7] Her early concern that her first volume of poems did not include enough war poems has obscured the range of her interests not just in World War I and II, but in wars of every kind from the Napoleonic Wars of "Casabianca" to the wars of colonization in "Brazil, January 1, 1502." "Wars are everywhere in *North and South*," Susan Schweik has argued in her study of American women poets and their treatment of World War II (234), pointing to the war imagery that floods Bishop's poetry of every subject. Stein's extensive war writing has also been largely neglected, and yet her involvement in World War I brought her to the attention of the popular press, eliciting poems for *Vanity Fair* and *Life* and changing her conception of her audience, the possibilities of a style suitable to that audience, as well as her own sense of herself as a public personage. War continued to interest her as she repeated her involvement with a second wave of American soldiers in World War II and moved on to comment even on atomic warfare.

On the subject of war, these three poets had different ambitions, different resources, different constraints; but each of them sought to speak not only *to* the public but also *for* the public. Rich claims that she took her ambition from Emily Dickinson. She writes, "More than any other poet, Emily Dickinson seemed to tell me that the intense inner event, the personal and psychological, was inseparable from the universal; that there was a range for psychological poetry beyond mere self-expression" (*OLSS*, 168).

Elizabeth Bishop learned the same lesson from a much lesser poet. Commenting on Frank Bidart's first book, she wrote: "Just possibly, Frank Bidart has achieved, in his first book, exactly what all young poets would like to do: he has discovered and brought together a set of images, emotionally disturbing, apparently disparate, but in combination having the uncanny power of illuminating the poet's personal history and History itself, literary life and plain Life, at the same time" (Schwartz and Estess, 307). Gertrude Stein always associated her experimental writing with the novelty of life in the twentieth century, reminding teenagers in a late speech: "What you are going to do I don't know any more than anyone else. But I created a movement of which you are the grandchildren. The contemporary thing is the thing you can't get away from. That is the fundamental thing in all writing" (*GofM*, 489).

Connecting their life with Life, these poets turned from war as a subject to the social and political conditions in the larger world around them in order to write not about history, as their male contemporaries did, but about geography. From Stein's *Geography and Plays* to Bishop's *Geography III* and finally to Rich's *An Atlas of the Difficult World*, these three poets have concentrated on maps and locations as sources of creative speculation. Geography—the extremely public places they attempted to map— oscillates in their poetry with the extreme privacy and secrecy of the personal lives they also detailed. One hides the other, especially in Bishop, whose success in poems of description seemed to be all that critics noticed about her work until fairly recently. In a different way, Rich's politics and her interest in drawing an atlas of the difficult world have been read into her poetry, drawing attention away from its more conflicted intimate revelations. Stein, called the "Mother Goose of Montparnasse," made much of her actual physical location in the Rue de Fleurus as well as in the regions she traveled during her war work, depending on the particularity of her descriptions to obscure the life she lived. This interest in geography and in the social and political issues that geography raises for these poets proved them to be, in quite different ways, worldly women, circulating in the larger culture outside the woman's sphere of the domestic and senti-mental and outside, too, their own expressions of love and erotic desire. Moreover, place is related to their most intimate identity. Judy Grahn suggests that "the definition of *place* itself has been central to what we [as lesbians] have done," acknowledging the naming of place in early feminist works. Such a practice "helped push Lesbianism out into the world, a hostile world at times, a 'jungle,' but nevertheless we were perceived, and perceiving ourselves as out of the house, out of confinement. In our lives, we have felt greatly without place, and continually out of place," Grahn concludes (42).

Revealing perhaps her own attitude toward place as well as those of Stein and Rich, Bishop describes Darwin in a letter by noting, "heroic observations, almost unconscious or automatic—and then comes a sudden relaxation, a forgetful phrase, and one feels that strangeness of his under-taking, sees the lonely young man, his eye fixed on facts and minute details, sinking or sliding giddily off into the unknown. What one seems to want in art, in experiencing it, is the same thing that is necessary for its creation, a self-forgetful, perfectly useless concentration."[8]

Looking at the radical experimenter, the polished formalist, and the deliberately unliterary, I shall examine how each poet developed a style that could be "self-forgetful," just as it could also articulate the emotions of formidable—because painfully formed—selves. Although their circum-stances have differed, each one of these women poets has had the leisure for the "perfectly useless concentration" that such art requires. Theirs is not the art that is driven by madness or pain nor is it the art of the possessed creator. Each one of these poets has chosen art and devoted herself to the discipline of "heroic observations."

As the following chapters will indicate, a public lyric voice developed in these women first in private. Stein's poetry was largely unpublished in her lifetime. She had, as she announced in a prefatory message to her *Selected Writings*, a need to "be historical"; but her poetry served other purposes. She turned to poetry from her early narrative writing in order to write about her desire for Alice B. Toklas, and, in the privacy of that coded writing, she found an experimental form that would allow her both to blatantly announce her passion and express her misgivings about its trans-gressive nature. As she was exploring these subjects, she was also witness-ing World War I, and at first she simply included it as a subject in her love poetry. From this subject, she moved eventually to a poem in which she articulated her solidarity with the patriarchy and her confidence in her own ability to write "patriarchal poetry." Nonetheless, poetry also continued to provide a private language for Stein as she could write simultaneously the accessible prose of *The Autobiography of Alice B. Toklas* and another autobiography, the inaccessible "Stanzas in Meditation," a very long and difficult poem in which she embedded the difficulties in her relationship with Toklas.

Although her poetry had no public audience, she worked to create a public voice, confident that in the future she would be recognized as a genius. Because she wrote, as she admits, for herself and strangers, Stein has been able to be most private and most public at once. Writing for herself, she wrote daily, often recording simply the events of her day as well as her passions, her disagreements, her purchases, her food, for example, and simply filed away the endless reams of poetry. Writing for strangers, she acknowledged an unknown and perhaps future audience that would recognize her experimental writing as new and revolutionary.

Writing at the beginning of the century in Paris, Stein enjoyed a freedom that was denied Bishop, who began writing in the much more repressive mood of the 1930s and under the influence of the strict discipline and watchful eye of Marianne Moore. Victoria Harrison traces Bishop's ambivalence about representing the tensions, pain, desire, and passion of intimate relationships in her early work: "As Bishop was writing her first two books of poetry in the 1930s and 1940s, she was discovering just how much her subjects could lean over into each other's territory, without becoming too possessive, too dependent, or too revealing of their affection, just how much she could revise cultural assumptions without making her poems unpublishable, and just how close her poems' images could be to her own experiences, without seeming 'indecent' to her readers" (73).

The 1930s also cast up for Bishop a world of political activity that provided subjects for her early poetry. Although she resisted the pressure to write political poetry, she published frequently in *Partisan Review*, for example, where her work was surrounded by political writing, and her poetry, if not partisan, was at least concerned with the public issues of poverty, of race, and, in her Key West poems, of class. As the country moved toward war, so too did she turn to war as a subject. Later, in her Brazilian years, she lived in the middle of a revolution in a household immersed in politics, and she wrote again of poverty, race, and class, as well as social injustice. Writing often in traditional verse forms, Bishop could still explore lives that were marginal, dispossessed, alien. She brought to social and political issues the precision of a lyric voice that had been tuned to clear and exact expression. By the time she began to write more auto-biographically toward the end of her life, she had developed a lyric style that could be personal without being intimate, intimate without being confessional.[9]

But her lyric style remains indirect when she writes about her love or erotic desire. Pronouns remain vague, sexual identity remains blurred, as Bishop expresses her love. More often, however, she did not write about love's ecstasy and passion's fulfillment so much as she evoked its bitterness, its loneliness, and its pain. If Stein presents herself as the husband and Toklas as the wife, she celebrates nonetheless their grand passion and complete pleasure in the physical acts of sex. Bishop, by contrast, identi-fies herself and her lover as part of one person, neither dominant nor sub-missive, but even more intricately linked than partners or sisters. None-theless, even in this relationship, she views love's betrayal, loss, and grief as the dominant experiences of her intimate relationships. Inverted as she presents it, her love is far from perfect and rather too exactly a reflection of the miseries in the world around it.

In traditional verse form, Bishop could express political sympathies with marginal elements in society from maids to drunkards to impover-ished children. Although she maintained a kind of public propriety in her social life and consistently claimed that she had no interest in political writing, she was more liberal than Stein in her social and political views, supporting reform in Brazilian politics and trying to sympathize with the student revolutions in the 1960s when she returned to America. As the chapters ahead will suggest, Bishop added a seriousness and integrity to the woman's public lyric voice. Unlike Stein who was treated as ridiculous, Bishop gained the admiration and attention of serious poetry readers.

Rich lives in a different world from Stein and Bishop. The legal re-straints against lesbianism in the first decades of the century (although easily overlooked by women in Stein's cultured Parisian circle) and the social restraints that prevented Bishop from coming out in midcentury have not entirely lost their force in the last decades of the twentieth century; but, by coming out, Rich moved to release herself and others from them. I shall focus here on what she has discovered about herself and the world in this process, how she negotiated with the constraints on her own creative energies that she assumed by taking on the responsibilities of a public voice. Starting by expanding the idea of lesbianism to all women's friendships with women, Rich removed it from the exotic and the exclu-sively erotic, centering women's relationships first in the bond between mother and child and then in the bond between sisters and concentrating her attention on the place of women, even lovers, in the quotidian world, rather than in a purely erotic relationship. As she has sought to come out of the privacy, even duplicity, of what Stimpson calls "the lesbian lie," Rich has come into a world of her own history, emotional attachments, and political longings, a world that she now sees as irremediably "difficult." Drawing an atlas of such a world, Rich spins out dreams beyond that of a common language.

Politically, Rich has been an important force not only in the women's movement, but also in supporting lesbian and gay rights, civil rights, and in opposing war, political oppression, and violence. More liberal than Stein and more engaged than Bishop, Rich has brought the women's lyric voice into public issues, and she has encouraged younger women poets to follow her. She has fulfilled Stein's ambition to be "historical." Not surprisingly, she has found that ambition demanding, double-edged, and not always exactly what she desired. Still, placed with Stein and Bishop, Rich illustrates how consistently twentieth-century women poets have worked over the same public issues and, in the process, enriched the resources of their own lyric voices.

The chapters ahead will explore each poet in turn as she wrote of love, war, and place. As the readings will suggest, each poet wrote largely in isolation from the others, as if she believed that in her own work there would be—in Rich's words—"a whole new poetry beginning here" (*FofD*, 268). The new poetry of Rich's poem arises from "two women, eye to eye / measuring each other's spirit, each other's / limitless desire" (268). But it is there, too, in Stein's "I want you to mean a great deal to me" (*YGS*, 35) or in Bishop's "where the heavens are shallow as the sea / is now deep, and you love me" (*CP*, 70). Beginning over and over to create the new poetry that would express their desire for women, these women poets learned how to draw into their work the widest circle of their concerns. Read together, their work suggests the imaginative power of each new beginning as well as the growing recognition of a lesbian public lyric voice.

1

Gertrude Stein
Living Was All
Loving

As Gertrude Stein's poetry began to be read by generations after her own, her critics became interested chiefly in the erotic coding she devised. Thus, as early as 1952, Edmund Wilson noted that Stein wrote about relationships between women that the standards of her era would not have allowed her to describe more explicitly. More recently, William Gass has explored what he identifies as the covert texts of Eve and Pandora that underpin *Tender Buttons*, arguing that evasiveness became a habit, a style, a method for Stein even when she was dealing with subjects for which it was unnecessary.[1] And, in an important early article, Elizabeth Fifer began to break Stein's erotic code, noting that "'Butter,' like cake and water, appears frequently as part of Stein's special food imagery for sex," for example ("Is Flesh Advisable?" 479). For Stein's first feminist readers, this coding was an achievement of her work against the patriarchy. For example, Marianne DeKoven, who oddly seeks to release Stein's work from all interpretable meaning, still praises her feminist revolution in terms that would appear to have consequences that admit of a social interpretation: "[h]er encoding of lesbian sexual feeling in her experimental work, her undoing of patriarchal portraiture in *The Autobiography of Alice B. Toklas*, the buried anger at female victimisation in *Three Lives*, and her overall, lifelong commitment to freeing language from the hierarchical grammars of patriarchy."[2] For other critics, her coding was an experiment with language in which she appeared to have "anticipated not only most of the linguistically experimental strain of modernism but much of post-modernism as well" (Nelson, 179). The Stein thus placed in the canon is a wonder woman, "quite impossible to naturalize and domesticate" (179) in Cary Nelson's words. This view, held curiously by her admirers and detractors alike, first kept her at the margins of the modernist movement and now, with the rise of feminist and postmodernist criticism, moves her to an advanced position within modernism.[3]

A harbinger of the feminist movement of the 1970s and 1980s or an early postmodernist Stein may have been, but her coded language served a more immediate need for the poet herself. It allowed her to conceal her subject from an audience unaware of the code and further afforded her an opportunity to switch codes or obscure references as her bravado battled with her uncertainties about what she was encoding.[4] If, as DeKoven suggests, lesbian erotic poetry had to be written in code, Stein struggled nonetheless even within the code to come to terms with her sexual identity and experience even as she worked to find a means of writing it.

As a lesbian, working in what Sandra Gilbert and Susan Gubar have identified as the first generation of writers who were self-consciously lesbian, she had certain reasonable reservations about revealing her feelings too directly and a deep anxiety about her sexual identity (2:222). Even much later in her career when she turned to theoretical writing, she was anxious to obscure the nature of her language experiments, presenting them as more abstract than they were. Thus, hiding behind the general experiments of the modernist movement, Stein uncharacteristically failed to take credit for her real and unique contribution to that period—an erotic poetry of considerable variety and power. But in her work, the modernist movement may lay claim to sensibilities in which imaginative and creative powers were perfectly aligned with emotional and erotic intensity.

It is strange that Gertrude Stein, who claimed so much for herself, did not want to assert openly the erotic source of her poetry, preferring to distance herself from it by retreating into abstractions of language experiments. In this, she simply acknowledged that poetry is always an experiment with language just as the language of all poetry is coded. But, as Geoffrey Hartman in talking about the codes of Oriental love poetry has argued, "the code is always in the process of being established. . . . The skill or will of the interpreter is essential: his skill in playing, his will to find or else impose a meaning" (135). And what happened to Stein is that even her first feminist readers took her seriously and concentrated chiefly on her experiments with nonreferentiality. That Stein wanted to obfuscate her code by claiming it to be an experiment suggests only that she aimed to keep her readers at bay, and she was unusually successful. Her contemporary readers did not understand the code, looking as they were for a completely different kind of language experiment, one more like that of Ezra Pound or T. S. Eliot that connected to history, to the transpersonal. Stein's coding of her personal experience simply escaped their notice.

Stein did not start out to write simply in order to experiment with language. She began to write in order to come to terms with the disappointment of her love for May Bookstaver and later to express the joy in her attachment to Alice B. Toklas. Her creative experiment may seem now to be an early example of *écriture féminine*, but it was first an effort to study, express, question, and celebrate a new love. Writing the female body, she was not engaged in celebrating a *jouissance* that was preverbal so much as she was enjoying a witty play with words. Behind it all, she was working through the conflicts of her own emotions and sexual identity. She may have chosen to hide within a radical experimentation in language simply to conceal the full nature of her subject. In her late lecture, "Poetry and Grammar," Stein claimed, "I too felt in me the need of making it be a thing that could be named without using its name" (*LA*, 236). And so the radical experimentation of *Tender Buttons*, often theorized within the known parameters of modernist experimentation with nonreferentiality and the absent subject, is not a style that abandons representation, but rather one that seeks to represent something that Stein does not care to name directly.

In exercising this restraint, Stein seems less anxious to pander to the taste of a large audience than to work her way through a complex of feelings that drove her simultaneously to celebrate her passion for Toklas publicly, to guard its secret in a kind of intimate and private code, to judge it, and to set it in the narrative of her life. Her description of her subject in

Tender Buttons as "queer," "not ordinary," "dirty" is the clearest pointer to its nature for conventional readers who would make the same judgment.[5] They reveal Stein's ironic treatment of her audience; but they also indicate her own ambivalence about her experiment, carrying, as they do, an erotic as well as a moral charge.

Stein's poetry conveys both her gaiety and her guilt. She wanted to express both what had not been said before and what could not be said. She was as committed to the second experiment as to the first. Thus, she developed a double language that may have worked to undermine the patriarchal structures of modernist culture but that had its own moments of despair, melancholy, and misogyny.[6] It was celebratory, subversive, and lively, but it was also self-denying. The privacy of Stein's coded language was a game that could exhaust as well as please its creator. She had to make it all up, and, though such a practice left her wildly free of all inhibitions, it arose out of the need for secrecy that was itself a major constraint.

Moreover, she had to chart her own course as she came into her sexuality. In her first novel, *Q.E.D.* (1903), the character who represents Gertrude Stein's own position in the disastrous triangle of female lovers says: "As for passion . . . you see I don't understand much about that. It has no reality for me except as two varieties, affectionate comradeship on the one hand and physical passion in greater or less complexity on the other and against the cultivation of that latter I have an almost puritanic horror" (*FQED*, 59).

Some four years later, in "Ada," a portrait of Alice B. Toklas, Stein wrote: "Trembling was all living, living was all loving, some one was then the other one. Certainly this one was loving this Ada then. And certainly Ada all her living then was happier in living than any one else who ever could, who was, who is, who ever will be living" (*GP*, 16).[7]

Telling about the composition of this portrait in *The Autobiography of Alice B. Toklas*, Stein records how excited she was in its creation, insisting that Toklas interrupt her supper preparations to read it immediately. She has Toklas comment: "I began it and I thought she was making fun of me and I protested, she says I protest now about my autobiography. Finally I read it all and was terribly pleased with it. And then we ate supper" (*SW*, 107). Then Stein admits, "This was the beginning of the long series of portraits" (107).

Thus, the composition of Toklas's portrait celebrates the decisive moment in Stein's development from a "puritanic horror" of passion to an acceptance of that passion and the "affectionate comradeship" of Toklas, and, in turn, that emotional development allowed her to start her life's project of writing portraits. This movement from the intimacy of her love for Toklas to the public world of portraiture is curious. After all, Stein had the example of her friends, the artists Picasso and Matisse, who could have launched her portraits, and, as she theorized later, she was also inspired to experiment with a new way of looking by developments in the cinema. But her deliberate decision to emphasize Toklas as the person who launched her into portraits is an open declaration of the importance of passion, both as a source and as a subject, to her experiments in writing.

Still, Toklas was not the first passion, nor was she the first inspiration for Stein's creative imagination. Love and writing were intimately connected in Stein's life from the beginning, as her earliest writing suggests in its effort to find a form suitable to explore, explain, and express her unrequited passion for May Bookstaver. Bookstaver worked on Stein's imagination in a way quite different from Toklas's influence, leading Stein to explore character, hers and others', and, as Leon Katz has argued in discussing Stein's apprentice work (*FQED*, ii), to consider the "root problems—what is writing? what is knowing? what is describing?"

From early in her career and long before she met Toklas, Stein turned to writing in an effort to work out satisfactory answers to these questions. Trained as a scientist, Stein thought of "writing" as "describing" and "describing" as the way of "knowing" what she needed to understand about herself. In this project, she started, again as a scientist would, by classifying characters as types. Such a classification, an improbable method of describing her own identity, did allow her to express her differences from Bookstaver since, as she discovered, they were contrasting character types—"Their pulses were differently timed" (*FQED*, 104). But classification posed problems in her narratives, as Katz has noted (*FQED*, xix). Character types and schematic patterns of relationships may be useful in distancing a writer from her personal troubles and disappointed love affairs; but they do not generate interesting narratives, and, as the contradictions of her method became more explicit, Stein began to abandon narrative for a different kind of composition and a completely different understanding of character. She began to see individual rhythms instead of types. Her new work began, as she explained some years later in "Portraits and Repetition," by "talking and listening . . . and in so doing I conceived what I at that time called the rhythm of anybody's personality" (*LA*, 174).

The transition from character types to personal rhythms was gradual, but it began once Stein became interested in the rhythm of someone else's personality. "Ada," the first portrait of Toklas, belongs to a transitional moment when Stein was still writing narratives along familiar schematic patterns.[8] Although a number of critics have singled out "Ada" as marking a new beginning in Stein's writing (perhaps because it is about Toklas), the portrait is new only in its positive identification with Ada.[9] This "portrait" is of a character type that Stein does understand, a person whose pulse she wants to see as similarly timed.

But even here, or especially here, Stein retains something of the "puritanic horror" against physical passion that she expressed in *Q.E.D.* For example, however insistent "Ada" might be about the fact that "living was all loving," the portrait depicts "loving" as merely "listening to stories" and "telling stories" (*GP*, 16). At one level, of course, this emphasis signals the importance of Toklas's companionship to Stein's writing and the significance of the dialogue between them, as Harriet Chessman has argued. At another level, describing love as merely listening to stories reveals a kind of Victorian prudishness in writing about their relationship. This reticence is evident too in the identification of Ada's lover only as "Some one" or "That one" or "this one." Chessman claims that identity is not important here because dialogue becomes a metaphor for "a certain form of relationship, where two 'ones' may be distinguished, yet where the boundaries may also become confused and even disappear" (65). And, it must be admitted, such confusion is evident even in Stein's account of this portrait in *The Autobiography*, which mixes up the pronouns so that the sentence—"I protested, she says I protest now about my autobiography"— is Toklas speaking both as "I" and as "she" (*SW*, 107).

In "Ada," two people, the lover and the beloved, can be distinguished, and perhaps they are not named because identity is too important to be mentioned here. Stein wanted to identify neither herself nor Toklas in this portrait, even when she did want to announce the exaggerated claims of their happiness. The anonymity here is part of a pattern of secrecy that will screen Stein's imaginative treatment of their relationship throughout her life.[10] Although she embeds the subject in *Tender Buttons*, treats it more directly in "Lifting Belly," and certainly acknowledges it as a fact in *The Autobiography of Alice B. Toklas*, the need to write about her love for Toklas without stating it directly is the central impulse of her work in all its stages. This double-talk in her language reflects deeply divided feelings.[11] For all her interest in self-promotion, Stein kept something of herself hidden. She was worldly, that is, she lived in the public world, inhabiting the house of culture as a whole, and she was also extremely secretive.[12]

Hiding her desire behind words that are affectionate and generalized in "Ada," Stein moved on to try a much bolder experiment in *Tender Buttons*. Shifting her focus from Toklas to herself, she explores the pleasure, especially the erotic pleasure, of her relationship with her new companion. Stein began by asking how much she could write what she meant, how much she had to hide it. Again, it was a portrait—"Portrait of Constance Fletcher" (1911–12)—that signaled this new effort.[13] From gerunds to direct statements, the movement in the second half of "Portrait of Constance Fletcher" is to an exploration of meaning and especially of what is not meant. After abruptly changing style, Stein writes, "This has not any meaning" (*GP*, 159). But, she goes on to explain the new way of writing: "This is all to prepare the way that is not the way to like anything that in speaking is telling what has come that like a swelling is inside when there is yellowing" (160).

Later, she admits, "That is not a disclosure. That is not the way for all of them who are looking to refuse to see" (*GP*, 161). It is, rather, a way of seeing something quite different and differently. In *The Autobiography*, she describes the change: "hitherto she had been interested only in the insides of people, their character and what went on inside them, it was during that summer that she first felt a desire to express the rhythm of the visible world" (*SW*, 111–12). And again, "They were the beginning, as Gertrude Stein would say, of mixing the outside with the inside. Hitherto she had been concerned with seriousness and the inside of things, in these studies she began to describe the inside as seen from the outside" (147).

In all these explanations both in this text and years later in her autobiographical and theoretical works, Stein displays a concern about meaning or disclosure that is new to her. Her interest in the outside, even the rhythm of the visible world, was also an interest in how much of the inside Stein could make clear to the outside, how much she could come out where the rhythm of the visible world might impede the rhythm of her personality. In "Ada," she had identified the inside with emotions; in *Tender Buttons*, the inside is more closely connected with her erotic experience. Writing about emotions, she could be quite direct because she wrote in very general terms. But when she began to describe the erotic impulse behind those feelings, she had to change her style.

Her self-consciousness about this change of style is evident in "Rooms," the final section of *Tender Buttons*, written in 1911 during the same period as "Portrait of Constance Fletcher." Here, Stein concentrates on her organization as she begins to test the limits of her revelation. It opens, "Act so that there is no use in a centre" (*SW*, 498), and this idea runs through

"Rooms" as Stein experiments with writing and simultaneously hiding what she means. The two efforts go on at once. At one level, Stein reworks the meaning of the center from its traditional association with stability to a new association with activity and free play.[14] At another level, she identifies the center of her passion for Toklas in the bedroom and writes a long warning to herself against exposing that fact. In this text, one meaning can cancel out or contradict another, even as it is reversing itself.

Stein writes, "Any change was in the ends of the centre" (*SW*, 498). She plays on that idea: "If the centre has the place then there is distribution. That is natural. There is a contradiction and naturally returning there comes to be both sides and the centre" (499). And suddenly the center becomes not the still point, but the place of division between two contradictory sides. It is a place of separating and ordering.

But, in a world where there is no contradiction, there is no need for such a center, and Stein suggests another way of positioning, as she creates this catalog: "A damp cloth, an oyster, a single mirror, a mannikin, a student, a silent star, a single spark, a little movement and the bed is made" (*SW*, 501–2). Here where the bed is made, as in the bedroom, this associative and contiguous grouping includes rather than separates things, as Stein explains: "This shows the disorder, it does, it shows more likeness than anything else, it shows the single mind that directs an apple" (502). Connecting it to the still lifes of Cézanne and Picasso, Walker claims that it is a "deliberate artistic model, not a naïve reproduction, of the 'real'" (135). More than that, it is the creation of "the single mind," the mind that is not divided, the mind that reveals itself in "likeness," the mind that, in its "little movement," is willing to make its bed and lie in it, beginning to identify its lesbian desire.

Stein approaches that possibility by suggesting immediately that "it is not very likely that there is a centre, a hill is a hill and no hill is contained in a pink tender descender" (*SW*, 502). As if she had revealed too much here, she moves to a series of explanations that does not do much to clarify or describe its subjects, but starts suggestively: "A can is," "A measure is," "A package and a filter," and finally "A cape is" (502). Each paragraph meditates on containment or covering and exposure, as if Stein had moved back in order to consider words themselves as containers, covering up as well as representing things. These paragraphs lead into a series of questions, including the question of the center: "Why is there a circular diminisher" (503).

Stein revises the meaning of "the centre," which she now claims is differently configured for "singularity": "the centre having spelling and no solitude and no quaintness and yet solid quite so solid and the single surface centred [*sic*] and the question in the placard and the singularity, is there a singularity, and the singularity, why is there a question and the singularity why is the surface outrageous, why is it beautiful why is it not when there is no doubt, why is anything vacant, why is not disturbing a centre no virtue" (*SW*, 505–6). By stages, disturbing the center, Stein has moved the "centre" from a point of division to a place of "singularity." And, more explicitly, she makes singulars into doubles, reordering language to express a center that does not divide or distract but combines similar words as in "Sugar any sugar, anger every anger, lover sermon lover, centre no distractor, all order is in a measure" (506).

Having succeeded in translating divisive "centres" into unified "singularity," Stein advises, "Dance a clean dream and an extravagant turn up, secure the steady rights and translate more than translate the authority, show the choice and make no more mistakes than yesterday" (*SW*, 508). Showing her own choice, as she translates authority by assuming it, she sets the center in motion: "A willow and no window, a wide place stranger, a wideness makes an active center [*sic*]. // The sight of no pussy cat is so different that a tobacco zone is white and cream" (508).

In this term of endearment and erotic pleasure, Stein uncovers her own desire to "translate the authority." "Rooms" is, in the end, one room—the bedroom—the center of a newfound passion, and the section demands to be read again as an extended covering up of its subject or acting, that is, pretending, so that there is no use in such a center.

Read again, "Rooms" appears obsessed with the admission, early stated, that "There is a use, they are double" (*SW*, 498). And, then, the identities of Stein and Toklas in their bedroom come out from hiding: Stein, "The author of all that is in there behind the door and that is entering in the morning" (499), and Toklas, "This makes no diversion that is to say what can please exaltation, that which is cooking" (499). Again, as if to be more clear, Stein writes, "The sister was not a mister" (499).

Their bedroom activities include "this which is no rarer than frequently is not so astonishing when hair brushing is added" (*SW*, 500–511), "the bed is made" (502), "there is some use in not mentioning changing" (502), "lying so makes the springs restless" (503), "Almost very likely there is no seduction" (503), "A window has another spelling, it has 'f' all together" (507), and "A pecking which is petting and no worse than in the same morning is not the only way to be continuous often" (509).

"Rooms" has often been overlooked in readings of *Tender Buttons* because the other two sections of the prose poem appear to be more interestingly experimental. But "Rooms" has its own power as an early and quite successful effort to find a language that could both express and conceal lesbian eroticism. The text is multiply reversible; on one side, it appears to be about centering or rather decentering, translating the language of authority into a language of singularity. On the other side, it is a celebration of the center in the bedroom that Stein shared with Toklas. But these two sides are themselves always changing under our eyes so that the simple phrase, "Act so that," can mean "go on so that" and "pretend so that" as well as "do not go on so that" and "do not pretend so that." The "centre," itself a point, a place, a moment, a table, a new place, is also a new moment.

Tender Buttons is a celebratory text that enjoys its private as well as its public celebrations. And it is an extremely witty example of Stein's continued interest in the inside even as she experimented with ways to turn the inside out, the outside in.[15] In this word play and quite apart from the idea of representation that any discussion of inside and outside entails, Stein is also entertaining the whole question of coming out, of what she could come out from or to, of where the outside begins and the inside ends. But within all this play, Stein expresses too her fear of a direct expression of eroticism. The word play itself allows her to take back as much as she reveals here of what goes on in the bedroom.

"Objects" and "Food," written simultaneously in 1913, appear to be more direct in their use of words, although they are, at the same time, more experimental. Opening with longer segments that look like the transitional style of "Rooms," these sections work toward a more radical deconstruction of language in brief segments composed of single lines. Still, the idea of the inside and outside—central to "Rooms" and important, too, in any referential use of words as well as in any expression of lesbian eroticism—persists. "Food" opens with a list of its separate segments and then moves to "Roastbeef," which appears to be set in the same bedroom as "Rooms," as Stein celebrates an "inside" of secret passion and an "outside" life of "meaning" or the writing that she did in the morning: "In the inside there is sleeping, in the outside there is reddening, in the morning there is meaning, in the evening there is feeling. . . . In feeling anything is resting, in feeling anything is mounting, in feeling there is resignation, in feeling there is recognition, in feeling there is recurrence and entirely mistaken there is pinching" (*SW*, 477).

Given the insistence here on "feeling," it is remarkable how much, even years later, Stein wanted to occlude the connection between her new life with Toklas and her writing. In "Portraits and Repetition," writing about this period, Stein claims: "All this time I was of course not interested in emotion or that anything happened. I was less interested then in these things than I ever had been. I lived my life with emotion and with things happening but I was creating in my writing by simply looking" (*LA*, 191).

Although the book does include some commentary on looking, especially on how some people cannot see even when they do look, *Tender Buttons* appears to be much more interested in emotions, especially those that had entered her life with Toklas, than Stein is willing to admit. If "Food" and even "Objects" describe, as Walker suggests, "a female world (circa 1912) of domestic objects and rituals—a world of dresses and hats, tables and curtains, mealtimes and bedtimes, cleanliness and dirt" (127), it is a world especially and specifically devoted to Toklas. Food was her department, and her physical presence is everywhere celebrated in this section. "Certainly the length is thinner," Stein writes, acknowledging Toklas's body by contrast to her own, "and the rest, the round rest has a longer summer" (*SW*, 477).

It "is so easy to exchange meaning," Stein claims, as she introduces her term for orgasm, "a cow absurd" (*SW*, 477–78). The passage rises to lyrical intensity where internal rhymes and repetition celebrate the passion of the two lovers: "Lovely snipe and tender turn, excellent vapor and slender butter, all the splinter and the trunk, all the poisonous darkening drunk, all the joy in weak success, all the joyful tenderness, all the section and the tea, all the stouter symmetry" (479). Here, references to size ("slender" and "stouter") and to food ("butter" and "tea"), mixed with feelings of both delirium and order, danger and pleasure, turn this passage into an encoded synaesthesia of desire where the lilting iambic meter of traditional love poetry conserves Stein's own subversive rhythm.

Against such passages as these runs the refrain, "It is not dirty," as if Stein had both to enjoy its illicit quality as well as convince herself that this passion she knew how to express in traditional meter was not, in some way, acceptable (*SW*, 479). It made her uneasy, and she felt she had to explain it, seeing her role as "Lecture, lecture and repeat instruction" (483), even when she had to concede, "What language can instruct any fellow." "What is the custom, the custom is in the centre," she declares, going back to her concern in "Rooms" (483). By contrast to "the custom," hers is "A bent way that is a way to declare that the best is all together" (484). Nonetheless, she acknowledges a need for self-censorship. She admits that "it shows a necessity for retraction" (484), although she goes on to celebrate "Wet crossing and a likeness," "a cow, only any wet place," and urges "to pay and pet pet very much" or "Cuddling comes in continuing a change" (486). Finally, "A cow is accepted" (486).[16]

But, however much "the difference is spreading," Stein's persistent use of the word "dirt" in "Objects" suggests that she wanted to emphasize the illicit quality of her "not ordinary" life, including what she imagined would be the public judgment of it. In discussing *Tender Buttons* in an interview in 1946, Stein claimed that "Dirty has an association and is a word that I would not use now" (*GofM*, 510). But it is a word she uses throughout "Objects": "Dirty is yellow. A sign of more in not mentioned" (*SW*, 463); "Dirt and not copper makes a color darker" (464); "if they dusty will dirt a surface" (465); "If there is no dirt in a pin" (467–68); "If the chance to dirty diminishing is necessary . . . why is there no special protection" (468); "a disgrace, an ink spot, a rosy charm" (471), for example. And it seems to bring up the very associations she claims she wants to cancel in her 1946 interview. Also, the persistence of "dirty" and "dirt" admits into the erotic experience of this text a severe and unbalancing judgment. If *Tender Buttons* is a celebration of lesbian desire, it is a celebration that is always being undercut even as it is enhanced.

As an erotic prose poem, *Tender Buttons* is much more openly expressive than "Ada," however much it can conceal in its openness. Even its title appears to advertise the female body and to underscore the tenderness in her passion for Toklas. Freeing herself from narrative, Stein was able to celebrate here an erotic life that had, as yet, no plot; simultaneously, she was able to display the polysemy of language.

Stein's many efforts to explain *Tender Buttons* in her later works emphasize its experiments in abstraction, in looking, and in ridding herself of nouns, finding words for a thing that was not the name of the thing. In "Poetry and Grammar," she writes: "And so I went on with this exceeding struggle of knowing really knowing what a thing was really knowing it knowing anything I was seeing anything I was feeling so that its name could be something, by its name coming to be a thing in itself as it was but would not be anything just and only as a name" (*LA*, 242).

She expresses the same idea differently in "Portraits and Repetition": "I became more and more excited about how words which were the words that made whatever I looked at look like itself were not the words that had in them any quality of description" (*LA*, 191). Again in "Poetry and Grammar," citing the example of Shakespeare who in the forest of Arden created a forest without mentioning the things that make a forest, she notes in a passage quoted earlier in this essay: "Now that was a thing that I too felt in me the need of making it be a thing that could be named without using its name. After all one had known its name anything's name for so long, and so the name was not new but the thing being alive was always new" (236–37).

Judy Grahn traces this effort to Stein's identity as a lesbian writer: "Writing out from the base of a woman to woman relationship considered taboo in the world, and translating this everyday personal experience into a literature that no longer overtly contains the taboo experience yet covertly contains it in great detail was a lifelong preoccupation of Gertrude Stein. . . . She began perceiving and treating words as individual bricks that have a free-floating meaning of their own, unattached to the automatic clichéd meanings they have in sentence form" (62–63).

As Stein herself became more distant from the text, as in the 1946 interview, she became more general in her explanations, explaining, "PEELED PENCIL, CHOKE" as "That is where I was beginning and went on a good deal after that period to make sound pictures but I gave that up as uninteresting" (*GofM*, 511). But "Rub her coke" picks up a number of other references to rubbing as sexual play or masturbation in *Tender Buttons* that prevents that phrase from being read merely as a "sound picture." So even as late as 1946 Stein still engaged in concealing the erotic nature of her language. Grahn is perhaps too optimistic in her assessment of Stein when she writes: "She removed all the expectation: this is good, this is bad, this is indifferent. In her sentences each word is indifferent, is good and is bad. Each word is evil, is a landlord, a heroine, is saving. And so she was able to use the substance of her inner life, her home life, her personal life and those of *all* her friends, not merely the socially acceptable ones. And because she had freed the language of all possible judgment there is no way to read her work and to judge her life in any terms except her own" (64–65).

Stein probably hoped that that would be true, but, as her very late theoretical comments suggest, she was never sure that she had succeeded. Nor did she ever work free from her own expectation that some things were good, some bad. Over and over, in *Tender Buttons*, she moved from explicitness to unintelligibility and even authorial self-correction as she mused on how much she could say, how much she must obscure what she said. She entertained these possibilities not as an abstract idea; she was writing, after all, at a time when censorship was enforced and when the author of an "obscene" work could be tried. By generating a certain amount of nonsense in her sense, Stein opened herself up to caricature and critical attacks; but, like Virginia Woolf, who was to pass off her study of bisexuality, *Orlando*, as a joke, Stein was also able to protect herself in this way from the public censure that, for example, Radclyffe Hall would suffer on the publication of *The Well of Loneliness* a decade later.[17]

As a prose poem, *Tender Buttons* owes something to the classifications of Stein's apprentice prose as it also looks toward the expression of erotic experience that was to be more fully explored in her poetry. In making this transition, she works from a "no since" or nonsense or prohibition to discover what is "real" for her or, as she puts it, "Pain soup, suppose it is question, suppose it is butter, real is, real is only, only excreate, only excreate a no since" (SW, 496).

This idea of relettering or excreating by providing a list of new definitions drives the next stage of her writing. This stage begins with "Lifting Belly," which develops through a lengthy series of definitions, this time of that one phrase, lifting belly. Unlike the varied elements in "Objects" or "Food" that are defined in Tender Buttons, the single phrase calls up definitions that are so diverse and extensive that they defy explicit reference. Thus Stein plays with all efforts to contain "lifting belly" in any single meaning and simultaneously creates and "ex-creates" names for erotic experience in her continuing effort to name it and to leave it unnamed.

Nonetheless, unlike the opacity of Tender Buttons, "Lifting Belly" is persistently referential, not just defining the activity of lifting belly, but commenting also on a whole array of daily events. In his notes to the poem, Virgil Thomson claims that the poem "is not a hermetic composition but a naturalistic recounting of the daily life" (BTV, 63). Written in Mallorca, Paris, Perpignan, and Nîmes during the years 1915, 1916, and 1917, according to Thomson, the poem records daily events and specific references to all these places: to Mallorca where Stein and Toklas went to sit out the war, to the Battle of Verdun, the purchase of the Ford automobile, the purchase of an antique Spanish desk imported to Paris with sausages in it, and the photograph taken of Stein with her car, among other things. Thomson calls the poem "a diary" and "a hymn to the domestic affections" (64).

Diaries and hymns have two independent purposes—the one to record events of the day and the other to celebrate special events—and Thomson is accurate in pointing out this double purpose. This odd combination in "Lifting Belly" reveals another effort on Stein's part to mix modes so that she will not be caught in the explicitness she obviously relishes.[18] The "hymn to the domestic affections" mixes the erotic and the everyday, sexual pleasures and the humdrum. Like the references to "dirt" in Tender Buttons, the daily events of "Lifting Belly" deflate, if they do not judge outright, the passion of the poem. For example, right after the declaration "Pussy how pretty you are," Stein writes: "That goes very quickly unless you have been there too long. / I told him I would send him Mildred's book. He seemed very pleased at the prospect" (YGS, 17). And then the refrain returns:

Lifting belly is so strong.
Lifting belly together.
Lifting belly oh yes.
Lifting belly.
Oh yes. (17)

Stein states explicitly:

Kiss my lips. She did.
Kiss my lips again she did.
Kiss my lips over and over and over again she did. (19)

Then she follows it with statements that blur the situation and relocate it
in the idle chitchat of daily life:

I have feathers.
Gentle fishes.
Do you think about apricots. We find them very beautiful. It is not
alone their color it is their seeds that charm us. We find it a change.
(20)

Noting this rendering of an intimate situation that veers into a language of indirection, Chessman argues: "In this way, Stein attempts both
to call into her writing the female body and love between women more
directly than in *Tender Buttons*, and to avoid reproducing the structures of
representation in which the female has been constrained" (101). But the
conventional structures of representing women are reproduced here freely,
both in the idealizing and in the controlling of the beloved, both in the
flattery and the commands. If Stein experiments at all in "Lifting Belly," it
is not in the way she represents women but in the way she refuses to
privilege sex over other activities. Lifting belly is there; so is the need to
have a Ford.

Setting moments of intimacy in the routine activities of a life in this
poem, Stein defies the conventional decorum of erotic poetry.[19] Absent
from Stein's poem is the idealizing, even fetishizing, of sexual intercourse
that marks Ernest Hemingway's style, for example. The earth does not
move for Stein's lovers. Sex is part of their daily life; like the "apricots," it
is "beautiful," it has "charm," and it is a "change"; but, perhaps, this
juxtaposition suggests, it is no more beautiful, no more charming, no
more different than apricots.

The persistence of a pattern of love talk followed by either specific and
incongruous references to daily life or nonsense suggests Stein's uncer-

tainty about the exaggerated and direct celebration of sex she was describing as an everyday reality. Even in this hymn where "lifting belly" starts line after line in an obsessive repetition and where the brevity of the lines would appear to set off the phrase as if it had special significance, the adjectives used to describe it flatten it out. Called "kind," "dear," "good," and even "my joy," "rich," and "perfect," "lifting belly" is given such a general description that it might refer to any experience.[20] Normalizing "lifting belly" in this way, Stein lifts the taboo on the subject by repeated mention.

If the general adjectives she uses do not point in any particular direction, neither do the earnest declarations of passion lead to an erotic narrative.[21] The ongoing activity of lifting belly, kissing, cuddling, "Caesars" or orgasms, sexual contact, declarations of love, is the same at the beginning as at the end of "Lifting Belly." The poem has no intensity in its language, few verbal climaxes, and little quickening of details. And because the clutter of other concerns in this poem has the same value as sex, Stein appears to be making the case for the naturalness of lesbian eroticism, for its dailiness, its ongoing nature, its steadfastness. The only contrast to "lifting belly" is the war, as Stein writes:

> Lifting belly is so strong.
> I said that to mean that I was very glad.
> Why are you very glad.
> Because that pleased me.
> Baby love.
> A great many people are in the war.
> I will go there and back again.
> What did you say about Lifting belly.
> I said lifting belly is so strong. (*YGS*, 8)

Again, Stein writes, "Lifting belly is anxious. / Not about Verdun. / Oh dear no" (10).[22] Placed in opposition to the war: "Lifting belly is peacable [*sic*]" (14), although it is consonant with patriotism, as Stein writes:

> We used to play star spangled banner.
> Lifting belly is so near.
> Lifting belly is so dear. (14)

And again, "Lifting belly is so kind. / She was like that. / Star spangled banner, story of Savannah" (29). It fits into military life: "Lifting belly is notorious. / A great many people wish to salute. The general does. So does the leader of the battalion. In spanish. I understand that" (19). And:

What shall you say about that. Lifting belly is so kind.
What is a veteran.
A veteran is one who has fought.
Who is the best.
The king and queen and the mistress.
Nobody has a mistress.
Lifting belly is so kind. (21)

Here it would seem that the war is linked to the heterosexual love triangle of "The king and queen and the mistress" and distinct from the passion celebrated in "lifting belly" as "kind." But the distinction does not hold, and, as the poem develops, the military and Stein's passion are brought together most notably in her use of "Caesar" as a code for orgasm:

Big Caesars.
Two Caesars.
Little seize her.
Too.
Did I do my duty.
Did I wet my knife.
No I don't mean whet. (22–23)[23]

The proximity of passion and war is underscored even in this amicable relationship as one letter of the alphabet is all that distinguishes the sex act from murder, love from duty. And soon, sex and war are not distinct at all. Making "Caesar" "plural" (26), Stein fuses sex, patriotism, war, in "Lifting belly say can you see the Caesars. I can see what I kiss" (30).

The poem concludes in the declaration of "Lifting belly enormously and with song" (54) and then the questions:

Can you sing about a cow.
Yes.
And about signs.
Yes.
And also about Aunt Pauline.
Yes.
Can you sing at your work.
Yes.
In the meantime listen to Miss Cheatham.
In the midst of writing.
In the midst of writing there is merriment. (54)

Uniting "signs" of her passion ("cow") and of her war work ("Aunt Pauline"), Stein assures her interlocutor that she can include the full range of her experience in her song and that she can enjoy it in all of its "merriment."

In the end, then, affirming her ability to sing about both a "cow" and "Aunt Pauline," Stein erases the division that she might have appeared to have drawn between her private passion and the public war. It is not that she cannot distinguish between the two, not even that they are similar; it is rather that Stein refuses divisions of all kinds in "Lifting Belly." She can play with divisions, even sexual ones, such as, "Darling wifie is so good. / Little husband would. / Be as good. / If he could" (YGS, 49). She can divide war from passion, the everyday from the erotic, the public world from the intimacy of her relationship with Toklas; but, in the course of "Lifting Belly," she undermines all these divisions. The poem ultimately is a hymn to sameness and singularity, to lesbian eroticism that arises from, as it generates, "merriment."

The desire to celebrate is the dominant note in Stein's early work inspired by Toklas from "Ada" through *Tender Buttons* to "Lifting Belly," and it drives the constant experimenting with form. Her experiments started with narrative and moved to poetry. First writing a prose poem, she then moved on in "Lifting Belly" to poetry composed of short lines, which she explains:

> Think of how you talk to anything whose name is new to you a lover a baby or a dog or a new land or any part of it. Do you not inevitably repeat what you call out and is that calling out not of necessity in short lines. Think about it and you will see what I mean by what you feel.
>
> So as I say poetry is essentially the discovery, the love, the passion for the name of anything. (*LA*, 234–35)

Describing a much later period in her writing that seems equally pertinent to her erotic poetry, Stein says, "In writing this poem I found I could be very gay I could be very lively in poetry" (*LA*, 243). She concludes, "I decided that if one definitely completely replaced the noun by the thing in itself, it was eventually to be poetry and not prose which would have to deal with everything that was not movement in space" (245).

Although she carried her experimental writing beyond poetry into plays, mysteries, and novels, she found that her first experiments with finding a language to express her erotic experience led her to poetry where she could be not only "gay," but where she could simultaneously discover and hide the name of "anything." From the anonymity of "Ada" to the double language of *Tender Buttons* to the naturalizing context of "Lifting Belly," Stein worked deliberately both to express her erotic life and to censor it.

Feminist and postmodernist readers at the end of the century in which she began to write—perhaps Stein's first receptive readers—have been particularly alert to her experiments with *l'écriture féminine*, with writing the body, with undoing hierarchical relationships and language—in short, with the expression of her erotic life. They have been less aware of Stein's self-censorship, the sexual anxiety that drove her tireless experimental writing, the self-judgment that undercut even her most exaggerated celebrations of her sexual power.

Placed in literary history as the first of the modernists, Stein will appear a more complex, if no less revolutionary, figure. She was one of the few modernist poets of love and erotic experience. Along with Hart Crane, she demonstrates how important the modernist experiments in language were to the free expression of lesbian and gay desire even as these same experiments seemed designed to fragment the speaker and restrict the expression of heterosexual desire. But, even within that freedom, Stein was moved to question and undercut her own erotic expression. Like Crane and also like many lesbians of her time, she was given to self-erasure as often as to an open expression of *jouissance*.[24] In this, she seems more easily naturalized as a modernist than a postmodernist. Whatever her work may have anticipated for the postmodernists, Stein shares with her contemporaries both an interest in radical experimentation with language and a conservative reservation about a too open or too personal expression of her experience.

2

Gertrude Stein & the First War She Saw

"Lifting Belly," the love poem that Gertrude Stein wrote in the years 1915 to 1917, is set in the context of the war. "Baby love. / A great many people are in the war" (*YGS*, 8), Stein remembers. A decade later, when again Stein takes up the subjects in "Patriarchal Poetry," it would appear that both love and war are merely functions of the patriarchy.

First, patriarchal poetry is identified with patriotism, as Stein admits: "Patriarchal poetry is the same as Patriotic poetry is the same as patriarchal poetry is the same as Patriotic poetry is the same as patriarchal poetry is the same" (*YGS*, 116). Then, both the patriarchy and patriotism appear to honor the kind of love celebrated in "A Sonnet," addressed "To the wife of my bosom" and followed in the long poem by the certification that "Patriarchal poetry makes no mistake makes no mistake in estimating the value to be placed upon the best and most arranged of considerations of this in as apt to be not only to be partially and as cautiously considered as in allowance which is one at a time" (124).

Although a contrast in form and subject to the rest of "Patriarchal Poetry" with its endlessly repeating title, the sonnet verifies the values of the patriarchy where the wife must validate the husband even as she is praised:

> Her virtues her beauty and her beauties
> Her charms her qualities her joyous nature
> All of it makes of her husband
> A proud and happy man. (*YGS*, 124)

The husband is completely devoted, dedicating "The Sonnet":

> To the wife of my bosom
> Whose transcendent virtues
> Are those to be most admired
> Loved and adored and indeed
> Her virtues are all inclusive. (124)

Although the sonnet's conventional celebration of the wife's virtues may sound parodic, it echoes Stein's sincere description of the beloved in "Lifting Belly," which is similarly adulatory: "Lifting belly is so strong. I love cherish idolise adore and worship you. You are so sweet so tender and so perfect" (19).

The "husband" and "wife" motif in "Patriarchal Poetry" is also taken over from "Lifting Belly" where Stein writes:

> Lifting belly is so kind
> Darling wifie is so good.
> Little husband would.
> Be as good.
> If he could. (*YGS*, 49)

Read in light of its connection to "Lifting Belly," then, the sonnet celebrates a love that coincides with both the values of the patriarchy and with Stein's own, and it forces a reconsideration of Stein's attitudes toward the patriarchy. Moreover, if, as she writes, patriarchal poetry is the same as patriotic poetry, we should remember that Stein herself spent the decade between "Lifting Belly" and "Patriarchal Poetry" writing war poetry that was patriotic. This poetry also places Stein in a more cordial relationship to patriarchal/patriotic poetry than we might have first imagined. In addition, at this time, she was writing works that would be published in *Useful Knowledge*, a book about America and about her pride in being an American. She commented, "Writing about Americans comes to be very much what is natural to any one thinking that it is pleasant to be one."[1] Thus, in the context of all of Stein's poetry written during this period, "Patriarchal Poetry"—so easily understood by Stein's most recent readers as antihierarchical, deliberately anticanonical, and opposed to univocal meaning—yields up such meaning less willingly.[2] It does not stand alone as the single expression of Stein's attitude toward the patriarchy, nor is its meaning quite so singular as its repetitive calling upon patriarchal poetry would seem to be.

Perhaps Stein's relationship to the patriarch of her family is one thing, her ideas about patriarchal poetry another. According to Lisa Ruddick, the rage that Stein felt against her father, distanced in *Three Lives* (1909), was identified with and directed against him in *The Making of Americans* (1925). In killing off her father in that long work, Stein also did away with the nineteenth century and invented the modern novel, in Ruddick's view (55).[3] But, in turning to poetry and to the new subject of her love for Alice B. Toklas and the early years of their new life together (which they spent as volunteers for the American Fund for the French Wounded in World War I), Stein was able to take a new position toward the patriarchy and toward patriarchal poetry insofar as its two major subjects are love and war. First, her relationship with Toklas allowed her not only an identification, if only parodic, with a patriarchal marriage but also access to a celebratory subject. Second, the joint war work of Stein and Toklas extended that identification to Stein's place in society. In the war, she could think of herself as doing the work of the patriarchy, and she could also exercise her maternal feelings in caring for the young soldiers. Thus, she was freed from the narrow confines of her role in her family of origin and allowed to occupy a wide range of psychological positions.

Quite apart from her personal experience, poetry that could be called patriarchal was her chosen genre. She wrote it. In fact, it is not too much to say that she invented patriarchal poetry for the twentieth century. While Ezra Pound was studying the Troubadours and T. S. Eliot was detailing the impotence of J. Alfred Prufrock, Stein was writing poetry on the patriarchy's own subject—war.

Between "Lifting Belly" and "Patriarchal Poetry"—one long poem ostensibly about love and the other about the patriarchy although both about both—lies a decade in which Stein wrote patriotic poetry. This poetry, like her war experience, was almost unique both among women and men writing about World War I. It differed from the war poems Wallace Stevens wrote at home haunted by the statement of the poet Jean Le Roy, "I am sorry for the man who has not seen this war."[4] And it differed as well from H.D.'s poem addressed to her soldier-husband, "I envy you your chance of death" (319). Living in France and seeing the war at closer range, Gertrude Stein had no occasion to envy anyone. In fact, her war experience was considered so unusual that she was able to publish war poetry in such popular magazines as *Life* and *Vanity Fair* at a time when she was having great difficulty in placing her work in avant-garde journals.

Claiming that the real Stein was funnier in every way than the imitations of her style that had been published when *Tender Buttons* came out (*SW*, 161), Stein urged the editor of *Life* to print the original. He agreed and published two things, one about Woodrow Wilson and one about her war work. Although she admitted that "Mr. Masson [the editor] had more courage than most," in fact, publishing in *Life* was the ultimate recognition by the patriarchy itself (161). "Relief Work in France" appeared in the January 1917 issue of *Life* entirely set in upper case, as the anxious and uninformed editor explained: "*Miss Gertrude Stein sends us this contribution from Paris, and it has been set in the style of type in which Miss Stein's verses usually appear*" (*R*, 13).

Of course, "Miss Stein's verses" did not usually appear in any style of type partly because they were often devoted to the taboo subject of her passion for Alice B. Toklas and partly because they were written in what was considered a hermetic style that even editors of little magazines were reluctant to publish. The exception was her experimental prose poem *Tender Buttons*, which had been published by the poet Donald Evan's private press.

Stein's war poetry was a quite different experiment. First, its publication in popular magazines provided Stein with a potential audience for essentially the first time, and that fact changed her writing. Second, much of it was in short form, a new and unusual choice for her. Brevity had never marked Stein's work. In choosing the short poem to describe her experiences in the war, she was treating such moments as discrete, abandoning the idea of completeness that she had absorbed from her scientific training and expressed in her lengthy early works and abandoning too her habit of writing continuous works without regard to form.

For this new experiment, she had to confront new problems in the limitations of form itself. In her early work, she had written every day without much concern for the discrete text; her long works run on, changing styles freely. By choosing the short form, she accepted the convenience of form, acknowledging not only the boundaries of the text but also the limits of war as a subject. For her, war appeared to be an anecdote, not a complete history, although paradoxically she devoted much of her career to writing about it. At the same time, her new useful role in the war effort allowed her a new sense of identity or rather an awareness of the boundlessness of her connection to the world. She began to see herself not only as a nurturing and maternal figure, an image latent perhaps in her early writing and now available as an imaginative strategy as well, but also as an active participant in the essentially male war effort.

Perhaps for all these reasons—her new awareness of an audience, her new form, her new sense of identity—her war poetry is also an experiment in writing in the more lucid style that she was to use again some twenty years later when she wrote *The Autobiography*. The hermetic style of *Tender Buttons* had been useful to conceal as she expressed her erotic attachment to Toklas. Its secretive style perfectly expressed the open secret of Stein's newfound passion. By contrast, war was both public and an adventure, an event to explain, an experience to advertise. It was a man's world, and she wrote about it in the accessible style she might have wanted to identify as a man's style in the same way that she wrote *The Autobiography of Alice B. Toklas* in what she might have imagined as Toklas's style. On the subject of war, she composed by situation and event, as well as by melodic sounds, in response to requests for a poem as well as in response to remarks she heard and registered. Her work as a driver for the army hospitals brought her in contact with a whole new generation, the young soldiers, and a new vocabulary, and a new idea of censorship, all of which found their way into a poetry of passionate commitment and experience.

Although Suzanne Clark does not discuss Stein in her book on sentimental modernism, she might have considered Stein's war poetry as an expression of sentimental modernism especially where Stein articulates the sense of maternal power that became part of her war experience. Like Emma Goldman and Kay Boyle, whose expressions of maternal identity Clark does discuss, Stein presents the image of the strong woman, capable of adventures but also of helping and healing, devoted to the community and to a communal effort. The maternal Stein had always been a part of her identity, but for the woman known as the "Mama of Dada," this new maternal role was not an occasion for public derision. It had rather a more practical side, but one that was not without its sentimentality or a wide appeal.

Again, her experience was not simply sentimental and maternal. It was, in fact, quite different from the experience of women as described by Sandra Gilbert and Susan Gubar in their treatment of this period: "when their menfolk went off to the trenches to be literally and figuratively shattered, the women on the home front literally and figuratively rose to the occasion and replaced them in farms and factories" (2:271). Whereas those women were released from the home to work during the war, Stein, who had never felt imprisoned at home, found in her war work a way to express those deeply embedded maternal feelings usually associated with home. More than that, whereas women who sent their sons and lovers off to war with encouraging words faced a complex of emotions—liberation and guilt, freedom and fear, erotic pleasure and censure, pride and envy—Stein seems to have experienced only the more positive of these emotions.[5] Her war poems are singularly unconflicted in their concern for the wounded, in their sense of the worthiness of her own tasks, and in their enthusiasm for the adventure.

Unlike the average woman's experience, her experience was also different from that of the men who wrote about the war.[6] She was not a combatant and faced none of the fears and traumas that the war soldier knew; still she was there, she saw the suffering, she was a witness. If she was not a combatant, neither was she a pacifist. She questions neither the cause nor the effect of the war. Her war poetry indicates the complexity of her relationship to the patriarchy and to the gendered issues of her time; it also suggests the difficulty of classifying any war poetry by gender.

The poem that appeared in *Life*, "Relief Work in France," has five short sections that swivel toward the questioning American audience and back toward the questions of the French wounded. It is an effort to describe her activity as simply as possible and, at the same time, to use her knowledge of both the French and the Americans in order to serve as a cultural ambassador. Leaving out only the connectives, she is informative, opening with "The Advance": "In coming to a village we ask them can they come to see us. We mean near enough to talk; and then we ask them how do we go there. / This is not fanciful" (*R*, 34). For two women starting off in a vehicle, which one of the women did not know how to drive and the other did not know how to back up, into an unknown area of a country at war, the work was indeed "not fanciful." As she explained it almost twenty years later in *The Autobiography of Alice B. Toklas*, when they were sent to Perpignan in the south of France, they had never been farther than Fontainebleau in the car "and it was terribly exciting" (*SW*, 163–64).

The second section of "Relief Work in France" turns to the French wounded. "In the meantime what can we do about wishes?" the speaker asks, and the French soldier responds, "What are you doing for my niece?" and is answered, "Baby clothes. / And milk." Then to both audiences the speaker says, "The right spirit. There are difficulties, and they must be met in the right spirit" (*R*, 34). In the last section, "Again," the speaker seems to be uncommonly patient toward her questioners, assuming the tone of the travel guide: "Are the French people healthy? / I think them healthy." "That is a question I meant to ask. / It is answered" (35).

Certainly the editor of *Life* had reason to wonder at the non sequiturs, the non-narrative quality of the text, the sketchiness of the details, even the format of the piece as a poem. But, in the context of her earlier writing, these war poems are uncharacteristically explicit, revealing Stein trying to explain to the patriarchy that part of the war she saw. Her statements both to her American and her French audiences are those of an apologist for the existing order.

"Relief Work in France" launched Stein on a new kind of writing. Absent from it are those experiments that would separate her from her audience—the effort to find "words that made whatever I looked at look like itself," as she said in *Lectures in America* (*LA*, 191), or to "describe not only every possible kind of a human being, but every possible kind of pairs of human beings" as in *A Long Gay Book* and *The Making of Americans* (148). The war poem's short, pointed, descriptive style reflects a new attitude toward the world she witnessed. Although Stein claimed in "Composition as Explanation" that the "war may be said to have advanced a general recognition of the expression of the contemporary composition by almost thirty years" (*SW*, 521), her war poems seem to have returned her to the nineteenth century where, she claims, "explaining was invented" by English men "living a daily island life and owning everything else outside" (*LA*, 40). Explaining the war was her subject. Somewhat like those English writers, Stein as a war poet was isolated within the foreign country where she lived, and that metaphoric "island" existence allowed her the vantage point of an outsider from which she could "own" imaginatively what she saw.

Her war poetry was different from her own early writing and also different from that of other American writers. It does not inveigh against the moneylenders and the politicians as Ezra Pound's does nor lament the dead as Wallace Stevens's does nor detail the ravages of war as T. S. Eliot's does. Nor is it an account of her private anguish as are H.D.'s war poems. Stein's attitude is rather like Walt Whitman's in his Civil War poetry; her war poems are the work of a compassionate tender of the wounded even if they lack Whitman's pictorial style and direct evocation of the scene. But, unlike Whitman and also unlike most of her contemporaries, Stein does not express any doubts about the rightness of the war effort.

Still, when her poem "The Great American Army" was published in *Vanity Fair*, its editor was no more certain than the editor of *Life* of what Stein was attempting. To the poem published in June 1918 he appended this note: "Gertrude Stein, the first and most representative of the so-called Cubists in prose, has, since the outbreak of the war, been living in France and working in war relief as an ambulance driver. Few American women have taken a more active part in the conflict than she. During the past few weeks, the continued arrival of our troops in France has inspired her to compose this poem" (*R*, 13).

Although Stein did title later poems "Cubist," as we shall see, "The Great American Army" is hardly such a work. Rather, it is as patriotic as any patriarchal poem could be, celebrating "The Great American Army," which may be—like the acorn the speaker finds—"Green / In the center. / No, on the end," but which is nonetheless ready to serve (*R*, 36). "And what must *we* do?" they ask, and again, "What do the boys say? / 'Can we?'" (36). The coming of the young, eager, willing Americans inspired a patriotic fervor in Stein. In her close-up view, she expressed nothing but affection and admiration for them. Later, she was to write: "Gertrude Stein always said the war was so much better than just going to America. Here you were with America in a kind of way that if you only went to America you could not possibly be" (*SW*, 174).

The coming of the Americans was the subject of her next war poems. But when the editor of *Vanity Fair* published "J.R.," "J.R. II," "The Meaning of the Bird," and "A Deserter" in March 1919, he commented, "*Whether or not you like her art form—or lack of it, rather, whether or not you understand the cryptic meaning of her verses, there she is, and there is her influence, and there are her changes, and there they will remain*" (*R*, 13). Whatever her influence, "J.R." and "J.R. II" are too brief and cryptic to be completely meaningful, although they do establish the speaker's position in the war, "In the midst of it. / And the respected fields" (38). And to the question in "J.R.," "Did you have the pleasure of an American" (38), "J.R. II" responds, "We had fish and Serbs and pleasure" (38). This enigmatic combination had an earlier expression in *How Could They Marry Her?* (1915) in which Chapter VIII opens, "I wish to find an experienced nurse to leave immediately with our party for where the Urgent Fund for Serbian wounded is establishing a base hospital under the Serbian Government" (27). The next chapter starts with "Boiling. / Ardent fishes" (27).

The connection between fish and Serbs obviously had some private significance to Stein, who uses them to underscore "pleasure" even in the war.

The other two war poems in *Vanity Fair* mark a change from the plain style of these earlier poems to a play with rhymes that insist on the artifice of the poem and its textual boundaries. Not about the French war wounded but rather again about the Americans, "The Meaning of the Bird" is a poem about Nîmes where Stein spent part of the war. It opens with a list of infinitives describing common and uncommon acts ("To play baseball" or "To have feather hair") and then slides into a kind of compulsive rhyming:

> And to do that
> Is Nimes
> As she seems
> With United Statiens
> With feathers for tens
> Of thousands
> Who love ice creams
> Alas there is none in Nimes. (*R*, 39)

A quite different short poem, "A Deserter," was written, she informs us in *The Autobiography*, on long trips through the countryside to bring into Nîmes the soldiers and officers who had fallen ill of "the spanish grippe" (*SW*, 174). It is about the aptly named "Narcissus Deschamps," a deserter whose two brothers were killed in the war. He deserts and is caught. The story is told in poetic form, then repeated in prose, as if Stein were meditating on its point, perhaps because, as she writes, "I cannot forget Narcissus Deschamps" (*R*, 40). "Simple Narcissus flung in a flower. / It does sound like that," she opens the poem (40). But the story is no myth, and its meaning to Stein is not so clear as the story of "Simple Narcissus." The love here is not erotic but familial. Its meaning is expressed not in the lush language of Stein's erotic poetry but in an economy of language that moves toward the simple conclusion, "We know him," in a new tone of seriousness (40). The wartime activities that Stein often represented as high adventures are solemnized here.

Nonetheless, even with a new audience and a new subject, she was not always so solemn and direct. Stein could take an interest in the formal opportunities that the poem presented to her. Even when she was asked for a contribution to the bulletin of the American Fund for the French Wounded, she was not willing to descend to a bulletin style, however much she might have been expressing the sentiments of the fund. Rather, she sent the bulletin "Our Aid," which it did not print:

In the middle.
All around
And the wedding.
It is bound
To release the middle man.
And we can be left to fan.
What.
The nearest of kin
We have met many of them. Some look like Leon Bonaparte others
    look like brothers and some just like children.
And all of them.
All of them are worthy of a caress.
The little English that we know says, We cannot miss them. Kiss
    them.
We meet a great many without suits.
We help them into them.
They need them to read them to feed them to lead them.
And in their ignorance.
No one is ignorant.
And in their ignorance.
We please them. (*BTV*, 184–85)

As an occasional poem, "Our Aid" teeters back and forth between lines
of internal rhyming and flat statement ("No one is ignorant"), suggesting
two voices—that of the poet and of the bystander, that of the wound tender and of the cynic, that of Stein herself and of someone like Hemingway
who took a more jaundiced view of the war. But, paradoxically, though the
internally rhyming lines may seem trivial, in fact they are not deflated by
the sober voice saying, "What" or "And in their ignorance." Rather, the
disjunction strengthens the sincerity of the rhyming sentiment.

The desire to be absolutely clear in her description of the war effort is
made parodically evident in "The Work" (1917), which was in fact published in the bulletin of the American Fund for French Wounded. She
provides a running commentary on her meaning in the text itself:

I see a capstan.
This meant that we knew the direction.
I see a straight, I see a rattle, all things are breathing.
This means that I had learnt to go down hill. (*BTV*, 189)

And again, by way of explanation, she repeats herself:

Soldiers like a fuss.

Give them their way.

This is meant to be read they like a fuss made over them, and they do.
(193)

Or "Please then and places. / This is apropos of the fact that I always ask where they come from and then I am ashamed to say I don't know all the Departments but I am learning them" (193). But in the context of Stein's work, this effort, which may appear to play with the obtuseness of the audiences she knew she would have in the bulletin, may be seen as another use of her favored forms of expression, repetition and insistence.

For all her pleasure in the experience and expression of her war work, she was quick to state, "It is not a joke. / A war is not a joke" (*BTV*, 192). What she saw of the war were homesick, wounded, needy young boys, and she opens "The Work" with "Not fierce and tender but sweet. / This is our impression of the soldiers" (189), ending with, "I finish by saying that the french soldier is the person we should all help" (194). "The Work" is studded with notes that "This is an interview" or "Please be an interview," as if Stein were responding to a request from the bulletin to give an eyewitness account.

A poem about the war, "The Work" is also a tribute to the French, to their cuisine, their kindness, their gentility even in time of war. Like a cultural anthropologist, Stein makes many observations about the natives and their country: "it is reasonable to be well fed and they are in France. It is astonishing how well everything works" (*BTV*, 189); "we were always meeting people and that it was pleasant" (190); "Of course there were hotels and many of them were most sympathetic" (191); "We do not understand the weather. That astonishes me. / Camellias in Perpignan. / Camellias finish when roses begin"; "It is astonishing that those who have fought so hard and so well should pick yellow irises and fish in a stream" (194).

What interests Stein is the humanity of the soldiers and their compatriots. Hers is not the war poetry of the combatant nor entirely of the patriot. Because she is writing about helping the wounded of another country, she is free from some of the stereotypical reactions to the war, free from jingoism as well as from pacifism. "We are not mighty. / Nor merry. / We are happy" (*BTV*, 193), she comments, and the context makes it clear that "happy" signifies the willingness to rise early and visit hospitals. Such happiness came from being useful rather than mighty, although it did not assuage Stein and Toklas when they came up against real battlefields in Alsace where, Stein wrote later in *The Autobiography*, "To any one who did not see it as it was then it is impossible to imagine it. It was not terrifying it was strange. We were used to ruined houses and even ruined towns but this was different. It was a landscape. And it belonged to no country" (*SW*, 176). A French nurse told Stein, "c'est un paysage passionant, an absorbing landscape." Even the few people there seemed strange: "one did not know whether they were chinamen or europeans" (177). The strangeness of the real war forms a contrast to the hominess of her work behind the battle lines, and Stein, always alert to landscapes, is struck by it. But she does not linger on this description, going on immediately to mention her car's broken fan belt.

Despite the intrinsic interest of her experience in the midst of the war, the poetry that she wrote did not become part of the war poetry in America. If the editors of *Vanity Fair* and *Life* and even the bulletin of the American Fund for French Wounded were willing to publish Stein's war poetry, the literary journals were not. Her positions were too advanced and her expressions too new for the 1914 war issue of *Poetry* with its pacifist message and the assurances expressed by Carl Sandburg's "Among Red Guns" in its refrain, "Dreams go on."[7] Stein was also more current than Ezra Pound, who had reasonable reservations about the *Poetry* war issue, but tried a variety of expressions of his own war emotion, universalizing it through myth in "The Coming of War: Actaeon," published in the March 1915 issue of *Poetry*, "translating" from T. E. Hulme's conversations about his war experience in "Poem: Abbreviated from the Conversations of Mr. T. E. H." (1915), wondering in "Near Perigord" whether Bertran de Born's canzon was inspired by love or war, and finally raging against the politicians in the Hell *Cantos*.[8]

Living in France and working for the American Fund for the French Wounded, Stein's ideas and attitudes were distant from the concerns of Americans viewing the war from the other side of the Atlantic. Moreover, she brought to the war certain preoccupations that again separated her from her fellow American poets. Like all war poetry, Stein's was informed by subjects that had concerned her in earlier work.

One such subject was the question that she posed in all her early work about her relationship with Toklas: how much could she say? In Europe and at the front, Stein found that this was exactly the question that the war censors addressed. Revealing the details of the public war was as taboo as revealing the details of her private erotic life. The poet writing about either subject had to exercise restraint. In writing about her erotic experience in *Tender Buttons*, Stein had resorted to puns, word play, nonsense, and coded language to express and simultaneously conceal her subject. In "Why Win Wings. On a Hat" (1918), Stein uses another method of simultaneous disclosure and concealment by acknowledging without naming the experience. The unmentionable act appears to be a private one, although the need to remain silent about it is a need that will appear again in her war poetry:

> We had it to-day.
> And we were pleased.
> We can not be nervous.
> All the drink saw it.
> We did not say the taste.
> We are satisfied.
> We cannot conceal.
> Then you say.
> Necessity.
> Can we be careful together.
> Can you mention a dog.
> She will not let me finish. (*BTV*, 205)

Whatever "we" had today, it is over, and it is not to be mentioned in its mentioning. If it is to be the subject of the poem—"We cannot conceal"—it is also to be something shared intimately, but not revealed—"Can we be careful together." If it is over, it is also ongoing as its first and last lines indicate—the first in Stein's playful perversity announcing the end and the last declaring its endlessness.

The question of what can be said and when and if it can be said is, in fact, the topic in several poems that Stein wrote when she was in Nîmes at the end of the war. For example, "In the Middle of the Day, Part II" opens with "Can we say that. Can we say that," and the reply is, "Do not mean presently. / Then when can we mean" (*BTV*, 206). Again, "In Their Play" concludes: "It is this that we are able to say. / Can we say to-day / Can we mean to be elfish" (207). And "Can you Speak" opens, "Can you speak / Teaches. / When can you please me" (209).

The reverse of censorship also interested Stein as, during the war, she picked up statements that could be placed in poems. For example, "A Poetical Plea" (1917–18) (*BTV*, 195), Thomson notes, is about an American officer who " '*at everything his eyes lit on*' always said '*I would like a photograph of that.*'" Opening with "I would like a photograph of that said Captain Dyar," Stein goes on to suggest that *her* war, unlike Captain Dyar's, was no mere substitute for the Grand Tour but a matter of pure need, and her plea is at least as political as poetical: "I need the money to give away. / To the mutilés and the reformés" (195). The two desires—for photographs and for money—both lead to the statement, "But you must not be stupid," and to the conclusion:

> In this way we must.
> Excuse me.
> In this way they must
> You excuse me. (195)

In this way, she distances herself from Captain Dyar, using repetition not to bind the poem together, but rather to keep the two speakers apart. But Captain Dyar's remark stayed in Stein's memory to be used again in "American Biography and Why Waste It," where she interjects into an aleatory composition: "I would like a photograph of that said Captain Dyar. / What he saw of them made him see that" (*UK*, 169).

Like the found poem in Stein's repertoire of everyday experience that could be expressed in the war poem is the occasional poem written to commemorate some event. Because these poems, too, were limited so definitely in subject, they posed particular problems of form for Stein. She entertained those limits as part of her subject, admitting in one poem, "I can answer any question" (*BTV*, 186), and claiming in another, "I do not like to close. / But you must" (188).

The rigidity of military order is the subject of "Decorations," describing a fourteenth of July parade in Nîmes in which American troops participated. Stein writes: "If the general goes first they all follow him. If the captain goes first those follow him. If the officer goes first they go behind him. If the iron wire is torn they go if not even though they be the children of everything they do not need to go" (*BTV*, 185).

As if to verify this position, the speaker says, "This was said to me." But even within the hierarchy of war, the whole question of what to believe becomes pertinent, and the speaker advises, "The best way to go is to believe in reading" (*BTV*, 185). As if that position were too simple, a dialogue ensues: "You are making fun of me. Not at all. I am literal. I say they do not drink coffee there. / I do not wish to write down what I hear" (186). Whatever the speaker hears, she is convinced that the American and French soldiers "will sing together and one will be won together. This is what we think" (186). Although she might entertain some uncertainty about the situation, asking, "Did I make a mistake about decoration," her impulse is nonetheless to assert, "I know the meaning of decoration," "I can answer any question," and "I believe what I hear" (186–87).

In "Decorations," although she is writing about the order and hierarchy of war, Stein breaks out of the simple and self-explanatory style of her other war poems by including any number of private references to Degal-lay, Leon, Henry, Willy, Ezeroum, Trebizonde, Erzingan, Edwstrom, Mr. Gilbert, Mr. Louis. Her own poetic order is casual as she moves through oddments of meaning: "What was the life of the bee. / I forgot to mention trumpets. Whistles are known. / Sit in the chair with the pleasure of seeing the old women mutter" (*BTV*, 185). The poem ends, "Not this again. / Knot this again" (187), as if the speaker knew that she would have to repeatedly tie up the loose ends of a situation that would never end.

Stein's interest in representation and order appears again in the poems "A League" and "More League," originally titled "Two Cubist Poems. The Peace Conference I." The importance of Cubism to Stein's work has been detailed by Jacqueline Vaught Brogan, but these two poems are Cubist only in the illogic of their organization.[9] "A League," which opens the series "Three Leagues," displays a Cubist playfulness:

> We gather that the West is wet and fully ready to flow.
> We gather that the East is wet and very ready to say so.
> We gather that we wonder and we gather that it is in respect to all of
>   us that we think.
> Let us stray.
> Do you want a baby. A round one or a pink one. (*UK*, 84)

The next poem, "More League," reports "A vote all around," "We refuse, I refuse" and finally, returning to the baby image of the first poem, "Is there a mother." Next in "Events" is "The President and the President / And he says he is not dead," and Stein's wish that with his death there would be a new order: "We believe in further wishes." By the time Stein took up the subject of the League of Nations, she had moved from reporter to analyst, and, as she writes in "Woodrow Wilson," "History is told and the rest is to unfold and the rest is to be retold and the rest leaves us cold" (109).

As her war experiences receded into her own history and as Cubism itself became a remoter moment in that history, Stein moved into a new style and new subjects. Though "Patriarchal Poetry" may be, as she wrote, "the same as Patriotic poetry," the poem itself is not about the subject that elicits most patriotic poetry—war. It is rather

> Patriarchal Poetry at peace.
> Patriarchal Poetry a piece.
> Patriarchal Poetry in peace.
> Patriarchal Poetry in pieces. (*YGS*, 133)

It is about peace among other things. Despite its title, the poem is not "patriarchal" in the sense that it is written about, by, or to the patriarchy. It is rather a commodious poem receptive to many subjects and interests, and perhaps, in that sense, it is "patriarchal" in fostering a whole family of concerns, in including everything.

In his introduction to the poem, Virgil Thomson writes: "*In 1927 Miss Stein remarked to me that she was writing a long piece to be called 'Patriarchal Poetry.' 'There are all these emotions lying around; no reason why we shouldn't use them' she said*" (*BTV*, 251). According to him, Stein was immersed at this time in the neo-Romantic movement "of which the chief originality lay in the restoration of personal sentiment, of emotion, to a major place in art's overt subject matter." In addition, she was working during this period constantly on grammar and rhetoric. She was later to claim that paragraphs are emotional, and, Thomson claims, "*Patriarchal Poetry*" is "*significant for its research into the paragraph both as a literary form and as a carrier of pure emotion. The structure of emotion is its theme*" (251–52). It counts on repetition for its power, much as Romantic music does.

Ulla Dydo traces some of the details of "Patriarchal Poetry" to the *cahiers* in which Stein wrote or Toklas copied her work, noting that the word play between "patriarchal" and "patriotic" derives from the title of one of these *cahiers* in the series *Chants Patriotiques*. In addition, she notes, "their origin and their history patriarchal poetry their origin and their history" (*YGS*, 115), which seems to fit perfectly in the context of patriarchal poetry, also echoes the subtitle of *The Making of Americans: Being a History of a Family's Progress* and is a literal translation of *son origine and son histoire* from the title of a notebook in the series *Chants Patriotiques* ("Reading the Hand Writing," 92). But, despite the playful and aleatory origin of "Patriarchal Poetry" that Dydo traces here, she concludes, in another comment on the poem, "In 1927 she wrote a piece entitled 'Patriarchal Poetry,' which implied that patriarchal poetry, along with other hierarchical systems, was dead and needed to be laid to rest," and then she quotes the passage about peace and pieces cited above ("Gertrude Stein," 56).

Dydo goes on to argue that "Patriarchal organization is vertical, hierarchical and fixed. The landscape of Stein's world is horizontal, democratic and fluid" ("Gertrude Stein," 57). Stein writes, "There never was a mistake in addition" (*YGS*, 106). Certainly, "Patriarchal Poetry" is a long and inclusive poem, perhaps full of emotion but full, too, of a variety of commentaries in which Stein identifies with the patriarchy. In the beginning, the speaker (if the poem can be said to have a speaker) is "Wishing for Patriarchal Poetry" (107), and in the end, the speaker "Having patriarchal poetry" concludes, "Patriarchal poetry and twice patriarchal poetry" (146), apparently harboring no antagonism toward the genre.

Stein's "Patriarchal Poetry" is associated with much that she admires. For example, she associates it with days of the week and with her coded term for orgasm, writing, "chose one day patriarchal means and close close Tuesday. Tuesday is around Friday and welcomes as welcomes not only a cow but introductory. This always patriarchal as sweet" (YGS, 110). And immediately, she thinks of patriarchal poetry in terms of food: "Patriarchal poetry and ham on Monday patriarchal poetry and pork on Thursday patriarchal poetry and beef on Tuesday" (111). Between these two connected paragraphs is what may appear to be the pompous language of the patriarchy but which actually includes a justification of the word "cows" that Stein used for orgasm and that is transformed into beef in her long paragraph about food: "Patriarchal in investigation and renewing of an intermediate rectification of the initial boundary between cows and fishes. Both are admittedly not inferior in which case they may be obtained as the result of organisation industry concentration assistance and matter of fact and by this this is their chance and to appear and to reunite as to their date and their estate. They have been in no need of stretches stretches of their especial and apart and here now" (110–11). Even in the patriarchy, Stein argues, "Both are . . . not inferior." The connection too between "cows" and "beef" in the paragraphs on days of the week and on food suggests that, however "Patriarchal" the investigation may be, its end is to "reunite" flesh with flesh, "stretches of their especial."

Moreover, in noting "Their origin and their history" and admitting that "Patriarchal poetry makes no mistake" (YGS, 115), Stein goes on to comment on something quite outside that origin and the patriarchy—the doubling of two people, an apparent reference to her relationship with Alice B. Toklas since she concludes, "I double you, of course you do. You double me, very likely to be. You double I double I double you double. I double you double me I double you you double me" (115) with "When this you see remarkably" (116), a play on her frequent refrain, "When this you see, remember me."

Toklas is not the only person mentioned in the poem. Shortly after this passage, Stein writes, "Does she know how to ask her brother" (YGS, 117), and continues: "These words containing as they do neither reproaches nor satisfaction may be finally very nearly rearranged and why, because they mean to be partly left alone. Patriarchal poetry and kindly, it would be very kind in him in him of him of him to be as much obliged as that" (117). The problems between the brother and Toklas may be the subject of the next long passage of the repeated "Let her be" that concludes, "Never to be what he said" (121).

Letting *her* be what she wants to be, Stein moves back into the family again in order to define patriarchal poetry: "Patriarchal poetry she said what is it I know what it is. . . . I know what it is it is on the one side a to be her to be his to be their to be in an and . . . at first it was the grandfather then it was not that in that the father not of that grandfather and then she to be to be sure. . . . To be sure not to be sure to be sure correctly saying to be sure to be that. It was that. She was right. It was that" (*YGS*, 124).

Patriarchal poetry, so defined, belongs to "her" as much as to him. It is "she" who is right, who knows what patriarchal poetry is, and, I want to suggest, it is she who writes it. The passage above is followed by the sonnet, then more commentary on patriarchal poetry, and finally the statement, "To like patriarchal poetry as much as that is what she did" (*YGS*, 125). If, as she goes on, "Patriarchal poetry makes it a master piece like this," it is Stein's own work that exemplifies it and "master piece" is soon translated into "peace," "Patriarchal Poetry as peace to return to Patriarchal Poetry at peace" (133).

Although Stein appears to dissociate herself from patriarchal poetry, claiming that "When this you see remember me should never be added to that" (*YGS*, 134), she goes on, in fact, to connect herself with "Patriarchal Poetry intimately and intimating that it is to be so" by suggesting, "Even what was gay" and, "Like it can be used in joining gs" (135). Later, she adds, "A line a day book. / How many daisies are there in it. / Patriarchal Poetry a line a day book" (140), referring perhaps to her "A Birthday Book" (1924). Thus, she can announce, "Patriarchal Poetry reclaimed renamed replaced and gathered together" (140–41). Asking "Is it best to support patriarchal poetry Allan will patriarchal poetry," Stein answers, "Patriarchal Poetry makes it incumbent to know on what day races will take place and where otherwise there would be much inconvenience everywhere" (142).

Finally, it is not just convenient information that patriarchal poetry has; it is "Patriarchal Poetry in pieces. Pieces which have left it as names which have left it as names to to all said all said as delight" (*YGS*, 145). It may be "Dinky pinky dinky pinky dinky pinky dinky pinky once and try. Dinky pinky dinky pinky dinky pinky lullaby," but "Patriarchal poetry has to be which is best for them at three which is best and will be be and why why patriarchal poetry is not to try try twice" (146). "Patriarchal poetry and twice patriarchal poetry," the poem concludes (146).

Although the poem itself is generously inclusive in its definitions of patriarchal poetry, readers have been able to extract single lines in order to summarize its point as, for example, Ruddick does in citing the line

"Patriarchal Poetry is the same" and suggesting that such poetry is the creator of "Univocal meaning," "one of the illusions and oppressions of patriarchal thinking" (197). From this reading, Ruddick can generate an elaborate interpretation of Stein's work that fails, among other things, to take into account the extent to which Stein identified with patriarchal poetry, supported it, considered even that she was writing it.

Although the term "patriarchal" may concentrate certain specific political meanings for feminist critics in the 1990s, Stein did not appear to understand the word in the same way. For her, patriarchal does not seem to be one part of a binary opposition; rather, it is all-inclusive. Patriarchal poetry is not, in Stein's mind, poetry written by or for the patriarchy; it may be rather poetry as the originator and generator of meaning. When Stein told Thomson that there were "all these emotions lying around; no reason why we shouldn't use them" in the long poem she was writing, she may have been indicating her interest in the neo-Romantic painters who were turning to emotion as the subject of art; but she may also have been suggesting something about the structure of the poem she was writing as varied, aleatory, accommodating.

At the same time, Stein was interested in introducing a variety of emotions in the poem, including her feelings for her father, her grand-father, her brother, as well as for Toklas. She also wanted to cover the full range of emotions from patriotic to erotic, from familial to spousal, from war to peace, in a text that would be compendious enough to allow her to use whatever she had at hand. She was interested, as she wrote in "Composition as Explanation," after the war "in an equilibration, that of course means words as well as things and distribution as well as between themselves between the words and themselves and the things and themselves, a distribution as distribution" (*SW*, 521). She goes on to suggest that equilibration and distribution are interesting when "using everything and everything alike and everything naturally simply different has been done" (522). In "Patriarchal Poetry," Stein demonstrates her powers of equilibration and distribution.

But such equilibration as Stein practiced in "Patriarchal Poetry" was not to last in the world she witnessed, and a little more than a decade later the world was again at war. In an article published in the *Atlantic Monthly* in November 1940, she explains how frightened she was: "We were spending the afternoon with our friends, Madame Pierlot and the d'Aiguys, in September '39 when France declared war on Germany—England had done it first. They all were upset but hopeful, but I was terribly frightened; I had been so sure there was not going to be war and here it was, it was war, and I made quite a scene" (*SW*, 615).

This event turned Stein back into war as a subject, and, between 1940 and her death in 1946, she wrote four major works: "The Winner Loses: A Picture of Occupied France," quoted above; a novel, *Mrs. Reynolds*, written in 1940–43 and published as volume two of the Yale editions of her work in 1952; her war diaries, *Wars I Have Seen* (1945); and *Brewsie and Willie* (1946), a series of conversations between American nurses and soldiers in liberated Paris. Although these works have been attacked for what critics have perceived as their superficiality and shallowness, their restricted perspective, their provinciality and triviality, they are a depiction of the way one elderly woman experienced the war in occupied France. Maria Diedrich argues of Stein's work here: "She strove to replace universal HIStory by a personalized and individualized HERstory. In doing so, she not only forced her readers to review critically and question the paradigms of their discourse and to abandon canonized expectations of coherent sense, but she also induced them to perceive the diversity as well as the immediacy of experience. At the same time, she shattered the belief that an event like World War II can still be reconstructed according to the rules of what Jacques Derrida was later to call logocentrism, that is, the cultural hegemony of sense—rationality, linearity, and hierarchical order."[10]

These comments were anticipated by Stein's own awareness, expressed in "Composition as Explanation," that "Everything alike naturally everything was simply different and this is and was romanticism and this is and was war" (*SW*, 521). She goes on to explain the importance of war to her modern composition: "And so the art creation of the contemporary composition which would have been outlawed normally outlawed several generations more behind even than war, war having been brought so to speak up to date art so to speak was allowed not completely to be up to date, but nearly up to date, in other words we who created the expression of the modern composition were to be recognized before we were dead some of us even quite a long time before we were dead. And so war may be said to have advanced a general recognition of the expression of the contemporary composition by almost thirty years" (521). Stein came to this conclusion in 1926. It has taken almost seventy years for her readers to draw the same conclusion.

The patriotism of Stein's World War I war poetry and even her interwar "Patriarchal Poetry" gave way to pacificism as she witnessed World War II. Diedrich claims: "Surrounded by aggressive patriotic slogans that called men to arms against fascism, that challenged women to sacrifice their sons, brothers, husbands, and lovers on the altar of democracy, Stein and her neighbors, men and women alike, are depicted in her writing as living the conviction that anything, any compromise, any truce, albeit difficult and embarrassing, is preferable to war" (104). Thus, Diedrich counters denunciations of Stein's experience in World War II—her silence on anti-Semitism, her apparent sycophancy and opportunism as she, an American Jew, remained safe in occupied France. Acknowledging that Stein "repeatedly begins to discuss the question of the holocaust and always breaks off abruptly," Diedrich asks, is it "not an honest portrayal of the human mind recoiling from knowledge, of the Jew afraid of losing her protective shield, of an avowal that she is unable or unwilling to continue? Is silence a form of applied polemics?" (102). Surely, Stein was not the only Jew confronting the Holocaust who chose silence, but for a writer given to words, such a choice reveals the intensity of her response. What else had ever silenced Gertrude Stein?

From her earliest poems written during World War I to her late prose about World War II and reflections on atomic warfare, war as a subject dominated Stein's imagination, and yet it was a subject that she always tried to fit into her daily life. Just as she situated her early love poetry against the war that was raging around it, later wrote poetry about the experiences she and Alice B. Toklas had in their volunteer work for World War I, and even after the war accommodated patriotic poetry in a wide-ranging long poem, so too her writing about World War II was aimed at providing a view of daily life during war. As Diedrich notes, "The men's view of an increasingly dubious *ars moriendi* is replaced by the woman's matter-of-fact account of the everyday heroism of survival" (90). Stein concludes "The Winner Loses" with confidence: "I had my own private prediction, and that was that when I had cut all the box hedges in the garden the war would be all over. Well, the box hedge is all cut now today, the eighth of August, but the war is not all over yet. But anyway our light is lit and the shutters are open, and perhaps everybody will find out, as the French know so well, that the winner loses, and everybody will be, too, like the French, that is, tremendously occupied with the business of daily living, and that that will be enough" (*SW*, 637).

The business of daily living was always exciting for Stein, and she participated in some of its most turbulent moments in war-ridden twentieth-century Europe. She was anxious to celebrate neither its violence nor its victories, neither its sorrows nor its heroisms. Rather, she wrote as a woman taken up at first by the adventure of serving the wounded in World War I, then moved by the young soldiers she came to know there. Turning to poetry to write about World War I, Stein interrupted her early long prose writings as if war itself were to be only a brief interval in her lifelong experiment in composing the twentieth century. But war was to remain her subject, as late in her life she returned to prose to chronicle World War II. In the epilogue to *Wars I Have Seen*, she writes: "It is pretty wonderful and pretty awful to have been intimate and friendly and proud of two American armies in France apart only by twenty-seven years. It is wonderful and if I could live twenty-seven more years could I see them here again. No I do not think so, maybe in other places but not here" (*SW*, 694).

She sounds like a patriot here, although she also could write, "the war is over and this certainly this is the last war to remember" (*SW*, 693); what she finds so wonderful and so awful is not the military prowess of the American armies so much as the young men themselves and her own friendship with them. They said, "Write about us," she claims, and, throughout her war writing, that was her purpose.

3

G Is for
Geographical

Perhaps it was because she was an American and lived so long abroad that Gertrude Stein had an interest in geography or place. Or perhaps, to repeat Grahn's view, it was because she was a lesbian. Geography fascinated her throughout her career, and it is an interest that she shares with Elizabeth Bishop and Adrienne Rich. The poetry of place has found its expression in minor forms—the pastoral, the georgic, the topographical poem of the eighteenth century—and so the interest of women poets in geography might appear to confirm the time-honored suspicion that women are minor artists. Not for them the epic. But it is exactly this hierarchy of genres that Stein demolishes in her lifelong fascination with geography. In her early collection, *Geography and Plays*, she mixes genres, including poems, prose poems, essays, portraits—all presumably under the general heading of geography—along with her plays. In an essay introducing the collection, Sherwood Anderson praises this mixture of genres: "Here is one artist who has been able to accept ridicule, who has even forgone the privilege of writing the great American novel, uplifting our English speaking stage, and wearing the bays of the great poets, to go live among the little housekeeping words, the swaggering bullying street-corner words, the honest working, money saving words, and all the other forgotten and neglected citizens of the sacred and half forgotten city" (8). She did write what she called novels, plays, and poems, but Anderson is right in locating her interest chiefly in the city of words. In this sense, all that she wrote can be called lyric poetry. She does not change voice when she moves through genres in *Geography and Plays*. For example, in the opening poem, "Susie Asado," she writes:

> Sweet sweet sweet sweet sweet tea.
>   Susie Asado.
> Sweet sweet sweet sweet sweet tea. (*GP*, 13)

In an essay, "In the Grass (On Spain)," she continues:

>   Kiss a turn, close.
>   Suppose close is clothes, clothes is close.
>   Be less be seen, stain in burr and make pressure.
> This is bit. (80)

In "Accents in Alsace: A Reasonable Tragedy," she writes: "Sweeter than water or cream or ice. Sweeter than bells of roses. Sweeter than winter or summer or spring. Sweeter than petty posies" (415).

All written in a brief period and about her commitment to Toklas, this poem, essay, and play may be viewed simply as the product of a single voice arbitrarily divided into genres. But even in the long course of her career as she continued to think about geography, when Stein moved beyond poems into other genres to detail scenes, to write plays or travel essays, to describe an audience, her interests, as we shall see, always came back to considerations that started in her poetry. Thus, even when she appears to try out various genres, Stein does not make a great distinction among them, always speaking in her own lyrical voice.

Stein's interest in geography, along with that of Bishop and Rich, has been little noticed. Indeed, even poets such as Marianne Moore and Elizabeth Bishop, two of America's great observers of geographical facts, have appeared for a long time to be detailers of the merely eccentric. In an effort to offset this view, recent reevaluations of the work of women poets have minimized this interest in geography in favor of their radical revisions of history. For example, new interest in H.D.'s poetry is directed at her mythic and historical discoveries rather than at her startling geographical relocation of all history in *Helen in Egypt*. And, despite the fact that she designated her interest in geography in the titles of two volumes of her work, Gertrude Stein has been acclaimed for her experiments with time rather than place, for her interest in the "continuous present" rather than for the way she ordered her world through geographical notations.

Such an emphasis on Stein's experiments with time connects her with the High Modernists; but her interest in geography would tie her to women poets both of her generation, such as Marianne Moore and H.D., and of a later generation, such as Bishop and Rich, whose work fastens on location, even if it cannot be entirely split off from history. Elizabeth Bishop could write, "More delicate than the historians' are the mapmakers' colors" (*CP*, 3), although she too linked geography and history. Geography and the "continuous present" provided Stein with a different approach to history, removing her from strict attention to its narrative sequences and turning her instead toward history as composition, as movement in space. Geography encouraged the redrawing of a map that historians might have fixed too firmly, the creation of a history in a reconfigured geography. For women writers, these possibilities proved irresistible.

Geography figures in the titles of at least two of Stein's books: her early collection, *Geography and Plays* (1922), and her later *The Geographical History of America, or The Relation of Human Nature to the Human Mind* (1936). And in *Useful Knowledge*, a collection of her writings on America, she concentrates on particular geographical locations, always identifying them in opposition to other locations, as in "Wherein the South Differs from the North," "Wherein Iowa Differs from Kansas and Indiana," "The Difference between the Inhabitants of France and the Inhabitants of the United States," and "Near East or Chicago." It is in the first of these essays that Stein describes her interest in geography as a place for exploration:

Not only but also the explorer should be able to know how to and also to recognise the spots he has seen before and which he will recognise again as he occupies as he successively occupies as he occupies successively the places he recognises and not only that he occupies them successively but also that he will later be able to make maps of the region which he has traversed. Such is the duty of an explorer. In short it depends upon him in short he is to realise that he is to acquire knowledge of the directions of the direction of a direction of previous visits and successive visits. It becomes necessary therefor [*sic*] that he indulges in active plans and map drawing and also in constant observation and relative comparisons. In this way he easily finds his way. (*UK*, 32)

For Stein, who interestingly enough describes herself as the explorer in masculine terms, the "spots he has seen before and which he will recognise again" are not just places on a map, although they are that, but also Wordsworthian "spots of time," places to which she will return in time and at different times. They are "spots" also of light and of a "difference in the light" that can be seen—"A little observation as to the impression made upon one by observing the difference in the light and heat made by artificial light and the sun, also the difference made by the impression as to how it all had happened" (31). They are "spots" of insight and illumination, "Expectantly shining, as is easier than that and not always fairly presentable" (32).

Making maps of the region she has traversed recently, Stein is trying to chart the direction of her emotional life as she began her relationship with Alice B. Toklas, the direction of her experiments in writing as she moved away from narrative and toward poetry, as well as the direction of her actual travels before and during World War I. The immediate source of this writing may have been her wartime experiences traveling in the south of France where she met American soldiers from all over the United States, an experience that drew her attention to the political differences that have a geographical base in American history. Also, in Elizabeth Fifer's view, Stein is writing about the "geography" of her sexuality, a geography that has to do with the dominance of a conquered territory where Stein represents the warmer, more emotional South, and Alice B. Toklas is the colder, more intellectual North (94).[1] Fifer goes on to claim that "These maps are puzzles, mazes, dangerous journeys. Their very inaccessibility only emphasizes their fragile and vulnerable nature. Even so, the explorer might enjoy the difficulty of the terrain" (94). Maps are, then, another way of coding Stein's erotic experience, a means of pointing the way without giving away the secrets.

This sense of geography as a mapping of unknown and perhaps un-knowable territory parallels Stein's sense of language as itself a surface presentation of the multiple possibilities of her experience that, like a map, can be read backwards and forwards, up and down, in no particular sequence. Stein's experimentation with language is itself a placement of words in space. Her early commentators were quick to pick up her own language in order to describe her writing in geographical metaphors. For them, the metaphors had to do with displacement of words or their replacement in new contexts. In his introduction to *Geography and Plays*,

Sherwood Anderson writes: "There is a city of English and American words and it has been a neglected city. Strong broad shouldered words, that should be marching across open fields under the blue sky, are clerking in dusty dry goods stores, young virgin words are being allowed to consort with whores, learned words have been put to the ditch digger's trade" (7). Stein's experiments are, in Anderson's estimation, cleaning up the environment: "For me the work of Gertrude Stein consists in a rebuilding, an entire new recasting of life, in the city of words" (8).

William Carlos Williams praises Stein along the same geographical lines. In "The Work of Gertrude Stein," an essay published in *Pagany* in 1930, he writes: "Having taken the words to her choice, to emphasize further what she has in mind she has completely unlinked them (in her most recent work) from their former relationships in the sentence. This was absolutely essential and unescapable. Each under the new arrangement has a quality of its own, but not conjoined to carry the burden science, philosophy and every higgledy-piggledy figment of the law and order have been laying upon them in the past. They are like a crowd at Coney Island, let us say, seen from an airplane" (116). And, of *Useful Knowledge*, Williams notes: "Stein's pages have become like the United States viewed from an airplane—the same senseless repetitions, the endless multiplications of toneless words, with these she had to work" (119). Stein's contemporaries here praise her for the experiments they imagined the modernists and particularly they themselves were perfecting—Anderson's release from decorum and Williams's detachment from conventional usage.[2] But their geographical metaphors are true to Stein's own inclinations.

Stein herself explains how she became interested in location through her war work in "The Work," where she writes, "Please then and places. / This is apropos of the fact that I always ask where they come from and then I am ashamed to say I don't know all the Departments but I am learning them" (*BTV*, 193). And again, in her poem about the war, "I Expressed My Opinion,"

> In Iowa
> In Idaho
> In Illinois
> In Tennessee
> Indeed
> In there.
> And what did they say.
> They said they don't like puzzles.
> We give them jam. (210)

Stein herself draws the connection between experimental writing and experimental geography in "Scenery":

Call a man a mountain Shasta.
Answer.
Mount Shasta or Mount Blanc or a mountain in the South. I can
    make geographical tastes.
We have decided upon so long.
We used to make a joke. (217–18)

In *The Autobiography of Alice B. Toklas*, Stein describes her interest in the American soldiers whom she met in Nevers: "It was quite a thrilling experience. Gertrude Stein of course talked to them all, wanted to know what state and what city they came from, what they did, how old they were and how they liked it" (*SW*, 170).

In the garage in Nevers where she was getting her car fixed, she met two American soldiers whom she called "California" and "Iowa." And at this time, she claims, she conceived "the idea of writing a history of the United States consisting of chapters wherein Iowa differs from Kansas, and wherein Kansas differs from Nebraska etcetera" (*SW*, 170). "She did do a little of it which also was printed in the book, Useful Knowledge," she adds (170). Thus, the conventional civility of greeting a compatriot is converted into an understanding of place in American history.

Connected with this source of her interest in geography was also her attitude toward her early scientific training. In her writing before the war, she had relied on that training to classify and describe what she saw. But she soon gave up that ambition because, as she explains in "The Gradual Making of *The Making of Americans*," although "science is continuously busy with the complete description of something . . . with ultimately the complete description of everything" (*LA*, 156), she was not interested in describing everything because that would depend on telling everything she knew, whereas she preferred to "let come what would happen to come" (158). And so she changed from her habit of scientific description which she connects with history to an interest in creating time as a space of movement. In this, she was, she declares, quintessentially American: "a space of time is a natural thing for an American to always have inside them as something in which they are continuously moving" (160–61). Conceiving time as "space" is an American habit because American history has stretched out in space moving westward as land opened up in successive waves across the continent. The closing of the American frontier took place just a few decades before Stein wrote *The Making of Ameri-*

cans, and William Gass has connected Stein's understanding of American history with that of Frederick Jackson Turner, who developed the thesis that the open frontier determined the course of American history (11). Thus, in thinking about the making of Americans, Stein came to an interest in the space of America.

When she visited America in 1935, she began to experience America geographically or naturally as a space in time. Traveling from east to west, she wrote an article for the *New York Herald Tribune* in which she stated: "And then we went west and then I began to begin to know what I now do know about the physical aspects of the land, the water is a part of the land, it is not land and water it is water in the land, that is what makes it American. And this is what makes it so real and so strange and so detailed and so there and so romantic" (*New York Herald Tribune*, April 6, 1935, 13).

Geography became a fascination for Stein also because she lived in a foreign country and during a time of war. As she writes in *Paris France* (1940): "It really takes a war to make you know a country, I had only known Paris until 1914 and then I learned to know France, and now once again living here all winter in a provincial French town I once more realise that a war brings you in contact with so much and so many and at the same time concentrates your isolation" (*PF*, 72).

In addition, living in France provided her with a second country. As she explained in *Paris France*, "After all everybody, that is, everybody who writes is interested in living inside themselves in order to tell what is inside themselves. That is why writers have to have two countries, the one where they belong and the one in which they live really. The second one is romantic, it is separate from themselves, it is not real but it is really there" (*PF*, 2). She goes on, "Of course sometimes people discover their own country as if it were the other . . . but in general that other country that you need to be free in is the other country not the country where you really belong" (2–3).

Living in France, then, Stein had the two countries necessary for a writer; she also had a heightened sense of the geography of the actual country, of geography as a distinctive category in which to locate herself and others, of geography as a "spot of time." It was a subject that interested her throughout her career, starting with her most abstract treatment of it in her writings of 1913 in *Geography and Plays* to the more accessible *Paris France*, the loving tribute to France she wrote before World War II.

In the new edition of *Geography and Plays* (1993), Cyrena N. Pondrom lists the essays with geographical titles under the classification "Concrete, alogical style, celebrating the 'simply different,' stressing selection from the lexicon" and identifies the style as "'lively words' style; uses prose format, non-sensical 'sentences'" (lvii). Still, in discussing works from this period, Pondrom concentrates on the portrait, "Braque," rather than the number of essays that are not portraits but geography: "France," "Scenes. Actions and Dispositions of Relations and Positions," "In the Grass (On Spain)," "England," and "Americans"—all written in 1913, the same year as "Braque." In this, Pondrom simply follows earlier critics of Stein who have tended to emphasize the portraits of her early period and, in fact, Stein herself, who emphasizes her portraits in the series of lectures explaining her work that she gave in America in 1935 after the publication of *The Autobiography of Alice B. Toklas*. One can only conjecture about Stein's reason for choosing to emphasize her portraits in her comments on her early work; perhaps it had to do with her desire to link her own experiments with the experiments in the arts, with portraiture as a literary experiment. It may also be that because she continued to write portraits throughout her career, she could tie her work together by concentrating on them. And it may be that Stein, ever interested in publicity, could attract attention to her portraits by their subjects—Picasso, Matisse, Braque, for example—whereas her interest in geography was too general, too abstract, to be immediately attractive to the general audience she was addressing.

Nonetheless, having published *Three Lives* and *Tender Buttons*, Stein chose to emphasize not portraits but geography in the title of the first general collection of her work that she selected for publication. *Geography and Plays* divides in two with an emphasis on geography in the first half followed by plays in the second half of the book. The essays at the beginning of *Geography and Plays* that name geographical locations or identities—"France," "Americans," "Italians"—are distinctly not descriptions that particularize countries or nationalities; but, as they are placed together, they point to Stein's interest in something more abstract even than her experiments in portraits. If in her portraits she was trying to capture the "rhythm of anybody's personality," as she said (*LA*, 174), in these essays she appears to be interested in finding a location, setting directions, and naming the differences between one place and another, as she writes in "France": "What is up is not down and what is down is not reversing and what is refused is not a section and what is silenced is not speaking" (*GP*, 27). Again, "In cross and across, in that show and wide there is the sensory statement that there is night rule and a winter rule and even the chamber is empty and watches why are watches lighted," or "Excuse the point that makes a division between the right and left that which is in the middle in between. Surprise an engagement, surprise it so that an agreement is all the time" (37). But directions are hard to establish, and differences may be subtly drawn, as she notes: "A pleasant little spot to have gold. The same spot is used for silver. The gold is the best way to keep it. The silver is the way to keep silver" (38).

If all this appears to have little to do with France, it does have to do with directions, divisions, oppositions, although in "Americans," Stein argues, "A gap what is a gap when there is not any meaning in a slice with a hole in it. What is the exchange between the whole and no more witnesses" (*GP*, 39). She can also ask, "What is a hinge. A hinge is a location. What is a hinge necessarily" and state, "A and B and also nothing of the same direction is the best personal division there is between any laughing" (40).

"Americans" is also about words as divisions and additions as she plays with sounds in "Icer cream, ice her steam, ice her icer ice sea excellent, excel gone in front excel sent" (*GP*, 42). Again, she plays with the name of the country itself as:

America a merica, a merica the go leading s the go leading s cans, cans be forgot and nigh nigh is a niecer a niecer to bit, a niecer to bit. (43)

And Stein continues with this word play:

To irregulate to irregulate gums.
America key america key.
It is too nestle by the pin grove shirr, all agree to the counting ate ate pall. Paul is better.
Vest in restraint in repute.
Shown land in constate. (44)

In making up words, dividing words, playing on words, Stein is also playing with the idea of America as a state, "irregulate," "constate."

The next essay, "Italians," dates from 1908 to 1910 and belongs to Stein's early repetitive or intensive style (*GP*, lvi), although it too is interested in the differences among "them," as it develops its point:

Being different each one from any other one of them and this being a completely simple thing, being each one of them not needing being one going on being living if any one has been listening and being all of them listening, and all of them being living is something that gives any one of them gives all of them a way of being one doing anything any one of them are doing so that any one can be quite certain that it is a thing that is being existing and again and again every one can be looking and again and again can be certain that that thing is a thing completely to be existing. (57)

Beyond these first essays on nations and people, *Geography and Plays* continues with "A Sweet Tail (Gypsies)" and "I Must Try to Write the History of Belmonte," vaguely Spanish subjects, and then another geographical piece, "In the Grass (On Spain)" which opens, "Occident all Spain and the taste" (*GP*, 75). It is also in the "alogical style" where "Spanish cut that means a squeeze and in place of water oil and water more. Mine in the pin and see cuttle cuttle fish call that it is that it is sardine, that it is in pelts and all the same there is paper in poles paper and scratches and nearly places" (76).

Suddenly "In the Grass (On Spain)" moves to a story of "paper in poles," perhaps the writing of her relationship with Alice B. Toklas as a "pole." Food imagery proliferates here: "Any roast is not leading"; "A melon within then"; "A little return bitten with a cake set white with ink"; "A peach a peach pear" (*GP*, 76–77); and, finally, "What you call them what you call them say butter butter and let us leaves and a special a realteration lace a realteration lace" (81). Looking back, it becomes clear that this geography of "realteration" is a geography of difference—"being different" in "Italians," "irregulate" in "Americans," "in place of water oil" in "In the Grass (On Spain)."

The food imagery in this Spanish story picks up hints from "France," especially butter, which has a sexual reference for Stein: "Butter is not frozen, this does not mean that there is no bravery and no mistake" (*GP*, 32); "The likelihood of dipping and drawing and digesting and drinking and dirtying not dirtying smoking, the likelihood of all this makes such an order that every discussion is simultaneous" (33); "A lime is in labor, a lemon is cooler, a citron is larger, a currant is redder, a strawberry is more vexed, a banana is straighter" (35); "Cut a slice to show a pear" (38). "Americans" starts out with "Eating and paper" and goes on to develop its own food imagery, also drawing on the sexual reference of butter: "When the butter cup is limited and there are radishes, when radishes are clean and a whole school" (40); "Win, win, a little bit chickeny, wet, wet, a long last hollow chucking jam, gather, a last butter in a cheese, a lasting surrounding action" (41); and then again a reference to Toklas, whom Stein called a "Pole": "Poles poles are seeds and near the change" (44). In their food imagery, these essays on countries seem to draw on the same source of inspiration as *Tender Buttons*, where food is linked to erotic experience.

The interest here in geography is also a way of using actual locations to express nonsensically the variety of her love and sexual desire for Alice B.

Toklas, as she writes in "In the Grass (On Spain)": "Spain is a tame name with a track a track so particular to shame, a track a little release in sold out casts a little next to saleable old cream. Able to pass" (*GP*, 80). And she concludes, "A Spanish water and a coop shape mine and legs and reed ridiculous red, and little lively hue, little lively hue and copper, little lively hue and copper up" (81).

In "England," the essay that follows, Stein opens with an insistence on the importance of food, arguing first that one should "Cane sour asparagus and do not season with reason" (*GP*, 82). But butter is the predominant image, obsessively present in the opening pages: "A pleasant taste and plenty of butter" (83); "there is butter, a whole city is not subdued it is iniquitous" (84); "Butter which is every where has a little table" (84). But the essay soon moves away from food and on to abstractions, although Stein combines the idea of food and land, announcing: "A land is not more seen than a beefsteak and a beefsteak is wasted" (86); "A bloom on a red thing means that there is a single country. An apple offered means that there is no disgrace" (87). Here, too, as in the mention above of dirty, Stein includes with her erotic references her sense of "disgrace" and shame.

Written in 1913, as her relationship with Alice B. Toklas was beginning to be fixed and war was declared, "England" is also about the importance of geography to war where "Nothing is perplexing if there is an island. The special sign of this is in dusting. It then extends itself and as there is no destruction it remains a principle" (91). War carries over into "Mallorcan Stories" with its mention of "McKinley's eagle. / Pope's prayers for peace. / Pins and needles ship" (96).

As the collection *Geography and Plays* moves toward the plays, Stein does not neglect her interest in geography, titling the next essay, "Scenes. Actions and Disposition of Relations and Positions." Concentrating on what scenes are not, Stein seeks to dispose entirely of positions, writing: "To have the land behind when there is no sea has that to do which is not settling that which is more than free. It is so natural that the opinion is there" (*GP*, 107). Again, "A page of no addresses does not mean a mistake it means that there are places where the whole family is glad to eat together" (117). But where are those places? Stein wants to locate them and dislocate them simultaneously, stating, "there is a little square center and no center, . . . the same thing is the place unset, the same time is tomorrow, there is no date to marry" (118). Keeping both location and lack of location open, the essay concludes: "It does not mean that, it means that the time and place and more is so satisfied that there is no place, and any place is no vacation. . . . There is that establishment when there is no land and any land that shows the line is that and is one. Any extra way is the way of speaking. There is no use in no more" (121).

Here, in locating herself by negating place, Stein employs multiple forms of negation to create a mood of dissociation.[3] It is a favorite device that Stein uses in her experimental writing to create a sense of lack or indifference that is at odds with the forward movement of the writing itself so that the language seems intentionally misleading.

And yet, working against this element of dissociation, Stein was at pains to situate her plays. Moving from poems to so-called plays, she does not change voice or themes so that the division between genres seems irrelevant except that a play is identifiably a public utterance, completely dependent on audience. Again, in the titles of the plays, Stein indicates an interest in geography—for example, "For the Country Entirely" and "Mexico." And even "Pink Melon Joy," her celebration of lesbian eroticism, mentions "Maps. / I am thinking" (*GP*, 376). In part, thinking about maps is for Stein a contemplation of how she can map out her emotional experiences. She returns again and again in this long poem to geography as if that order would give her some hint of how she might order her own world. She writes: "Let us consider the french nation, let us watch its growth its order its humanity its care, its elaboration its thought its celebrated singing and nearly best nearly best with it. Let us consider why we are in authority, let us consider distribution, let us consider forget me nots" (369).

Then, she is emboldened to write, "I mentioned gayety" (*GP*, 369). Gayety is itself a country, as she admits, "I am just gradually beginning to get to look around" (370). Or gayety is the wish for a country, as she writes: "By nearly wishing for a country by nearly wishing for a country, by this you will spoil her. Do you. Do you ask for Greek. Do you deny Spain. Do you not praise England. Do you prize England. I said that I believed in the country and that I was silent in the city" (370). "Pink Melon Joy" acknowledges at the end, "I looked for the address"; but it concludes, "Would you have another. / What. / Kiss" (376). The search is for the location, the country, where such kisses are possible.

Geography and Plays ends with brief commentaries on Stein's war work, again identified by location. She describes: "We were taking a trip. We found the roads not noisy but pleasurable and the shade there was pleasant. We found that the trees had been planted so as to make rows. This is almost universal. // In coming to a village we ask them can they come to see us we mean near enough to talk and then we ask them how do we go there" (*GP*, 399).

"Lands of Nations. [Sub-title And Ask Asia]" and "Accents in Alsace: A Reasonable Tragedy," "The Watch on the Rhine," "The Psychology of Nations or What are You Looking At" conclude *Geography and Plays* with notes on geography and the war, on places she saw. In "Accents in Alsace," Stein writes, "The names of cities are the names of all. / And pronouncing villages is more of a test than umbrella" (*GP*, 415). Alsace was a valuable location for anyone interested in geography since it had been annexed by France and then by Germany so that its accents were constantly changing, becoming actually "A Reasonable Tragedy" or a tragedy that derives from the unreason of politics. According to Ulla Dydo, Stein made use of the mixed language of Alsace to express her love for Toklas in this play, offering the work as a birthday present to Toklas (*SR*, 314).

Stein had little to say about *Geography and Plays* in *Lectures in America*, where she seems interested in that collection only as it forms a progression with *The Making of Americans* and *Tender Buttons* as a period marked by "the strictness of not letting remembering mix itself with looking and listening and talking" (*LA*, 196). Although she maintained her interest in looking, in trying to see things as if for the first time and not as if she were remembering how she should see them, she claims that she became "more and more excited about how words which were the words that made whatever I looked at look like itself were not the words that had in them any quality of description" (191). But, as this survey of *Geography and Plays* suggests, she was doing more than looking in this period. The geographical essays are also reflections on her desire for Alice B. Toklas, her erotic play, her wartime experience, as well as her travels in new and strange countries. Geography became a repository for all kinds of feelings, mentioned randomly, mentioned again not in successive order, just as the eye ranges over a map backward and forward, up and down.

Geography is also connected in Stein's mind with scenes, the scenes of the plays she was beginning to write as well as the scene of the theater with its audience. In the series of four lectures she gave in March 1935 when she returned to the University of Chicago, Stein did begin to articulate ideas about geography and nations as they relate to her audience. Lecture four opens: "After all anybody is as their land and air is. Anybody is as the sky is low or high, the air heavy or clear, anybody is as there is wind or not wind there. It is that which makes them and the arts they make and the work they do and the way they eat and the way they drink and the way they learn and everything" (*N*, 46).

This statement with its expression of the most regressive determinism appears totally out of character for Stein, whose experimental writing was always designed to detach people from their comfortable and accustomed ways of seeing and being. But Stein launches out from this comment to consider that she has been bothered by reading two books that are interesting but will not be read in five years, and that brings her to answer the question of whether or not she writes for an audience. She responds with the inquiry, "What is it to be an audience," and answers, "That is to say can does any one separate themselves from the land so they can see it and if they see it are they the audience of it or to it" (*N*, 51). It becomes clear that Stein is concerned here, as elsewhere, with showing her audience how to see things not in "prepared" ways but newly. For her, if each generation had something different to look at, it is "that composition is the difference which makes each and all of them then different from other generations" (*SW*, 513). These interests came together as Stein turned her attention to play writing where the time and space of a scene was a matter of new composition, as she explains in her lecture on "Plays": "I may say that as a matter of fact the thing which has induced a person like myself to constantly think about the theater from the standpoint of sight and sound and its relation to emotion and time, rather than in relation to story and action is the same as you may say general form of conception as the inevitable experiments made by the cinema although the method of doing so has naturally nothing to do with the other. . . . The fact remains that there is the same impulse to solve the problem of time in relation to emotion and the relation of the scene to the emotion of the audience in the one case as in the other" (*LA*, 104).

Stein's awareness of the "problem" of scene may have derived from the quite different "theater" of war, as she explains in "Composition as Explanation" when she argues that "Nothing changes from generation to generation except the thing seen and that makes a composition" (*SW*, 513). She then recounts the remark of Lord Grey that when the generals talked about the war before the war, they talked about it as a nineteenth-century war although it was fought with twentieth-century weapons. "That is," Stein writes, "because war is a thing that decides how it is to be when it is to be done"; it is "prepared" like old-fashioned writing and not like experimental writing, "a thing made by being made" (513–14).

Connected with her interest in scene is also a concern for the audience of her writing and particularly the emotion of this audience, specifically Toklas. In the new composition for this audience, Stein was also attempting to solve the problem of how to include emotion in the abstraction of a composition or how to find an audience beyond Toklas who would "rescue" the emotions she was relating through scenes, as Fifer notes

(*Rescued Readings*, 60). In "A Sonatina Followed by Another," a long poem, written in Venice in 1921, in which Stein encodes her passion for Toklas through associations of the landscape, she moves to obscure the too open revelation of her sexual relationship—"No I was personal. In the french sense" (*BTV*, 5)—by being quite specific about her address— "Address me to number thirteen rue San Severin and St. Anthony" (5). Or again, she follows "Why is pussy like the great American Army. Because she buds so many buddies" by "And now I want to explain again the difference between the South of France and Brittany. In Brittany they have early potatoes. In the South they have early vegetables" (6).

Stein continues this description at length and then adds, "I address my caress, my caresses to the one who blesses who blesses me" (*BTV*, 6). Here, acting as her own censor, Stein uses the specificity of geographical details to dislocate or draw attention away from the private expression of passion. It is a form of coding.

Again, in "Annex to No. 2 / Sonatina Followed by Another / Not Yet Sat But Walking," Stein continues describing the scene, this time in Normandy, as "In the forest by the sea in feathers, two white feathers have decorated Normandy," and continues, "We are spending our honeymoon in Normandy" (*BTV*, 18). But eventually she feels she cannot go on, and she writes: "This is a list of my experiences. I cannot describe beauty. I cannot describe a square, I cannot describe strangeness. I cannot describe rivers, I cannot describe lands. I can describe milk, and women and re-semblances and elaboration and cider. I can also describe weather and counters and water" (21).

She does, of course, continue, "I suddenly see the scene. And the scene sees me" (*BTV*, 26). And she goes back to crossing sexual revelations with geography: "Then we'll go on. / In different countries ploughed fields are softer than in others. In different countries in different countries can you guess by the F" (26). The long poem concludes with the speaker locating herself in her own country: "How I can have the air of here and there and I say it to you I say it to you I love my own little jew" (31).

Once more in *Capital Capitals* (1922), Stein turns to geography for her subject; here, the capital cities of Provence—Aix, Arles, Avignon, and Les Beaux—form the subject of the play that Virgil Thomson was to set to music for four male voices and piano in the spring of 1927. Stein composes in terms of four capitals because, she writes: "We have often been inter-ested in the use of the word capital. A state has a capital a country has a capital. An island has a capital. A main land has a capital. And a portion of France has four capitals and each one of them is necessarily on a river or on a mountain" (*SR*, 416).

In a chorus of the four voices of the capitals, Stein develops notions of the landscape and the weather because, as she admits, "I feel a great deal of pleasure of satisfaction of repetition of indication of separation" (*SR*, 426). This play is really a play on words, a theatrical performance that adds to the voice and theme of her lyrics an audience that came to interest Stein.

But, far from Provence, it was her own country that formed the basis of *Useful Knowledge*, the first selection of her writing to be published in America after *Geography and Plays*. In the opening, "Introducing," Stein indicates her awareness both of her own new construction and of her audience's reluctance to accept it: "He was a young one and he was clearly understanding this thing and he was certainly often very clearly explaining this thing. . . . Some one might be thinking that he might be more successfully than doing some other thing but really not any one thought he should not be doing the thing he was doing when he was doing the thing" (*UK*, 1).

Thus, Stein creates her own audience for a writing about America that included many other "things." Although she selected the pieces in this collection because they reflected the theme of America, they range over other interests as well, opening with a love note to Toklas, "Farragut or A Husband's Recompense," an account of their lovemaking and their quarrels and their settling "on the hill" where "I said is it likely that I am stubborn" (*UK*, 15). In "Part Two: How Farragut Reformed Her and How She Reformed Him. 'Oh that frightens me,'" Stein moves from their quarrels to her desire to be "natural," and so she concludes, "That's a good thing to talk about, apples. Apples and cows" (18). This leads into "Wherein the South Differs from the North," which opens "An agreement in it," as if the quarrels of the preceding selection had been settled. As the South is "As fat as that" (20), Stein seems to be associating herself with the South and to be identifying someone else as "North," since "North used to the same. The north used to see the same" (19), an indication that North is also a woman or that North sees in the "prepared" and not the new way. North and South argue and move but eventually settle down "Feeling an attraction the or center center of course," "North and south nestles" (29). In the end, North and South marry or "Come to Mary, a name. North a name come to Mary. North. Come to Mary. South" (37). The poem masks the emotional drama by reference to geographical differences that divided American history and also divide her peacetime activities in Paris from her wartime in the south of France.

In the next essay, "Wherein Iowa Differs from Kansas and Indiana,"

Stein abstracts the states from references to people and relocates them in an effort to "Otherwise seen and otherwise see and otherwise seen to see, to see otherwise" (*UK*, 38). In this geography, there are degrees of distinction as in "Iowa means much," "Indiana means more," and "Kansas means most," or "This is the difference between those three" (38). But there are still questions, as Stein claims: "A question is made to state something that has not been replied to there. / Is Iowa up or down. / Is Indiana down and why. / Is Kansas up and down and where is it." "These are questions only because no one thinks of three things at one time" (39), she states. In matters of composition and of geography, Stein prefers to compare not three but two things as in the next essays, "The Difference between Inhabitants of France and the Inhabitants of the United States of America," "Near East or Chicago: A Description," and "Business in Baltimore." In "Scenes from the Door," Stein returns to consider the war and again the geography of the war, as she writes in one of the scenes, "Red Faces":

Can you give me the regions.
The regions and the land.
The regions and wheels. (78)

And in "America," she writes, "Once in English they said America. Was it English to them" (80).

Stein's attention turns to Americans as she writes about compatriots—"Allen Tanner" and "Emily Chadbourne," "A Valentine to Sherwood Anderson," "Van or Twenty Years After. A Second Portrait of Carl Van Vechten," "Emmet Addis the Doughboy: A Pastoral," and "Woodrow Wilson," which ends, "When you make an ending you end the ending by realising that no truth is repeatedly read" (*UK*, 113). Still, surveying the landscape of her country, she writes, combining Walt Whitman and John Keats: "Going from San Francisco and Oregon and leaving out all who won any and all of us are pleased to say leaves, leaves are dry, grass grass is wet, creeks creeks are rushing and birds birds whistle" (113–14).

Commenting on her own writing in "American Biography and Why Waste It," Stein asks: "Do you see any connection between yes and yesterday, I will repeat this, do you see any connection between yes and yesterday. There is a way of recording an arbitrary collision but in inventing barbed wire and in inventing puzzles there is no arbitrary collision. Not at all" (*UK*, 162). Arbitrary collision is what fuels much of what Stein writes as she develops her sentences by playing with rhymes: "but they they were there and they met to declare, what, the air, to the air and by the air. Here is not there. Everywhere is not there nor is it here nor there. I declare and they declare. And the air. We do not recognise an heir. So there" (166–67).

At the same time that Stein was writing the essays of *Useful Knowledge*, she wrote "geography." Ulla Dydo claims that "Geography is never simply about location, scenery, and the space of the earth, though it includes these. It is about the arrangement of words in compositional space, the disposition of elements from inside" (*SR*, 467). Stein writes, "Geography pleases me that is to say not easily. Beside it is decided" (468). For Stein, geography was interesting only as it was not decided, as she notes, "It is a very interesting thing to know that it is as new as it is to you" (469). And then, she makes up her own geographical notations that hide her designation of "B" or Baby or Toklas as "best," writing: "I stands for Iowa and Italy. M stands for Mexico and Monte Carlo. G stands for geographic and geographically. B stands for best and most. It is very nearly decided" (469). Although she warns, "I know how to wait. This is a joke. It is a pun," she also concludes, "Geography includes inhabitants and vessels. / Plenty of planning. / Geographically not at all" (470).

Stein drew on her recent trip to America in 1935 to write *The Geographical History of America, or The Relation of Human Nature to the Human Mind*, a meditation on the geography of America, on identity, literary masterpieces, and audience. The subject of her book aroused the attention of the Paris *Herald Tribune* to which she gave an interview, admitting that the book was based on personal observations of last summer's activities of three members of her household—Toklas, Pépé, the Chihuahua, and Basket, the poodle. The book sets up a distinction between human nature and a purer state of existence, human mind, which, commenting to a reporter from the newspaper, Stein explains by reference to politics:

> People have a peculiar attitude toward being governed, in that they allow themselves to be governed not by people who think but by people who have never thought in their lives. . . . Do you think men like Hitler and Mussolini ever think? . . . Not on your life. Human nature, not the human mind guides their actions, and the people, mind you, put up with it. And yet in every other kind of human relations the people demand the use of the human mind as well as human nature. Obviously nothing constructive can develop in government so long as the leaders are in a state of identity instead of entity.[4]

By the time *The Geographical History of America* was published in 1936, Stein's interest in geography had shifted away from her erotic relationship with Toklas, away from Europe, away from war, and toward her own reputation as a writer of masterpieces and her new awareness of her native country and of its politics. Nonetheless, as Gass points out in his introduction to the Vintage edition of the book, she retained here her earlier interest in the continuous present because "the present was the only place we were alive," and, "although, as William James had proved, the present was not absolutely flat, it was nevertheless not much thicker than pigment. Geography would be the study appropriate to it: mapping body space" (*GH*, 8–9). Gass explains her method:

> Just as the order of the numbers in a sum makes no difference, just as there is no special sequence to towns on a map, the mind and the masterpiece may pass back and forth between thoughts as often and as easily as trains between Detroit, Duluth, and Denver, and chapter headings are, in fact, only the names of places. Oral literature had to be sequential (like music before tape), but type made possible a reading which began at the rear, which repeated preferred passages, which skipped. As in an atlas, the order was one of convenience, and everything was flat. A geographical history rolls time out like that. (41)

In an earlier introduction, Thornton Wilder explained why a book purportedly about the creative act should be called *The Geographical History of America*:

> Miss Stein, believing the intermittent emergence of the Human Mind and its record in literary masterpieces to be the most important manifestation of human culture, observed that these emergences were dependent upon the geographical situations in which the authors lived. The valley-born and the hill-bounded tended to exhibit a localization in their thinking, an insistence on identity with all the resultant traits that dwell in Human Nature; flat lands or countries surrounded by the long straight lines of the sea were conducive toward developing the power of abstraction. . . . Consequently, a country like the United States . . . promises to produce a civilization in which the Human Mind may not only appear in the occasional masterpiece, but may in many of its aspects be distributed throughout the people. (49–50)

Stein claims to be writing "A description of how the land the American land the land in America looks and is flat is and looks flat" (78). She wants to know "What has excitement got to do with geography and how does the land the American land look from above from below and from custom and from habit." And again, "Are there any customs and habits in America there is geography and what what is the human mind" (80).

In a tribute to her homeland, she writes: "I know so well the relation of a simple center and a continuous design to the land as one looks down on it, a wandering line as one looks down on it, a quarter section as one looks down on it, the shadows of each tree on the snow and the woods on each side and the land higher up between it and I know so well how in spite of the fact that the human mind has not looked at it the human mind has it to know that it is there like that, notwithstanding that the human mind has liked what it has which has not been like that" (*GH*, 85).

Connecting America to the highest state, the human mind, Stein goes on to explain its effect on writing: "Why the writing of to-day has to do with the way any land can lay when it is there particularly flat land. That is what makes connected land with the human mind only flat land a great deal of flat land is connected with the human mind and so America is connected with the human mind, I can say I say so but what I do is write it so. Think not the way the land looks but the way it lies that is now connected with the human mind" (*GH*, 87). Stein associates the vastness of the country with the freedom to wander in creative thinking, and she asks, can "the map of the United States of America make wandering a mission"? (93). In a short play in *The Geographical History of America*, Stein has a chorus chant "The land is flat from on high and when they wander" and, again, "There is flat land and weather and money for the human mind" (109).

Land is important to the human mind rather than human nature because, as Stein writes, "Scenery if it did it before does not remember but human nature if it did it before does remember," and so scenery "has no beginning and middle and end" (*GH*, 217–18). And "There is no use in forgetting scenery when it is scenery because there is nothing to forget. / Once more I can climb about and remind you that a woman in this epoch does the important literary thinking" (220).

Stein's contrast between the human mind as independent of memory and connection and human nature as contingent and limited would appear to point to an interest in the transcendent and eternal. Instead, she associates the human mind with space, scenery, and geography and human nature with history and time. Time is connected with sequence, with beginnings and ends, whereas space or geography is connected with the whole or an aerial view that encompasses the whole where sequence has no consequence. In "How Writing is Written," Stein explains her point by reference, ironically, to the new century and its "different way of life": "The United States began a different phase when, after the Civil War, they discovered and created out of their inner need a different way of life.

They created the Twentieth Century. The United States, instead of having the feeling of beginning at one end and ending at another, had the conception of assembling the whole thing out of its parts, the whole thing which made the Twentieth Century productive. The Twentieth Century conceived an automobile as a whole, so to speak, and then created it, built it up out of its parts" (*GofM*, 489).

Composition in space rather than in time is the twentieth-century way of composing, as Stein illustrates by claiming that, during the war, the average doughboy standing on the corner was more exciting than any news about events. "Events had got so continuous that the fact that events were taking place no longer stimulated anybody," she claims (*GofM*, 493).

Time would always keep events continuous, and, once these events were written down, as Stein writes in another essay of this period, "What Are Master-pieces and Why Are There So Few of Them," it is "not true or too true," in short, it is not new. Stein goes on: "I once said that nothing could bother me more than the way a thing goes dead once it has been said. And if it does it is because of there being this trouble about time." "That is what is the trouble with time. That is what makes what women say truer than what men say" (*GofM*, 500).

It was the importance of geography and the new discovery of space in the twentieth century that interested her. In *Paris France* (1940), writing about twentieth-century painting, Stein claims: "These conceptions all have to do with the world being round and everybody knowing all about it and there being illimitable space and everybody knowing all about it and if anybody knows all about the world being round and all about illimitable space the first thing they do is to paint their conceptions of these things and that the twentieth century painting did" (*PF*, 61–62). By contrast, Americans think of the world as flat, and Stein wonders if that is "because of their continent." She states, "Russia and America do have a tendency to think the world is not round but it is" (45).

But when World War II came and Stein had a chance to meet more Americans in France, she began to change her opinions. They were different from the Americans of the last war; they were "men of the world," as she wrote in *Wars I Have Seen* (1945). She wanted to know how it had happened: "I asked so many of them about it, we had long talks about it, they all agreed that the depression had a lot to do with it, it made people stay at home because they had no money to go out with" (*WIHS*, 256). And they admitted that military service had something to do with it, along with the radio, and the quizzes on the radio "kind of made them feel that it was no use just being ignorant, and then some of them said crossword puzzles had a lot to do with it" and also the cinema. Whatever the cause, Stein claimed, "The conclusion that one came to was that it had happened the American men had at last come to be interested and to be interesting and conversational, and it was mighty interesting to see and hear it" (256).

Nonetheless, Stein recalls that after the last war she had wanted to write a long book or a poem about "how Kansas differed from Iowa and Iowa from Illinois and Illinois from Ohio, and Mississippi from Louisiana and Louisiana from Tennessee and Tennessee from Kentucky, and all the rest from all the rest" (*WIHS*, 249). "There is something in this native land business and you cannot get away from it," although, she admits, she notices it more in war when "you are all alone and completely cut off from knowing about your country." But, even in this late work written by a Stein as much created by her audience as creating her audience, she goes back to her old sense that

> After all every one is as their land is, as the climate is, as the mountains and the rivers or their oceans are as the wind and rain and snow and ice and heat and moisture is, they just are and that makes them have their way to eat their way to drink their way to act their way to think and their way to be subtle, and even if the lines of demarcation are only made with a ruler after all what is inside those right angles is different from those on the outside of those right angles, any American knows that. (250)

Writing as an American who had lived all her adult life abroad, Stein finally makes a place for herself, acknowledging what "any American knows" that outsiders are different. Her lifelong effort to examine the ways in which "G stands for geographical" settles at last on the simple way in which geography allows for difference.

In an article published in the *Atlantic Monthly* in 1937, Stein recounts a conversation she had with Charlie Chaplin on her trip to America:

> We talked a little about the Four Saints and what my idea had been, I said that what was most exciting was when nothing was happening, I said that saints should naturally do nothing if you were a saint that was enough and a saint existing was everything, if you made them do anything then there was nothing to it they were just like any one so I wanted to write a drama where no one did anything where there was no action and I had and it was the Four Saints and it was exciting, he said yes he could understand that, I said the films would become like the

newspapers just a daily habit and not at all exciting or interesting. ("Your United States," 467)

And earlier, on April 6, 1935, writing in the *New York Herald Tribune*, Stein had connected states with saints, claiming: "As I flew over them I felt that I did know really know when we passed from one state to another one of them I really was certain that I did know this thing and I wanted to write an opera about the states differing as I flew over them. It would make a very interesting opera states instead of saints" (13).

Although Stein never wrote that opera, her interest in states that did not do anything but differ in immediately recognizable ways was part of her search for a new way to situate her life. It was part of her effort to return drama to the condition of poetry, to deprive narration of its continuity by creating a space where nothing happened and time stopped. Beyond that, it was an expression of an interest in the iconic that she shared with Picasso, who painted her as a figure of absolute immobility, a figure to which nothing happened. Finally, her interest in geography was an interest in her own body, a site of difference and yet enough as it was.

4

Half Is Enough
Elizabeth Bishop's Love Poetry

In her recent study, *The Apparitional Lesbian: Female Sexuality and Modern Culture* (1993), Terry Castle writes, "The lesbian is never with us, it seems, but always somewhere else: in the shadows, in the margins, hidden from history, out of sight, out of mind, a wanderer in the dusk, a lost soul, a tragic mistake, a pale denizen of the night" (2). Castle is discussing how we as an audience perceive or fail to perceive lesbianism. Some of these same terms apply to a lesbian writing about her own love life. The personal experience is often occluded, hidden from direct view, there only between the lines to be decoded but only by those already in the know. Poets have chosen a variety of experiments for such expression: at one extreme is the radically disruptive and experimental writing of Gertrude Stein, for example, where, as Stein herself said, she wanted to describe the thing without naming it; at the other extreme is the apparent surface tranquillity and restraint of Elizabeth Bishop's poetry, which hides even as it hints at a history and an inner turmoil. So successful was Bishop at her experiment in keeping secret what she intended also to express that until recently, readers have either failed to hear what she as a lesbian had to say or failed to expose what they may have detected.

Ironically, Bishop has often been praised for her precise observational skills at the same time that she has been called to task for the extreme impersonality of her poetry. One of the first critics to suggest that Bishop had an "'underground' emotional personality," Alan Williamson still locates her in the familiar view of a poet who controlled her emotions, contending that "if Bishop characteristically distanced emotion, it was partly because emotion for her—and especially feelings of despair, loneliness, apprehension—tended to become immense and categorical, insusceptible to rational or, in poetry, to structural counter-argument" (96, 108). Concentrating on her feelings of anxiety, he finds that even in the "happiest poem" "An impersonal despair is still very near the surface" (Schwartz and Estess, 99–100).

More recently, critics have looked at Bishop as a poet with a wider range of emotions, but, again, as Victoria Harrison's survey suggests, the emotions are often identified as mixed, even negative—"contented or trustful boundary diffusion, dependency, assertions of independence, aggression, rejection and alienation, playfulness, competitiveness, and the concomitant fear of and desire for reenvisioned forms of intimacy" (44). For such a poet, especially sensitive to the social taboo of lesbianism, the open expression of emotion was impossible; passion had to be expressed in coded language, any recognition of her lover had to remain private even as she published it, aubades had to be buried and their celebration deflected. Given these restraints, Bishop's love poetry covers a remarkable range of feelings from tenderness and affection to bitter loss, from erotic desire to sexual affront, from preciosity to crude expression. As she developed, both her reticence and her desire to speak her love intensified. She is the great poet of love's secrecy, its hiding, and often of its bitterness rather than its sorrow.

In all the attention Bishop has recently received, her love poetry has been little remarked. Lorrie Goldensohn suggests even that there are only a few poems that talk about love (29). From one perspective Goldensohn might be right. Bishop's love poetry is often indirect, restrained, hidden behind other subjects. But, from another perspective, we may see that

Bishop wrote throughout her career about love or erotic attraction, about the secret signs and recognitions of lovers, often projecting desire onto the landscape or onto distant literary figures. That critics have overlooked these poems is testimony to Bishop's skills at concealment as well as evidence of a curious inattention to women's love poetry, in general, and to lesbian love poetry, in particular. The subject is a difficult one as Elizabeth Burns, a poet-critic writing her dissertation on Bishop, argues in *Letters to Elizabeth Bishop*. Quoting Bishop's diary on "the dangers of love poetry," Burns writes outside her own desire to censor the admission of her lesbian life, commenting, "When I thought, I am going underground to write about you, to write to you, I felt I had found a place, and I felt it was completely forbidden" (7).

One critic who imagines that, had Bishop lived in a later era, she might have become a love poet of startling power, has turned to Bishop's unfinished poems and drafts of poems for what they reveal about her interest in the expression of love and sexuality (Lombardi, 72–73). Citing one poem, in particular, "Vague Poem (Vaguely Love Poem)," Marilyn May Lombardi suggests that Bishop revised the image of the rose from the romance tradition and used it as a way of "visualizing the transforming powers of sexual pleasure" and celebrating "the impenetrable female body and the unimpregnating pleasure of lesbian sexuality" (74). Yet, even here in this unpublished poem far from the public's view, it seems to me that Bishop is fascinated with an image of secrecy, the rose crystal that hides rather than reveals its nature: "a rose-like shape; faint glitters. . . . Yes, perhaps / there was a secret powerful crystal inside," she writes about "the rose-red lump of apparently soil" that is presented to her. Later, the image returns:

> Just now, when I saw you naked again,
> I thought the same words: rose-rock; rock-rose . . .
> Rose, trying, working to show itself,
> forming, folding over,
> unimaginable connections, unseen, shining edges
> Rose-rock, unformed, flesh beginning, crystal by crystal,
> clear pink breast and darker, crystalline nipples
> rose-rock, rose-quartz, roses, roses, roses,
> exacting roses from the body,
> and the even darker, accurate, rose of sex.[1]

Goldensohn, too, thinks that this unfinished poem suggests that, if Bishop had been born thirty years later, she might have written brilliant descriptions of the sexual body (72). Defying both the conventional image of the rose as representing idealized love and the modernist desire to strip that image of its obsolete meanings, Bishop here uses the rose to evoke the "unimaginable," "unseen," "unformed" "darker" movement of erotic desire. Even here, in the presence of the naked body, it is the hidden and the secret that attract her. It is hard to imagine what Bishop might have been had she lived in a different era, but it is clear that the power of the poetry that she actually did write came from the almost intolerable restraints she placed on it.

Like Gertrude Stein before her and Adrienne Rich after her, Bishop is that unusual artist who writes for the broader culture love poetry that speaks directly to a lesbian audience. Her poetry can have two readings: the universalizing reading of the generally heterosexual culture and the particularizing reading that identifies its lesbian subtext. Thus, Bonnie Costello can argue that the iceberg in "The Imaginary Iceberg" is "a symbol of the eternal within the temporal world" when there is evidence, as we shall see, to suggest that the iceberg stands for secret and hidden passion (94). Perhaps the most acute reader of Bishop's work was, after all, Marianne Moore, who seemed to intuit, even when she disapproved of, the expressions of love or desire at which Bishop hinted. For example, she argued with Bishop over poems that seemed to veer too close to personal revelation, calling "Insomnia" "a cheap love poem" or objecting ostensibly to the unladylike language of "Roosters" but perhaps indirectly to its buried aubade.[2]

Bishop's writing has such a brilliant surface that it has forestalled inquiry into the depths it might cover, but she often writes openly about emotional power that is hidden in display. The early poem, "The Imaginary Iceberg," describes an iceberg which "cuts its facets from within," a being "self-made from elements least visible," that might stand as a model of both revelation and reserve for the poet herself.[3] Its opening line— "We'd rather have the iceberg than the ship" (CP, 4)—wipes out Williamson's suggestion "that the wonderful is something frigid, remote, self-sufficient" (98). The wonderful here arouses a startling desire. Yet the attraction has not been much remarked by critics who, like Williamson, have tended to restrict the full resonance of this straightforward assertion by connecting it to what they identify as the allegory that concludes the poem, "Icebergs behoove the soul."[4]

Nonetheless, the opening statement is not transparent. Detaching it from the poem's concluding assertion, we may notice that, although the preference for the iceberg appears to be simply stated, it is not clear what it would mean to "have" the iceberg, and the next line does little to illuminate the meaning:

> We'd rather have the iceberg than the ship,
> although it meant the end of travel. (*CP*, 4)

To have the iceberg is to be shipwrecked, it would seem, and it is a meaning amplified by a repetition of the first line and then:

> we'd rather own this breathing plain of snow
> though the ship's sails were laid upon the sea
> as the snow lies undissolved upon the water. (4)

Preferring shipwreck to safe sailing defies common sense, and to pursue that idea, the reader must explain away the iceberg as, for example, Bonnie Costello does in calling it "an idea of absolute autonomy" to which the mind is attracted but which it must abandon (92). But the "end of travel" might also signify the end of cruising after a lover, the end of searching for a responsive recognition.

Costello's allegorical reading is forced to overlook the poem's middle stanza, which indicates the iceberg's attractiveness. Perhaps to "have" the iceberg is something beyond shipwreck. The middle stanza explores that possibility, concentrating on having the iceberg through looking at it and being looked at in return. The stanza opens with the admission, "This is a scene a sailor'd give his eyes for," and closes with, "Its weight the iceberg dares / upon a shifting stage and stands and stares." The sailor looks; the iceberg looks. This exchange of glances between the sailor and the iceberg signals a secret recognition, and, although the imaginary nature is daring and excluding, it elicits an ardent desire. To "have" this iceberg is a challenge, and, in the last stanza, the poem's speaker recovers power and moves within, as if to "have" the imaginary iceberg from another angle. The poem ends with three lines, not just the first one which is most frequently quoted by itself:

> Icebergs behoove the soul
> (both being self-made from elements least visible)
> to see them so: fleshed, fair, erected indivisible.

"Icebergs behoove the soul . . . to see them" is a different statement from "Icebergs behoove the soul" and the meanings that can be spun out of that behooving. Far from Costello's "symbol of the eternal within the temporal world" (94), icebergs, imaginary and real, that require to be seen in terms that belong to the human body, as Bromwich notes (167), may not be so easily allegorized. The "soul," however powerful a term, appears only late in this poem and should not take over or at least should not overpower the originary image of the iceberg which may be like the soul, "both being self-made from elements least visible"; but, if it is like the soul, it is described in terms that emphasize the soul's mortal trappings, in being "fleshed, fair, erected indivisible."

In the poem's development, this iceberg is neither eternal nor soul-like. It is rather something we would rather "own," "prefer," and "see" (*CP*, 4). But, paradoxically, it has a will of its own and does not lend itself to such wishes. Rather, it "spars with the sun," "dares" its weight, "adorns only itself," and this intensifies the speaker's longing. Such desire for such aloofness might seem utterly destructive but for the fact that the aloof iceberg has its human side itself: it is a "breathing plain of snow" that "rises and sinks," stands on "a shifting stage," "cuts its facets from within," and "saves itself perpetually" (4). Like the speaker, it seems to battle some internal turmoil.

The perspective shifts in this poem from speaker to iceberg as the poem closes in on its subject. Drawing on an early version of Marianne Moore's "A Grave," "The Imaginary Iceberg" is, like that poem, concerned not just with the sea but with seeing and with what is hidden from sight or only slightly visible.[5] The attractiveness of the iceberg for the viewer in this poem, as for the poet, is that it keeps so much "within" while seeming to offer so much to see.

Its spectacle is theatrical and elicits a theatrical speaker in "a scene where he who treads the boards / is artlessly rhetorical" or the reverse, rhetorically artless, as in the final scene: "Good-bye, we say, good-bye, the ship steers off / where waves give in to one another's waves" (*CP*, 4). Blurred in the sea waves are the speaker's waves of farewell and another's waves (the iceberg's waves?), and suddenly the oddity of this emotive gesture presents itself. Who is waving to whom? What or whom has the speaker recognized in this iceberg? Seeing and seeing what is hidden from sight are the special gifts of lovers excluded from the common code of love's expression. In seeming to share these gifts with the iceberg, so insistently personified here, the speaker identifies the imaginary iceberg as an imagined lover.

The speaker sees an unusual model of decorum in the iceberg. Keeping much of its bulk hidden, the iceberg still displays a spectacular surface. There is much to see even as there is much that does not offer itself to view, and the speaker of the poem recognizes this double sign. Far from a symbol of the ideal or the eternal, the iceberg is pure theater, pure poetry, or a figure of pure attractiveness. It would be characteristic of Bishop's wit to make the iceberg an image of desire, especially of a desire that "adorns only itself." The ship, then, becomes a means of evading such desire, as Bishop was to write later in "Questions of Travel": "*Is it lack of imagination that makes us come / to imagined places, not just stay at home?*" (*CP*, 94). By contrast, not lacking imagination, the imaginary iceberg makes up for lacks elsewhere as its "glassy pinnacles / correct elliptics in the sky" or dares to confront the real as its "white peaks / spar with the sun" (4).

In celebrating the hidden or "least visible" adornment at the same time that it privileges sight over all other senses, this poem expresses a fascination for the privacy of special vision. Only something that is most intensely desired is what "a sailor'd give his eyes for"; it is the end toward which all travel will tend. The imaginary iceberg standing "stock-still" in a sea of "moving marble" is, like the Grecian urn, a "still unravished bride," the embodiment of desire never fading but never to be enjoyed either. But the iceberg is not an art object, and Bishop finds her "Cold Pastoral" situated precariously in the mutable world.[6]

Seeing everything that is there in the iceberg's image and the everything that is not, Bishop's speaker has revivified the empty world of Stevens's snowman, making it into a world of imaginative and passionate power, rife with meaning, significance, and signs. Seeing what is hidden in what is revealed, lovers in Bishop's early poetry participate in a private recognition of each other, reading meanings where the obtuse viewer sees nothing, endowing chance encounters with significance, uncovering hidden potential. The allegory may be of love's secret attractions.

Seeing takes on a special power in Bishop's poetry because, as Marilyn Frye argues, "What lesbians see is what makes them lesbians" (173). In the social world in which Bishop lived, where lesbians had generally to pass as heterosexuals, they could still recognize each other by what they often described as a "mystical intuition in which the eyes are the privileged vehicle of secret knowledge."[7] For example, Audre Lorde, in *Zami*, recounts her own experience with this secret knowledge: "Still, we were always on the lookout, Flee and I, for that telltale flick of the eye, that certain otherwise prohibited openness of expression, that definiteness of voice which would suggest, I think she's gay. *After all, doesn't it take one to know one?*" (180). Knowing one becomes a skill of reading enjoyed only by the in-group, and knowing one has nothing to do with certainty or definite identity. Rather, seeing is an erotic pleasure. Moving from this social context to poetry where there is a long tradition of seeing as believing, of the visible as an epistemological guarantee, Bishop has been able to write a double-voiced discourse that is both disarmingly revelatory about her secret knowledge and most explicit about her open knowledge.

A case in point is "Three Sonnets for the Eyes," an early poem that Bonnie Costello argues is "representative of her early insular treatment of the eyes as the center of an inwardly defined, timeless identity" (251 n6). It is actually an expression of an in-group recognition so revealing that the speaker feels that the utmost discretion is required of those lovers who, separating themselves from all others, exclaim in the first sonnet, " 'How blind / Are eyes!' " Again, in the second sonnet, the lover says:

> Look, here I am in here! you're warm—oh look again!
> I knew you knew all else there gaped in vain:
> Stared eyes dull, wide-winked, squinted wrong surmise
> And ours said nothing, nothing. (*CP*, 223)

But to the lovers, the eyes are love's "instant own translator" to themselves and so revealing that they fear exposure, welcoming evening that "overwhelms" and "fortunately covers / With lashes, lids of reticence, these eyes those lovers" (223). In the third sonnet, the speaker pledges undying affection through eyes that will outlast all other senses: "thy gravestone's graven angel / Eyes I'll stand and stare. The secret's in the forehead / (Rather the structure's gap) once you are dead" (224). This fascination with eyes in Bishop's love poems expresses the double desire to recognize love and to shield it from recognition by the dull eyes of the unprivileged viewer. Reticence and its opposite, eloquence, are both to be desired in this expression of desire. It is any lover's dream of privacy, of love's special language, of love's privilege, and, at the same time, it is particularly the lesbian lover's dream of excluding the heterosexual world, of preserving itself against intruders, and more clearly of enjoying its private erotic pleasure.

Devotion to a secret love had its darker side. When that love surfaces, it forces the speaker in "Three Valentines II" to admit: "I own / Surprise / To meet, when I meet you—or Love—your eyes" (*CP*, 226). She has been warned to "beware / My dubious security, / —Sure of my love, and Love; uncertain of identity" (226). This distinction between "my love" and "Love" calls up the speaker's sense of her distinct identity; her dubious security underscores the risk such an identity entails. When this poem appeared along with "The Map" and "The Reprimand" as the first poems Bishop published in book form, Marianne Moore wrote an accompanying note in which she seems to acknowledge the effort Bishop made to guard the private, arguing: "Mere mysteriousness is useless; the enigma must be clear to the author, not necessarily to us"; then she quotes the lines, "Such curious Love, in constant innocence" and "—Sure of my love, and Love; uncertain of identity" as having the right air (175). She concludes: "One asks a great deal of an author—. . . that he [*sic*] should not induce you to be interested in what is restrictedly private but that there should be the self-portrait; that he should pierce you to the marrow without revolting you" (176). Moore seems to have intuited Bishop's need for privacy and champions its deflection into an evasive self-portrait. Encouraging this aspect of Bishop's work on general grounds, Moore diverted interest, both her own and that of later critics, from the whole question of privacy in Bishop's poetry, although she could also detect and criticize it when it veered too close to revelation.

Moore admired Bishop's reserve. What Bishop appreciated about Moore was her interest in the riddling aspects of observation because, in a way more like Emily Dickinson than Moore, she found this riddling a necessary means of protection against unwanted revelation. In two poems sent in early letters to Moore, Bishop toys with this image of the eyes as powerful deceivers; in "Britannia Rules the Waves," "Queen Elizabeth had a dress of eyes, / Embroidered to embarrass courtiers" and "One ancient eye with veins, with whitened lashes, / Reproached Canute seated in an armchair" (*CP*, 203). Again, the riddle, "To Be Written on the Mirror in Whitewash," turns on the unseeing or unrevealing of the eye:

> I live only here, between your eyes and you,
> But I live in your world. What do I do?
> —Collect no interest—otherwise what I can;
> Above all I am not that staring man. (205)

In this poem, the mirror reflection refracts sight, "collects no interest" to itself even as it bears enough resemblance to "that staring man" that it needs to deny such an identity.[8] Here, as in "The Imaginary Iceberg," Bishop seems to be reminding that vigilant observer, Moore, that eyes are not always made for seeing. Such eyes are important images in Bishop's early love poetry, where they serve to express how the lesbian lover must often disguise emotion even as she signals a private recognition.

In the early work, eyes are not only adept at reading hidden signs, they can also fill up with tears as emotions erupt into a calm surface. In "The Reprimand," for example, Bishop attempts to deflect attention from the tears' source by insisting that they are only superficial, claiming they "belong / To only eyes; their deepest sorrow they wrung / From water" (*CP*, 228). But the source of such tears would not have to be denied if it were not at risk of being exposed. The tears turn up again in the odd and isolated "man-moth," whose eye "stares back, and closes up" "Then from the lids / one tear, his only possession, like the bee's sting, slips" (15). And, again, in "The Weed," a tear leads to a momentary vision:

A few drops fell upon my face
and in my eyes, so I could see
(or, in that black place, thought I saw)
that each drop contained a light,
a small, illuminated scene. (21)

This separation of tears from their emotional source indicates the necessary reticence of this love poet. The suppressed details here would lead to a narrative explanation that might undercut the poignancy of the single tear, the few drops. Bishop cuts off explanation, restricting sorrow to the tears' water or identifying eyes with "that black place" which does not give up its secret directly, although it hints of such secrets. Bishop balances uneasily between alluding to the unspoken and hiding it, between particularizing her experience and making it accessible to a universal reading. The surrealism of these poems allows for a certain unreality in both what Bishop imagines she can admit and what she feels she must conceal.

David Kalstone attaches the image of the eyes from "The Weed" to a notebook entry in which Bishop, looking at raindrops on the window, realized she could look into the drops as into so many crystal balls, and the strangest of all drops was a "lonely, magnificent human eye, wrapped in its own tear" (14). Kalstone concludes: "The monitory eye wrapped in its own tear seems an appropriately riveting image for Bishop's writing at the time: the odd combination of observation and alienation that makes her early poems, especially, different from Moore's" (14). Such eyes are hardly monitoring a world outside themselves. Their tears' internal source is hidden as the tears erupt without cause, spill without effect.

The "monitory eye" in Bishop's early work may, as Kalstone notes, observe as well as alienate its object. "The Gentleman of Shalott" seems to express this odd combination. "Which eye's his eye?" (*CP*, 9), the gentleman asks presumably of his reflection. But the source of the alienation is hidden within; this gentleman is deeply attached to himself as half and to half of himself even as he wishes to toy with his attraction rather than state it too directly.

Bishop's gentleman is looking in the mirror at himself rather than at the world of Camelot as Tennyson's Lady of Shalott did, and yet Bishop's use of Tennyson brings the lady's inverted world into this poem where it becomes the real world of which her gentleman's mirror is the inverted image. The inversions here are dizzying as "The Gentleman of Shalott" traces love's inversion. In this plot, vision that may be capricious and unclear is not undesired, as Bishop writes, "The uncertainty / he says he / finds exhilarating" (*CP*, 10). For Tennyson's Lady of Shalott, uncertainty is painful even if direct vision is self-destructive, fated to lead to death; for Bishop's gentleman, by contrast, vision is never quite direct. Requiring a "sense of constant re-adjustment" that "He loves," the gentleman finds his sight both other-directed and self-affirming. He sees himself in the mirror as he sees himself in the other; and so his question, "Which eye's his eye," does not seek an answer but rather a confirmation of identity.

There is something a little fey, even precious, about Bishop's gentleman that is reflected in the frequency of the feminine rhymes: "And if half his head's reflected, / thought, he thinks, might be affected" or "But he's resigned / to such economical design" (*CP*, 9), for example. The preciosity is evident, too, in the fussy self-consciousness with which he is presented, as in, "To his mind / it's the indication" or "He felt in modesty / his person was / half looking-glass" or "He wishes to be quoted as saying at present: / 'Half is enough'" (10). This is not the language of philosophical inquiry into the nature of the self, nor does it draw on the conventions of love poetry. In its insistence on the gentleman's modesty and precision, the language underscores his trivializing wishes and desires.

Yet Tennyson's lady is his obvious foil; and where Tennyson turns to melodrama to express her fate, Bishop moves in the opposite direction toward farce to delineate his. The poem's speaker both exaggerates the danger of this preening gentleman's doubled life, where "There's little margin for error," and deflates its significance to "If the glass slips / he's in a fix— / only one leg, etc" (9–10).

"The Gentleman of Shalott" is, in part, a joke, a takeoff on Tennyson's poem. But the poem can also leave Tennyson's poem far behind. The crack in this gentleman's mirror is something more ominous even than the curse imposed by evil powers; the split within himself also curiously splits him off from the rest of the world: "The glass must stretch / down his middle, / or rather down the edge" (*CP*, 9). The symmetrical world of this gentleman becomes unbalanced as the middle slips into the edge, and the haphazard nature of all physical coupling is underscored in "this arrangement / of leg and leg and / arm and so on." If Tennyson's lady dramatizes the melodramatic abandonment to love, Bishop's gentleman epitomizes its opposite, the farcical aggrandizement of self-love. But, its final line, " 'Half is enough,' " is more than farce. However disclaimed and hedged in by this gentleman's preciosity, it is a serious declaration of same-sex attraction, again tucked under so many other signs that it goes almost unnoticed.

The opening image of the eyes as well as the exploration of "uncertainty" in seeing and the reference to love implicit in the title tie this poem to Bishop's earlier work in which she attempts to express what Williamson has called her "'underground' emotional personality" (96). By contrast, "Casabianca" is about aboveground emotions that are not always so sympathetically expressed. Placed on the page opposite "The Imaginary Iceberg" in *The Complete Poems*, this poem calls out to be read as its opposite. It states simply and directly: love is the "boy stood on the burning deck," "the son," the "obstinate boy," "the ship, / even the swimming sailors," and finally "the burning boy" (*CP*, 5). Thomas Travisano claims, "Here love is synonymous with pain and seems to exist in a realm of high rhetoric, where it exacts pointless, self-destructive gestures of devotion" (*Bishop*, 33). But what is love that is both the steadfast boy and the escaping sailors, both the boy and the ship?

Against "The Imaginary Iceberg," "Casabianca" would appear to verify that poem's preference for icebergs over ships. If the iceberg stands on "elements least visible," the boy stands on the visibly burning deck, and, if the iceberg stands for hidden passion, the boy stands for openly declared devotion. In the end the boy is burning, the iceberg remains "erected indivisible." But in "Casabianca" love is so many things that it is finally nothing. The poem suggests that openly declared love is both banal and pointless by contrast to secret passion. Linked to its precursor poem by Felicia Hemans of the boy in the Napoleonic Wars who goes loyally down with the ship along with his captain-father, who is unconscious and thus unable to release the boy from his duty, "Casabianca" takes a very cynical view of love's constancy.

By contrast to the open declaration of steadfast love in "Casabianca," Bishop buries the subject in "Roosters," another war poem where she hints at love's cruelty. The secrecy of love's recognition in early poems such as "Three Sonnets" is played out here by the poet herself, who risks more on the subject of love because she has placed it in such a guarded position in a poem where she wanted, as she told Moore, to "emphasize the essential baseness of militarism."[9] (Moore had objected to the poem's bathroom language, and Bishop defended her "sordidities.") Betsy Erkkila calls this a veiled coming out poem (and that might have aroused Moore's antipathy), but its statement is so veiled that its revelation is difficult to notice (126).

Beneath the subject of war is what Susan Schweik has identified as a submerged aubade (231). It opens, "We hear the first crow" (*CP*, 35), with the admission that there are at least two people there in the room and perhaps in the same bed. The aubade does not celebrate love so much as reveal its affinity with war. Its anxiety is evident when the speaker addresses the roosters: "what right have you to give / commands" "and wake us here where are / unwanted love, conceit and war?" (36). And again, "how could the night have come to grief?" (39), or the ending "faithful as enemy, or friend." Schweik concludes that "it is not that 'Roosters' is ostensibly a war poem but actually a love poem; it is that the two here are impossible to tell apart" (233).

Unlike "The Imaginary Iceberg" where the hidden is a source of attraction, the private emotions hidden in this ostensibly public war poem are painful, but they too are powerful enough to make themselves felt even in a poem that diverges from them. Attention to them is deflected by both the brevity of their mention and by the confusion of the rest of the poem where there appears to be a split in the poem's ostensible subject between an opening attack on violence and a Christian message of peace and reconciliation. The message of the buried aubade is, as Schweik suggests, almost a countermovement to that theme since the aubade indicates that violence cannot always be evaded, is most intransigent in personal and sexual relationships.

In her second volume of poems, *A Cold Spring* (1955), Bishop explores this sense of the treachery of love by treating its erotic power. Williamson claims that in these poems Bishop expresses her sense that "reciprocal love is, almost metaphysically, impossible" (97); but her subject is passion not love, erotic power not romantic attachment. And the feeling of being trapped by her own erotic desire, overwhelmed by a moment of physical ecstasy that cannot be sustained, drives "Four Poems." "I / Conversation" bears out Williamson's judgment since there is no reciprocity in this private conversation. The poem starts with a situation, not a person. It is "The tumult in the heart" that asks questions, stops, "then undertakes to answer" (*CP*, 76). Like "The Gentleman of Shallot," the speaker here is either alone talking to herself or to someone who speaks in "the same tone of voice." "No one could tell the difference," she admits, between the asker and the answerer, between the "tumult in the heart" and when it "stops." But the conversations are "Uninnocent"; they "start" and then "engage the senses," and "then there is no choice," as if the speaker were fatally attracted by some physical passion.[10] Here, if the speaker is aware of the impossibility of reciprocal love, she is still more concerned with the uncontrollable power of her own erotic desire.

"I / Conversation" is not a conversation between two people, and "II / Rain Towards Morning" is not about the weather. Both poems describe that moment when the senses are engaged, leaving no choice but to submit to a momentary passion, and their titles name appropriately non-directive events in which the moment of abandon takes place. In "II / Rain Towards Morning," the speaker has a vision of a million birds ascending, breaking "The great light cage," and realizes that someone has "tried the puzzle of their prison / and solved it with an unexpected kiss, / whose freckled unsuspected hands alit" (*CP*, 77).[11] Unexpected and unsuspected, the kiss and hands are identified only after their effect has been described. The poem opens in a burst that paradoxically releases its meaning only gradually: "The great light cage has broken up in the air, / freeing, I think, about a million birds." The light at the beginning remains "alit" at the end as the cage of the world becomes also the cage of the self and "frightening" gives way to "brightening." But the potential ecstasy of this poem is strangely muted, held in check even as it is expressed, as if, like the birds, it might ascend never to return.

In the next poem, "III / While Someone Telephones," the speaker is again engaged in a conversation. She passes "wasted minutes that couldn't be worse" and hears "*nothing*," although she also waits for "the heart's release" and hopes in a strangely negative construction that "while the fireflies / are failing to illuminate these nightmare trees / might they not be his green gay eyes" (*CP*, 78). The qualifications here, negatives that enfold negatives, make it difficult to read this poem as a plea for the "gay eyes," for release from the "tension" of "*nothing*." As in the second poem where the ecstatic moment is muted, the negative constructions here hide the power of the "gay eyes" and the force of the adjective.

The final poem, "IV / O Breath," starts out as positively as the first poem with its "tumult in the heart." Here it is "Beneath that loved   and celebrated breast," but, like the tumult that keeps asking questions, this breast is "silent, bored really" "maybe lives and lets / live," but "why restrained / I cannot fathom" (*CP*, 79). Like the "unexpected kiss" of the earlier poem, here the breath on black hairs around the nipple is an image unexpectedly specific, made all the more enigmatic by the speaker's claiming, "what we have in common's bound to be there," "something that maybe I could bargain with / and make a separate peace beneath / within if never with." "Beneath," "within" are some of love's locations outside the obvious union "with" someone else which Bishop abjures here.

In these poems, Bishop deals with reticence, the very subject that her critics confront in discussing her poetry; but it is not the reticence of love that concerns her so much as the reluctance and vagaries of a responsive physical relationship. Not poems of vision where a single speaker might express her attraction, but rather poems of speaking, listening, waiting for a reply, these poems call the other into existence, longingly, in surprised satisfaction, in desperate uncertainty. They are poems of voice, of breath, of response and inspiration, in which the speaker must wait, answer her own questions, hope that nothing is not nothing, and believe that she could bargain. The moments celebrated here are imagined as "tumult" and "puzzle" and "clamor," not the language of love's bliss but of its erotic power, disruption, and confusion.[12]

What is remarkable about these poems is the disjunction between a reticence of expression and the specific physicality of the imagery that describes it. Although the conversation is restricted and the occasions are rendered obliquely, the physical presence of the beloved is evoked in details of startling specificity that are faintly unattractive.[13] The single detail calls attention to itself rather than to the whole body of the beloved for which it stands. This use of a synecdoche, absorbing all the attention as if it alone would suffice, is itself a form of visual and verbal restraint, collecting and containing everything in itself.

Bishop's erotic poetry does not give itself to its subject. It resists the very state that it explores as if a "kiss," when mentioned, must be qualified by "unexpected," a "loved" "breast" must be "silent, bored really." But, strangely enough, the poems do not pull back from revelations of physical details, even when this forthrightness does not extend to the elaboration of love's emotional power. Writing love poetry as a lesbian for a generally heterosexual audience, Bishop assumes the restrictions enforced by that audience even as she pushes against them to write poems of muted ecstasy, uncertain tumult, evasive escape.

"Insomnia," which ends with what appears to be a statement of direct affection, "and you love me," is such a poem which works by indirection to equivocate. Here Bishop is not controlling emotion; rather she hides it from too pointed revelation. Bishop is careful to conceal the direction the poem will take from its opening image of "The moon in the bureau mirror" (CP, 70). The special vision that mirrored reflections offer, the moon's endowment of the imagination, both are possibilities that Bishop cancels, as she goes on to develop the curious idea that the moon might serve as a model of determination for the insomniac, claiming that if the moon were deserted by the "Universe," "she'd find a body of water, / or a mirror, on which to dwell" (70). What drives this development is not clear. As Lorrie Goldensohn writes, "if the reader blinks twice the subject of this poem goes right on past" (30). Like the imaginary iceberg, this moon is both a natural fact and an imaginary one, a moon that "looks out a million miles" and also "(and perhaps with pride, at herself, / but she never, never smiles)" (70). Perhaps, too, the subject is carefully hidden because Bishop does not choose to provide a narrative setting for a desire and disappointment that could not easily fit into a heterosexual plot.

The moon that the insomniac sees in the mirror is, like the iceberg, self-sufficient and, as such, a model for the insomniac herself, who cannot sleep because she is not so certain of her world. "By the Universe deserted, / *she'd* tell it to go to hell," the speaker says of the moon, as if she, the speaker, equally deserted, might take heart from the moon's example. In this make-believe world of capitalized universes and italicized moons, the speaker feels encouraged to "wrap up care in a cobweb / and drop it down the well // into that world inverted" (*CP*, 70). But she does not live in an inverted world, and, in the straight world, she is doomed to sleepless nights, to a feeling of desertion, to a colloquy only with herself about the more carefree moon and the intimate world that never will be where "you love me" (70).

In a discussion of images of reflection in Bishop's poetry, Costello considers that the shifts in scale and perspective in "Insomnia" and other poems "opened up unsettling questions about the relation of inner to outer self, of imagination to reality, questions suggesting that representation offered only precarious and dependent shadows" (32). It might also be possible that for Bishop the question of representation was really a matter of disguise, of keeping secret even what was revealed, of confusing an easy understanding of the relation of inner to outer. Shadows might be more preferable than the clear light of day to Bishop's imagination. Underground emotions are never easily expressed or brought to the surface of her poetry; more frequently, they erupt or come into play by inversion rather than by revelation. Mutlu Blasing has argued, "Bishop's poetry as a whole overturns the hierarchical dualities of subject and object, inside and outside, center and periphery, original and copy"; here again it may be because the original was never to be copied, the inside never to be fully represented outside (105). As a result, the speakers of Bishop's poetry inhabit a reflected world where the authority of experience over representation brings up the question, "Which eye's his eye?"

Divining this aspect of Bishop's work, Elliott Carter chose the title, "A Mirror on Which to Dwell," for the musical arrangement of six Bishop poems.[14] Including "Insomnia," "O Breath," and "Argument," Carter emphasizes the fact that the subject of love for Bishop is always refracted through a mirror image, never quite direct. Still, recalling Moore's comment that "Insomnia" was a "cheap love poem," we may see that the subject was apparently too direct for her.

In the love poems of *A Cold Spring* there are moments of peculiar revelation, as in "A Summer's Dream," which seems to detail a world of domestic calm in a place with "a gentle storekeeper" and "our kind landlady"; but it is also a place whose "population numbered / two giants, an idiot, a dwarf" (*CP*, 62). It is a world of deviants where nothing is quite as it should be. Few ships could come to "the sagging wharf"; the idiot "could be beguiled / by picking blackberries, / but then threw them away" (62); and in this summer, "The bedroom was cold" (63). The outside does not reveal its inside in this boardinghouse "streaked / as though it had been crying" (62). Inside, the floors "glittered" and the "wallpaper glistened" (62). And deeper in the interior of this house where the bedroom is cold, the speaker finds "the feather bed close" (63). In this world slightly askew, the closeness in the feather bed may not offset the cold in the bedroom, and the two in this summer dream who are "wakened in the dark" may be awakened to the dark of day (63).

In this volume, also, Bishop appears to draw the images of other poems into a gloomier commentary on both love and the imagination, as in "Varick Street," where the refrain *"And I shall sell you sell you / sell you of course, my dear, and you'll sell me"* (*CP*, 75) provides a cynical commentary, especially in a stanza that draws on Bishop's earlier love poems about icebergs and moons:

> On certain floors
> certain wonders.
> Pale dirty light,
> some captured iceberg
> being prevented from melting.
> See the mechanical moons,
> sick, being made
> to wax and wane
> at somebody's instigation. (75)

The poem oscillates between this cryptic self-loathing of her own imaginative performances in "The Imaginary Iceberg" and "Insomnia" and reluctant relinquishment to a strained relationship. Thus, "Lights music of love / work on," and "Our bed / shrinks from the soot / and hapless odors / hold us close" (75).

Contrasting with this bitterness is the more tender mood of "Argument," where the speaker regrets an estrangement. "Days" and "Distance" "argue with me / endlessly / neither proving you less wanted nor less dear" (*CP*, 81), she says. Almost as a relief from the intimacy of this relationship, the desire in these late poems to connect with someone else at a less private level is the occasion for experimenting with a new form—the invitation of "Letter to N.Y." and "Invitation to Miss Marianne Moore." In the public eye of the latter poem, written for a special issue of *Quarterly Review of Literature* in honor of Moore's sixtieth birthday, Bishop could be more openly affectionate than in the private "Letter to N.Y." with its dedication to her friend, Louise Crane. Bishop could honor Moore by insisting thoroughly on herself, celebrating Moore not in the syllabic style that Moore reinvented for the twentieth century, but in imitation of a poem in a language far removed from Moore's and closer to Bishop's own interests, Pablo Neruda's "Alberto Rojas Jimenez Viene Volando."[15] Gilbert and Gubar note the eroticism of this invitation to "come flying," "Come like a light," "come like a daytime comet," "Mounting the sky with natural heroism" (1:211–12). Arousing a more passionate atmosphere ("a cloud of fiery pale chemicals" or "the glittering grandstand"), this invitation encourages a more female-centered world where "museums will behave / like courteous male bower-birds" (81). To be sure, Bishop highlights humorously Moore's peculiarity of dress (cape, hat, and pointed shoes) and does not treat entirely reverently her poetic particularities of vocabulary, meter, and grammar, but the tone appears lilting and celebratory rather than ironic.

The last poem of *A Cold Spring* marks a turn in Bishop's love poetry to celebrate the love for Lota de Macedo Soares, who was to center her life for more than a decade. But its tone of tenderness is as carefully modulated as the kindly ribbing tone of "Invitation to Miss Marianne Moore." "The Shampoo" is another kind of invitation—an invitation to accept one's self (even the affront of the most "amenable" "Time") by accepting love (*CP*, 84). Its gentleness is a new note in Bishop's poetry that will turn up again in this period (in poems such as "Manners" and "Manuelzhino"). A middle-aged love poem can slip easily into self-parody, but here the frivolity of the offer named in the title masks the seriousness of the affection and the advice not to be too "precipitate and pragmatical" (84). The graying hair can be recast in a lover's eyes into "shooting stars" "in bright formation" and suggest the possibilities of the romantic transformation that passion can work at any age (84).

In dedicating *Questions of Travel* to Lota de Macedo Soares, Bishop moves closer to acknowledging love's presence, and the volume has many different expressions of the poet's affection for this woman. As Golden-sohn has noted, however, Bishop's new life of affection and security in Brazil caused her to make "a decisive break from anything resembling what she described in Emily Dickinson's work as that annoying 'constant insistence on the strength of her affections,' that clinging to the female topic, love" (235). Nonetheless, her new companion became the beloved subject of a variety of poems. In "Manuelzhino," she figures as the indulgent, loving mistress, taxed beyond patience by her profligate servant. Hers is the house in "Song for the Rainy Season" that is "darkened and tarnished / by the warm touch / of the warm breath, / maculate, / cherished" (*CP*, 102).[16] Like "Uninnocent" in "I / Conversation" where the reader expects "innocent," the "maculate" here calls up and cancels "immaculate" and unsettles an easy reading of "cherished."[17] This is a house "Hidden, oh hidden / in the high fog," and, except for the "fat frogs" that "shrilling for love, / clamber and mount," all that goes on there is hidden too behind a protective covering that is described nonetheless in terms of physical closeness where "waterfalls cling" and "vapor" is seen "holding them both, / house and rock" (101).

But even in this context Bishop could treat a wholly new range of emotions. The "warm touch" could turn cold and cruel, and Bishop could write scathingly of its assaults. "Pink Dog" (published in 1979, but evident in early drafts dating from 1959 and perhaps written in 1964) takes the Carnival and the social and political corruption of Brazilian society as its subject. Concentrating on the naked ugliness of the diseased dog it addresses ("scabies," "hanging teats," "with or without legs," "depilated dog"), the speaker here appears to be moved by a fury that is physical, even sexual, in nature (*CP*, 190–91). As she urges the dog to disguise its ugliness by putting on mascara and dressing up, she imitates the misogynist society she seems to be castigating.

In "Pink Dog," the speaker projects onto the animal world the hysteria of a woman who has been sexually insulted. She finds a reflection of herself in the diseased dog and makes that dog stand for her own sense of misuse as well as for the outrageous violations against womankind in a misogynist society. The artifice of the poem's triple rhymes, the dressing up of poetic language in an adornment of form, appears to be the poet's collaboration with the oppressor, a bitter use of her own talents. The tone is acrimonious, the rage spitefully controlled, the sexual fury deadly. It is a poem that gathers the eroticism of *A Cold Spring* into the political interests of her later Brazilian poetry.

In her late poems Bishop turned away from the domestic themes of

Questions of Travel and worked toward the expression of emotions that marked the loss of that domesticity and the love that sustained it. These emotions are intensely felt, highly conflicted, and often severely distanced, as in "Crusoe in England," where Crusoe calls Friday "nice" and again "nice," "Pretty to watch; he had a pretty body" (*CP*, 166). The repetitions call attention to the desperation hidden in their generalized terms. Along with its understatements, Crusoe's language hints at how painful the loss has been, how confused Crusoe's affection for Friday has become, how close it is to erotic desire. This poem, like "Casabianca" and "The Gentleman of Shallot," plays with the literary reference it insists on making in order to free Bishop's own voice for direct statement. Like the gentleman of Shallot, Crusoe presents Bishop as cross-dressing, as if she found it easier to confess a man's passion for his own sex.

Loss became the subject of Bishop's late poetry, and she had the technical skill to render it powerfully. The form of the villanelle leads the speaker to the final expression of the emotion she has held back in "One Art," where "The art of losing isn't hard to master":

> —Even losing you (the joking voice, a gesture
> I love) I shan't have lied. It's evident
> the art of losing's not too hard to master
> though it may look like (*Write* it!) like disaster. (*CP*, 178)

Here love, even as it is particularized in voice and gesture, is reduced to the pain that must be mastered in its wake. It is named here because it has departed, as if it could only be named in departing.

"Sonnet," published after Bishop's death, returns to images of her middle period where she struggled to find a way of expressing without exposing the erotic impulse of her poetry. Here, in the sonnet form reduced to a dimeter line, which Costello rightly identifies as Bishop's antithetical use of poetic constraints to release more energy (241), Bishop summarizes the imagery of her earlier work:

> Caught—the bubble
> in the spirit-level,
> a creature divided;
> and the compass needle
> wobbling and wavering,
> undecided.
> Freed—the broken
> thermometer's mercury
> running away;

and the rainbow-bird
from the narrow bevel
of the empty mirror,
flying wherever
it feels like, gay! (*CP*, 192)

Like the birds of "II / Rain Towards Morning," the rainbow-bird here has been released from his cage, and the mirror of "Insomnia" is emptied of its images so that the inverted world is the real world at last. It is as if Bishop had to write a lifetime before, "divided" and "undecided" still, she could write "gay!" But long before she came to the ecstatic release of that exclamation mark, she worked to express the emotions of her own "creature divided." From the secrets that lovers' eyes could divine in her very early poems through the more tentative testings of love's powers and treacheries in the work of the 1940s to the celebration of domestic affection and its bitterest loss in her late poetry, Bishop moved through a wide variety of emotions, taking love and all its ramifications as a major subject of her poetry. If she has been little recognized as a love poet, it is because she was so successful in hiding the nature of her deepest emotion even as she openly declared it. In this, her poetry was a perfect expression of her life as a lesbian.

Citing Bishop's use of repetition or anaphora, Lombardi locates its inspiration in Stein's "A rose is a rose is a rose," claiming: "Like Stein before her, Bishop is interested in finding a form of writing that preserves the sense of vagueness and mutability she recognizes in the natural world. Without naming the body in either graphic or conventionally erotic terms, she conveys her sensual experience through her tender reiteration of certain talismanic words—words and phrases that gain their power through insistence, through playful echoing and reversal" (96–97).

It may be true that both Stein's circular use of the rose and Bishop's reiteration of rock-rose were efforts to renew and revive for their own uses the conventional symbol of love, but their love poetry remained quite different. Where Stein could write "I double you, of course you do. You double me, very likely to be. You double I double I double you double" (*YGS*, 115), Bishop could seldom express love's reciprocity. Even the self-duplicating gentleman of Shalott would conclude that "Half is enough." Nor is Bishop's celebration of the unidealized female body so affirmative as Stein's "One is right and so we mount and have what we want" in "Lifting Belly" (45). Even Bishop's most positive approach to the body is more restrained than Stein's; rather than mounting or lifting belly, Bishop engages in "The Shampoo" or "Conversation" or "While Someone Telephones." It is true that she could rivet her attention on startling physical details such as the masculine thumb in "The Thumb," but more typically she is far removed from physical contact, sleepless or waiting or unfulfilled.

Both Stein and Bishop wrote their erotic experience in code; both left some of their most revealing erotic poetry unpublished. They both expressed a certain amount of guilt about their sexual choice and their erotic experience. They both attempted to revise the romantic identification of women with nature—Stein by naming her experience in terms of the juiciest and most fecund fruit and, in the opposite extreme, Bishop by choosing lichens and crystals to symbolize the exploding energy of female sexuality. But, in the end, as love poets, the two are quite different. Stein always presents her lovers as part of a double, whereas Bishop often writes of the woman alone, abandoned, bereft, halved.

The difference is probably temperamental. Still, it owes something, too, to the progress of women's writing and self-awareness in the decades that separated the two. At the turn of the century, the woman poet had to express herself in the extreme if she were to express herself at all. In quite different ways H.D. and Marianne Moore were also driven to extremes of expression in finding their poetic voices among a generation of dominant male experimental writers. Stein's elaborate celebration of her love for Alice B. Toklas, even in the extreme nonsensical terms of *Tender Buttons*, was the prerequisite of expression. A milder, more subtle form of love poetry might have escaped notice entirely. By the time that Bishop came to write in the 1930s, she had the experience of not just Stein but Djuna Barnes, Virginia Woolf, and Amy Lowell, among others, to guide her. She enjoyed the expression of a fuller range of emotion than Stein. What she discovered, within the formidable restraints of her generation, was that this fuller range of emotions included fear, anxiety, guilt, and inadequacy. The woman writer with a publisher and a public ready to read her had still to deal with her own emotional limitations.

5

Bishop on
Conflicts
War, Race, &
Class

It was 1917 when Elizabeth Bishop was brought from Nova Scotia to the United States and there put into school where she was forced to pledge allegiance to the American flag and sing war songs that made her feel like a traitor, according to her report in "The Country Mouse" (*CPr*, 26). But the six-year-old found war itself and the war cartoons with "German helmets and cut-off hands" that her aunt was silenced from discussing in the household no more daunting than her own dislocation in her grandparents' home, she claims. The war was perhaps the only real link with her life in Nova Scotia, where she had seen soldiers who were, in contrast to the drab American soldiers, done up in "beautiful tam-o'-shanters with thistles and other insignia on them" and "wore kilts and sporrans" (28). Even the war songs were better in Canada, she remembered.

Identifying the style of Canadian patriotism, the military, even war, as stable knowledge to which she could cling in the general upheaval and confusion of her move to the foreign and unfathomable household of her American grandparents, Bishop presents herself as a confused child. This childhood confusion and her interest in different national styles of patriotism were to inform her poetry. In a number of different situations, she retained that child's judgmental stance.

Nationality and class rather than war are the alienating issues of Bishop's early imagination, and they figure prominently in the poems she would write about conflicts of all kinds—cultural, sexual, ethnic, and racial. She had a keen eye for the different national styles of war memorials, from L'Arc de Triomphe to the "shabby lot" of statues in Washington, D.C., which served her well as she surveyed the place of art—even poetry—in public life. Selecting the foreign patriotism of her childhood as a focus of the profound turmoil of her early life, Bishop reveals here neither fear of war nor sympathy for it, but rather a sense of patriotism as a theater that still seemed odd to her when she experienced it again as an adult.

Bishop lived in a century of wars, and war is everywhere in her poetry. It is almost always intertwined with a private suffering that appears quite unrelated to the conflict, as her early move from Canada seems unconnected to World War I, although, as we shall see, the outer and the inner wars are not so completely separate. Her attitude toward war may have been conditioned by her childhood sense of being an outsider, a non-patriot, a native of no country. In this, she presents an unusual example of the woman war poet. Whereas war for Stein had been a high adventure and patriotism a boisterous sentiment, Bishop looked on war and the military as an empty show and devotion to country as exploitative. Not treating the subject directly, despite the odd persistence of war as a subject and image in her poetry, Bishop chose to write about wars distanced both in time and place from her own experience: for example, the Civil War in "From Trollope's Journal," the Napoleonic Wars in "Casabianca," the Portuguese wars of conquest in "Brazil, January 1, 1502," or Robert Lowell's conscientious objection to World War II in "The Armadillo." Even in "Roosters," which attacks the baseness of the World War II militarism that she witnessed firsthand in Key West, she uses the distancing device of allegory and Christian myth. This strategy allowed her to write about war without being politically current, to parody war poetry without attacking those poets among her friends like Marianne Moore and Robert Lowell who were committed to writing it, and even to examine poetry's complicity with the theatrics of war.

Distanced as her poetry might have been from the wars she knew, Bishop invariably interjected into the subject of war and political upheavals some concern of her own—troubled sexual relations, conflicted love affairs, personal misery. Like Stein, she placed her love affairs in the context of the wars and the political turmoil that surrounded them; but, unlike Stein, Bishop often could not distinguish love from war. And, for obvious reasons, she shared none of Stein's patriotism. Nor was she to participate in Rich's perhaps equally patriotic furor with the politics of her native land. She may have railed about American politics in letters from Brazil to Robert Lowell, but she was as wary of expressing her ideas in public forums as she was of political poetry in general, commenting about such work during the depression to an interviewer in 1966, "I was always opposed to political thinking as such for writers. What good writing came out of that period really?" ("An Interview," 293), and in an unpublished review of Denise Levertov's work in 1970, "When has politics made good poetry?" (Millier, 301).

Neither Stein nor Rich would assume a simple attitude toward war. Stein took great pride in the American soldiers who came to France in both World Wars, expressing a kind of camaraderie with them, and Rich became an outspoken critic of American militarism, attacking as a feminist what she perceived as male violence. But Bishop had great difficulty in coming to terms with the subject and in situating herself within countries—both the United States and Brazil—toward which she felt divided loyalties. She was of two minds about political poetry. Writing in an age of politically committed poets, Bishop felt it necessary to apologize to her publisher for the lack of war poems in her first volume, fearing that "The fact that none of these poems deal directly with the war, at a time when so much war poetry is being published, will, I am afraid, leave me open to reproach" (MacMahon, 8). It is an odd fear, especially for a poet, who wrote one of the most powerful antiwar poems and also placed conflict not just between men as soldiers, but between lovers, between different classes and races, between servants and mistresses, at the center of so many of her poems. In fact, it is so odd that it seems to be one of the strategies behind which she hid so often in presenting herself as an ordinary woman. Her comment seems designed to identify her poems to her publisher as women's work, perhaps open to reproach because they do not deal with the men's subject of war and yet written by a woman savvy enough to know that war poetry was the topic of the day. War is, despite her disclaimer, often the topic of her poems.

Some of the most puzzling aspects of her first volume of poetry might be attributed to Bishop's ambivalence toward war as a subject which she seemed unable to avoid even if she did not treat it directly often. In her early poetry influenced by surrealism, war or warlike images abound. Since many of these poems are set in Paris, military monuments were everywhere available to her, and she filled her early poems with references to them. In "Sleeping on the Ceiling," the speaker imagines that it is so "peaceful" on the ceiling that it seems to be the "Place de la Concorde," ironically, despite its name, not a site of peace but rather of war, revolution, the guillotine. Yet not sleeping on the ceiling, the insomniac speaker cannot sleep at all, menaced as she is by private warlike horrors:

> We must go under the wallpaper
> to meet the insect-gladiator,
> to battle with a net and trident,
> and leave the fountain and the square. (*CP*, 29)

Leaving the fountain and the square of the Place de la Concorde, the very location of national upheaval, the speaker retreats into an inner world that is equally at war, however dated its weapons and mode of operation. This world returns in "Sleeping Standing Up" with its "armored cars of dreams" and "ugly tanks" that track the wandering children Hansel and Gretel (30). Dreams and reality alike are war-ridden in these poems.

It is in "Paris, 7 a.m." that Bishop turns directly, however surrealistically, to the war, beginning, "I make a trip to each clock in the apartment" and identifying the clocks with "Time" itself and "Time" with an "Etoile" (*CP*, 26). In Paris, L'Etoile is L'Arc de Triomphe, with the twelve avenues that radiate from it, commemorating Napoleon's victories and evoking imperial glory and the fate of the Unknown Soldier whose tomb lies beneath. In Bishop's poem, the hours of this Time/Etoile "diverge / so much that days are journeys round the suburbs, / circles surrounding stars, overlapping circles" (26) in a surrealistic meshing of time and space as imperial power emanates both outward from Napoleon's time to Bishop's own but also outward from the imperial city to the countryside. Locating herself in winter, the actual season of Bishop's Paris' stay, the speaker reinforces the reference to military action by noting that "Winter lives under a pigeon's wing, a dead wing with damp feathers." Death permeates the landscape of this poem, as the speaker, looking in the courtyard, finds "ornamental urns" on the mansard rooftops where "pigeons" take their walks, although strangely enough "the childish snow-forts" "could not dissolve and die" in this surrealistic picture. She asks, "Where is the ammunition, the piled-up balls / with the star-splintered hearts of ice?" Again taking up the associations of war, the speaker claims, "This sky is no carrier-warrior-pigeon / escaping endless intersecting circles"; rather, "it is a dead one" (26). She asks, "When did the star dissolve, or was it captured / by the sequence of squares and squares and circles, circles?" (27). The sequence of squares commemorating military victories and civic power has captured the star—both Napoleon and the "star-splintered hearts of ice" that have waged endless war—in timeless memorials that attempt pointlessly to keep alive the war dead (26).

Opening the poem with the clocks in which "some hands point histrionically one way / and some point others, from the ignorant faces," Bishop goes on to develop the connection between history and histrionics, between actual historical events and the theatrical performance of military commemorations, which end in city street plans or more pathetically simply in urns beside which only pigeons walk (*CP*, 26). It is as if Bishop, who reports reading Wallace Stevens's *Idea of Order* and *Owl's Clover* at this time (*OA*, 44–45, 48), was attempting to rewrite Stevens's statue and even to anticipate the still-to-be-written *Notes Toward a Supreme Fiction* with its decaying monuments. She appears so attuned to Stevens's writing that she even sounds like him in her comment to Moore about revisions she had made of "Paris, 7 a.m." in which she apologizes for being so obstinate but insists on "apartments," claiming, "To me the word suggests so strongly the structure of the house, later referred to, and suggests a 'cut-off' mode of existence so well" (*OA*, 46) or like the lives Stevens was to describe in *Notes Toward a Supreme Fiction* when he writes of "the celestial ennui of apartments."

Inspired by the clock collection in the apartment in which she lived in Paris, "Paris, 7 a.m." draws together various strands of Bishop's early interests. The history and histrionics of time itself dissolve into those vain civic and imperial gestures toward stopping time by creating fixed memorials or mapping space evident at L'Etoile or in squares that similarly commemorate moments in history. What appears to be a poem of surrealistic blending of time and space picks up hints from "The Monument" of how vainglorious memorials are, how perfectly dead the dead warriors remain despite efforts to memorialize them. If it is not exactly a pacifist poem, "Paris, 7 a.m." provides an ironic commentary on the vaunted permanence of military victory.[1]

When Bishop was working on this poem in 1936, she was very much aware of the ravages of the Spanish Civil War, writing to Marianne Moore: "The war in Spain is frightful. I wonder if you saw the amazingly pathetic pictures in the *Times* a few days ago—the wooden and plastic statues and crucifixes, all periods and quantities, dragged out of a church in Barcelona, lying so that at first one thought they were dead soldiers. There was something suspiciously dramatic about the arrangement, which makes it even truer to what I've heard about the Spanish character" (*OA*, 45).

Here, too, she emphasizes the histrionics of war reporting as if the Spanish character were no more trustworthy in this respect than the French had been in "Paris, 7 a.m." And, of course, in her willingness to identify *the* Spanish character, she engages in some histrionics of her own, not unlike Stein's pronouncements in her 1935 lecture at the University of Chicago about how "anybody is as their land and air is" (*N*, 46). In fact, Bishop may have had in mind Stein's interest in geography as she followed Stein's American tour. Bishop's resistance to the drama of the Spanish character also seems to echo Stein's antitheatrical drama, *Four Saints in Three Acts*, in which nothing happens.

Even as she was concentrating on this "suspiciously dramatic" treatment of war, Bishop was concerned about her own inadequacy in writing war poetry. Sorting through her work to find a poem that Horace Gregory might want to publish, she wrote in 1937: "I don't know who the other poets you are gathering are, or what the material is likely to be like—but in case it's all 'social consciousness,' etc., and you'd rather keep up a united front, I am sending 'War in Ethiopia.' Of course it is very out-of-date, and I am not sure whether my attempts at this kind of thing are much good, but I should like to have you see it, too, and tell me what you think" (*OA*, 55–56). Although "War in Ethiopia" has been lost apparently, this letter suggests that Bishop might have been consciously trying to write war poetry even as she was attacking its histrionics.

The impulse evident in "Paris, 7 a.m." to deflate the significance of war by pointing to the histrionics of its treatment found expression in two quite different early poems, "Wading at Wellfleet" and "Casabianca." They draw on nineteenth-century treatments of the Napoleonic Wars— the first on Byron's "Destruction of Semnacherib," the second on Felicia Hemans's poem—but they redirect the imagery from war to personal experience and, in the process, show up its pomposity. "Wading at Wellfleet" opens with Byron's "Assyrian wars" from the Bible which introduced "a chariot" "that bore sharp blades around its wheels"; but, in the modern world, the speaker finds this military image transformed into nature itself: "this morning's glitterings reveal / the sea is 'all a case of knives,'" and "The war rests wholly with the waves" (*CP*, 7). The quotation here is not from Byron, but from George Herbert's "Affliction IV" in which "my thoughts" are "all a case of knives," and so the knife imagery moves from the biblical war of Byron's poem through nature into the individual psyche. But, the speaker concludes, the "wheels" of this imagery "will not bear the weight," and they "give way." And so Bishop's poem undoes the threatening quality of its opening image, rendering it strangely inconsequential. Never tempted, as she was to write in "Santarém," to literary interpretations "such as: life/death, right/wrong, male/female" (185), Bishop does not divide her poems between militarism/pacificism, war/peace, but rather indicates how the two bleed into each other as the act of wading at Cape Cod participates in and then retreats from the elaborate analogy of its opening description. She was to repeat this technique in more successful form in "Roosters," where the arrogantly strutting militaristic rooster gives way to the humbling of St. Peter, as if militarism could be pacified by Christian humility.

Another early work, Bishop's "Casabianca," outrageously flouts its predecessor's sentimental celebration of willful military sacrifice. Imaging love as "the obstinate boy," Bishop subverts filial devotion as well as military discipline, making a mockery of Hemans's bombast as well as all war poetry where "the boy stood on the burning deck / trying to recite 'The boy stood on / the burning deck'" (*CP*, 5). Even the sailors who have escaped the burning ship would prefer their regular routine to any heroism or "an excuse to stay / on deck" as much as the "schoolroom platform" in which their patriotic deeds are commemorated. It is only common sense to prefer life to possible death. "Casabianca" seems to be stating the obvious; yet despite the openness of its reference and declarations, "Casabianca" is a poem that hides its meaning. Its chief interest here is the curiosity of Bishop's reference to the devalued work of that rare figure of the woman war poet. Perhaps, in her efforts to fend off her own sense of inadequacy as a poet, if not of war, at least of "social consciousness," she turned to Hemans as an example of how completely destructive to poetry such an enterprise could be. Reworking these nineteenth-century poems, in Susan Schweik's view, Bishop comments "not only on the language of war but, in exaggerated fashion, on poetry's promotional and disciplinary functions in modern Western war systems" (236). But if Bishop's position appears to criticize such poetic functions, it is curiously empty of any pacifist message, as Willard Spiegelman suggests in noting that she disarms the military apparatus of the poem without filling the void it leaves

(Schwartz and Estess, 60). Although the military floods her imaginative treatment even of topics far from war during this period of her life, Bishop often deflects the full force of its reference.

"Roosters" is the poem that treats the military most directly, and yet, even here, Bishop writes in fables; the roosters' "traditional cries," their "protruding chests / in green-gold medals dressed, / planned to command and terrorize the rest" (*CP*, 35) must stand for human cockiness and its attendant military expression as well. Years later, commenting on this poem to an interviewer, Bishop was afraid that it might be read too directly. She reveals, "I suddenly realized it sounded like a feminist tract, which it wasn't meant to sound like at all to begin with" ("'The Work,'" 320). Critics, too, have commented on its feminist attack on war, reading the turn in the poem's second half to St. Peter and Christian forgiveness as a transformation from the militarism of the poem's opening.[2] Arguing that it is a buried aubade as well as the most "fiercely vivid critique of male power and of militarism by an American woman poet during the Second World War" (217), Schweik details, in an elaborate and brilliant reading of the poem's dialectic movement, just how conflicted the poem is. She comments: "Drawing the Peter/crucifixion analogy *inward*—into the bedroom, that sphere of the private, the domestic, the feminine, the sexual, the dream—it implicates the woman speaker in psychic structures of conflict, violence, and betrayal formerly reserved for specifically male or vaguely generalized others" (231–32).

Despite the power of "Roosters," Bishop remained of two minds about writing on such subjects as war. In a letter to Frani Blough Muser, she notes her excitement over selling "Roosters" to the *New Republic* (*OA*, 87); but, at the same time, she writes: "The literary highlight of the Key West season at present is James Farrell, who *looks* tough, maybe, but is just like a lamb that can swear—no, a sheep would be more accurate. I am utterly disgusted with 'social-conscious' conversation—by people who always seem to be completely unconscious of their surroundings, other people's personalities, etc. etc." (87).

Nor did she feel any more comfortable with "social-conscious" poetry, it would seem. Writing about "Roosters" to May Swenson almost twenty years later, she was anxious to domesticate it and remove it from public reference, claiming that she worked on the poem over four or five years, but had started it in the backyard at Key West at 4:00 or 5:00 A.M. "with the roosters carrying on just as I said" (*OA*, 316). But, closer to the composition of the poem in her infamous argument with Marianne Moore about its details, Bishop reveals her fascination with and her insistence on its socially conscious and military details. Admitting that in the first part she was thinking about Key West, Bishop adds that she also had in mind "those aerial views of dismal little towns in Finland and Norway, when the Germans took over, and their atmosphere of poverty" (96). Claiming too that she wanted "Roosters" and not Moore's suggested "The Cock" as a title, she admits that she wished to repeat "gun-metal" and "had in mind the violent roosters Picasso did in connection with his *Guernica* picture." She explains, "About the 'glass-headed pins': I felt the roosters to be placed here and there (by their various crowings) like the pins that point out war projects on a map" (96). Thus, wanting to "emphasize the essential baseness of militarism," as she wrote to Moore, she wanted also to tie her poem to particularities of military reference. Although she writes a fable, she writes from an alert attention to the details of an ongoing war.

Oddly enough, the military that seemed everywhere evident in *North & South* disappears almost entirely from Bishop's next volume. Even writing from Washington, D.C., she does not respond to its monumental architecture as she had responded earlier to Paris. Her year as consultant in the Library of Congress was a difficult one for her personally, and it provided few subjects for poems (Millier, 219–27). Only "View of the Capitol from the Library of Congress" treats Washington as her surrealistic poems had Paris, and it is not a view but sounds of the Air Force Band that provide her with a perspective on the nation's military life (Millier, 223). Writing from the unusual experience of listening to band music that faded in and out of hearing, Bishop provides a sardonic commentary on the efforts of the "Air Force Band" insistently dressed in "uniforms of Air Force blue" "playing hard and loud, but—queer— / the music doesn't quite come through" (*CP*, 69). This ceremonial city is obscured by a more gigantic nature, somewhat like the threatening waves in "Wading at Wellfleet," as Bishop notes that "giant trees" silence the band and:

Unceasingly the little flags
feed their limp stripes into the air,
and the band's efforts vanish there. (69)

She urges:

Great shades, edge over,
give the music room.
The gathered brasses want to go
boom—boom. (69)

Again, as in the earlier Paris poems, the past—both natural and civic—overshadows the present, and the "*boom—boom*" of the Air Force Band seems a feeble attempt to declare its own glory or even assert its military presence.

It took Bishop some years to write two other poems about war and politics that her year in Washington, D.C., must have inspired. "Visits to St. Elizabeths" and "From Trollope's Journal" reflect a much later stage in her development and in her political awareness that was to be ripened by her long stay in Brazil. Still, even in her Washington year, the public role of poetry in time of war could not have escaped Bishop's consideration since part of her duties in the Library of Congress involved visits to Ezra Pound, then incarcerated at St. Elizabeth's Hospital for the Criminally Insane. The visits were trying for Bishop, as Millier reports (220–22), not just because Pound was a difficult patient, but also because Bishop, herself succumbing to bouts of alcoholism during this difficult year, could see in Pound's madness a frightening version of what might have been her own fate. Thus, her visits to St. Elizabeth's were also a confrontation with her own weakness and guilt, "the house of Bedlam" that both she and Pound seemed to inhabit and even to have built themselves.

Writing from the model of the nursery rhyme, "This is the house that Jack built," Bishop calls Pound "tragic," "talkative," "honored," "old, brave man," "cranky," "cruel," "busy," "tedious"—running the full range of his qualities; but in the end, she judges him:

This is the soldier home from the war.
These are the years and the walls and the door
that shut on a boy that pats the floor
to see if the world is round or flat.
This is a Jew in a newspaper hat
that dances carefully down the ward,
walking the plank of a coffin board
with the crazy sailor
that shows his watch
that tells the time
of the wretched man
that lies in the house of Bedlam. (*CP*, 135)

This indictment of Pound's self-deception and lies (and her own self-mockery) is Bishop's most sympathetic statement of the sufferings of war and concomitantly her most serious expression of doubts about the value of serious poetry. "This is a world of books gone flat" (134), she writes, as if "the poet" in Pound could not be separated from "the man" and his inadequacy. Time may have proved Bishop accurate in her judgment; but, when this poem was written, only a few years after the controversy over Pound's Bollingen Award and the poetic establishment's defense of art against political judgments, its criticism of Pound had a particular political charge, taking the unpopular side of the whole debate over the poet and the value of his poetry apart from his politics. Perhaps Bishop's sense of her own failures in the unhappy year she spent in Washington forced her to reflect on the civic duties of the poet. Certainly part of the impulse for this poem was her personal reaction to Pound as a difficult and irascible man. Still, the poem presents Pound as tragically irresponsible, not saved by his art and not just cranky but cruel as well. Written long after her year in Washington, the poem reflects too the political awareness of her years in Brazil where the artist was never safe from political involvement nor protected from his own rash acts as Pound had been.

Some time later still, she returned to Washington, D.C., as a scene and war as a subject in "From Trollope's Journal," which she told Robert Lowell was almost all a complete quotation from Trollope himself (*OA*, 387), even if it was also, as she claimed later on, "actually an anti-Eisenhower poem" (439). Although she may have used Trollope's commentary on the monuments, the sentiments are familiar again from Bishop's own early treatment of national monuments, although here they interject into the equation the whole question of race that might have come out of her experience in Brazil:

> As far as statues go, so far there's not
> much choice: they're either Washington
> or Indians, a whitewashed, stubby lot,
> His country's Father or His foster sons. (*CP*, 132)

The "sad, unhealthy spot" of the White House on Potomac's "swampy brim" is matched by Trollope's own throbbing "anthrax," and even the surgeon who attends him comes "with a sore throat himself" and "croaked out," " 'Sir, I do declare / everyone's sick! The soldiers poison the air' " (132).

As a commentary on war, "From Trollope's Journal" is almost as treasonous as Pound's World War II broadcasts. An attack on the sickness of the defenseless soldiers recuperating in Washington, D.C., from the ravages of the Civil War, the poem voices a pitiless indictment of the sickness of war. Even phrased in Trollope's English xenophobic reaction to America, the sentiments are repellently self-centered and callously unconcerned with the larger human sacrifices of war. Published in 1961, the poem expressed the antiwar sentiment of the time, although only a few years earlier it would have come under suspicion as radically anti-American.

Bishop's return to war as a subject and Washington, D.C., as a location in these two late poems brings with it some of the concerns of her life in Brazil that turned her toward politics and the military as a subject. In her early poetry from Brazil, she took on the cast of that country's history and politics, revealing her talent for caricature. From the Portuguese conquerors in "Brazil, January 1, 1502" to the hysterical military police in pursuit of a killer in "The Burglar of Babylon," Bishop treats the conquering army as well as the Brazilian military as objects of contempt. Comparing them to lizards, she belittles them further in "Brazil, January 1, 1502":

> Just so the Christians, hard as nails,
> tiny as nails, and glinting,
> in creaking armor. (*CP*, 92)

These "tiny" lustful conquerors are no match, however, for the native women:

> Directly after Mass, humming perhaps
> *L'Homme armé* or some such tune,
> they ripped away into the hanging fabric,
> each out to catch an Indian for himself—
> those maddening little women who kept calling,
> calling to each other. (92)

Nor are the soldiers tracking Micuçú in "The Burglar of Babylon" of any finer quality. They remain completely unequal to this "enemy of society" (112) who seems nonetheless at home among the poor of his own social class. Even with tommy guns in hand, they are nervous, shooting the officer in command in a panic, and Micuçú eludes them successfully until, shooting a soldier at close range and missing, he is finally killed. These scenes are cartoonlike in their exaggerated parody of South American incompetence in its lust for military power. And yet, like the exaggerated concern for the dog with scabies in "Pink Dog," the sentiments of these poems cover a severe indictment of the repressive political regimes that first colonized and then came to rule the country.

Bishop did not have to go to Brazil to see such strife. The racial discord between the white colonizers and the maddening Indian women and the class struggles between Micuçú and his captors may have come out of Bishop's Brazilian experience, but they are not new to her poetry. Despite her disgust with "social-conscious conversation," she was fascinated by that other war between race and class that characterized so much of the internal politics of her time. Her early poems from Key West often take as subjects such conflicts. Although she was a member of the dominant culture in the United States, a country that, despite its ethnic variety, has regarded ethnic groups as outsiders, Bishop had occasion from earliest childhood to consider herself an outsider, witnessing confrontations of class and race quite unusual in American life—for example, between the impoverished, if homogeneous, rural community of her maternal grand-parents in Nova Scotia and the richer society of her paternal grandparents in Worcester, Massachusetts, where she was moved as a child, or between servants and mistresses in her early adult life in Key West.

If she thought of herself as "a New Englander herring-choker blue-noser" in Brazil, as she told Lowell (*OA*, 384) (although, strictly speaking, she was not a New Englander but a transplanted Nova Scotian), she also had an interest in other classes and races, as if she could study in their conflicts something of her own conflicted identity. Adrienne Rich has claimed that her poems about servants and mistresses take the place of poems examining intimate relationships (*BBP*, 130). But, in fact, these poems about mistress and servant, landowner and tenant, white woman and black woman, indicate a strange interest in the intimacy in which these racial conflicts play out. Commenting on "Songs for a Colored Singer," the poem Bishop wrote in the 1940s with Billie Holiday in mind, Rich again questions this choice:

> This is a white woman's attempt—respectful, I believe—to speak through a Black woman's voice. A risky undertaking, and it betrays the failures and clumsiness of such a position. The personae we adopt, the degree to which we use lives already ripped off and violated by our own culture, the problem of racist stereotyping in every white head, the issue of the writer's power, right, obligation to speak for others denied a voice, or the writer's duty to shut up at times or at least to make room for those who can speak with more immediate authority—these are crucial questions for our time, and questions that are relevant to much of Bishop's work. What I value is her attempt to acknowledge other outsiders, lives marginal in ways that hers is not, long before the Civil Rights movement made such awareness temporarily fashionable for some white writers. (*BBP*, 131)

Rich wants to claim Bishop for a female and lesbian tradition that has tried critically and consciously to "explore marginality, power and power-lessness, often in poetry of great beauty and sensuousness" (135), and, at the same time, to acknowledge the problems inherent in an establishment poet taking on such a task.

Although other critics have judged Bishop less severely, Rich is correct in acknowledging the outsider perspective from which Bishop views these figures and the subservient situations in which they find themselves.[3] And yet, of course, they were very much a part of her life and circumstances. In some sense, they held her interest over a lifetime and in varying environments because she identified with them. So she writes too as an insider, knowledgeable about the marginal, the exiled, and the dispossessed in society because she was one herself. She knew the bonds, even chains, of attraction and repulsion between classes and races that linked lives that would be solitary and lonely without them. In taking up such subjects, Bishop was acknowledging a range of experience that she, as a solitary woman, even a lonely tourist, knew intimately; but, like Sylvia Plath's appropriation of the Jew in a Fascist society as a metaphor for her own condition as a woman, Bishop's poetic possession of the dispossessed is a problematic choice. She does not evince any of Rich's openhearted political sentiment about class exploitation. At the same time, she writes from a deep sensitivity to ties that blur the boundaries of race and class.

Violence is often at the heart of the lives of the Key West African Americans she treats. For example, "Cootchie," Miss Lula's maid, appears to be a person known only by the erasure of her identity; in life as in death, "black into white she went," first as a maid and then as a suicide "below the surface of the coral reef" (*CP*, 46). No dramatic monologue records her wordless life, and yet the nine-line stanzas provide an elaborate, artificial structure for this minimal life, working their rhymes to diminish "kitchen table" into "faces sable," "wax roses" into "losses," "grave" into "wave." In a kind of reversal of her early monument poems, Bishop suggests how form can accurately focus as well as needlessly expand expression. Yet, the unusual rhyme scheme (abcbcdefe) signals something of Cootchie's significance for the poet as for Miss Lula, who, unable to understand what has happened to Cootchie, still can "mark" her losses with the artifice of a "line" of "pink wax roses / planted in tin cans filled with sand" (46).

According to Thomas Travisano, Miss Lula ran the boardinghouse in Naples, Florida, where Bishop stayed on her first trip, and her black servant Cootchie told Bishop, "That's why I like coloured folks—they never commit suicide" (83–84). But, of course, Cootchie does commit suicide in the poem and causes both the poet and Miss Lula to commemorate her. Like the war monuments in Paris, Miss Lula's memorial is only a way of covering up experience, a very stylized way of holding in abeyance baffling circumstances. But the poem is titled "Cootchie" not "Miss

Lula," and the maid dominates the poet's sense of how artificial most art is, how little even the most elaborate artifice can rescue. "Black into white she went" is a powerful reminder of racial assimilation against which art cannot defend its subject.

How little the outsider can understand racial conflicts is evident in "Faustina, or Rock Roses," where the speaker observes Faustina tending the white woman in "a crazy house" (*CP*, 72). Another subject drawn from real life in Key West, she, too, is both victim and victimizer in a conflict of intimacy:[4]

> Her sinister kind face
> presents a cruel black
> coincident conundrum.
>   Oh, is it
>
> freedom at last, a lifelong
> dream of time and silence,
> dream of protection and rest?
> Or is it the very worst,
> the unimaginable nightmare
> that never before dared last
>   more than a second?
>
> The acuteness of the question
> forks instantly and starts
> a snake-tongue flickering;
> blurs further, blunts, softens,
> separates, falls, our problems
> becoming helplessly
>   proliferative.
>
> There is no way of telling.
> The eyes say only either. (73–74)

The question of "freedom at last" turns first to death and then to release from servitude, but whose death and whose release are the conundrum.[5] Is death of the mistress freedom for the maid or freedom from the maid's sinister kindness for the mistress herself? And what is the "unimaginable nightmare"? The visitor is as intertwined in the scene as those she surveys; she is "embarrassed" not for intruding into this privacy, but for being part of the disguise, for betraying her own stupefaction within which she may discover, if not concern, at least that she should be concerned. Taking this in, the reader too can see herself drawn into the poem, understand how her own view of what is going on may betray a voyeuristic curiosity rather than concern, a desire to know what the poem means rather than what death signifies in the lives of these two women.

This is not a poem of rich and poor so much as a poem of trust and protection spelled out in racial terms, where trust has always been intertwined with exploitation. The white woman whom Faustina tends lives in a decaying house where the floorboards sag and the bedroom is cluttered with ragged garments. She is not rich, nor is Faustina, complaining of the terms of her employment, either without resources or all suffering. "She bends above the other," the speaker says of Faustina, noting both her superior and her subservient position. The racial component of the situation marks an exploitation that works both ways.

What the visitor sees, if she sees at all, is the solidarity of mistress and maid, their interdependence, as a "dream of protection and rest" that may turn into a "nightmare" at any moment.[6] The fragility of such a relationship is all the more frightening because the women depend utterly on it. The speaker of the poem manipulates this fear by the mixing of such opposites as stupefaction and concern, sinister and kind, dream and nightmare. And this speaker, like the visitor, is no transparent observer; she is a kind of voyeur gasping for breath in the linguistically excessive "yes" in the opening lines ("Tended by Faustina / yes in a crazy house") and "oh" in the final lines ("and wonders oh, whence come / all the petals") (*CP*, 72, 74). In the "crazy house" of this poem, everyone is threatened (72). "Oh" turns easily into "O," into blankness and a cipher. "There is no way of telling," the poet concludes of this conflict (74).

Beyond Key West, Bishop saw other social conflicts fixed by race and class. In settling in Brazil in 1951, she had a new social system from which to draw characters and themes as well as a purchase on the society of her earliest childhood where the conditions of poverty did not preclude an important sense of identity and a code of conduct, as she writes in "Manners." But the conflict, as well as the intimacy between classes and races in Brazil, is the subject of "Manuelzhino," where both landowner and tenant are locked together in their relationship to the land: "Half squatter, half tenant (no rent)— / a sort of inheritance" (*CP*, 96), he is a human being who holds his tenure on the land with the same fragile claim that she does herself. Over account books, she says, "we dream together / how the meek shall inherit the earth— / or several acres of mine" (98). The irony of the last line does not completely undercut the biblical enjoinder to meekness which the speaker shares with her tenant.

Manuelzhino and his mistress are linked in many ways. She orders "pounds of seeds, / imported, guaranteed," and, with the same profligacy, he plants gardens that, she tells him, "ravish my eyes," edging "beds of silver cabbages / with red carnations" (*CP*, 96). She hands over money; he prays for her. Like a mother, she alternately puts up with his foolishness, yells at him, gives in to his "wistful / face" (97–98), teases him, and loves him all she can. Manuelzhino, the gardener, requires tending as much as he tends. But he is not without his own gifts. He provides her with a spectacle, a family, confidences, needs. In return, she does her part, providing him with an audience, money, as well as a protection that is familial, and needs that he in turn must fill.

In this relationship between mistress and squatter-tenant, there is something more than the "amused and affectionate condescension" that Goldensohn finds (193) or the "self-conscious whimsy" that Bromwich detects (168). Unlike the emotional tensions of "Faustina, or Rock Roses" that seemed so impenetrable, the speaker of this poem, identified as a friend of the poet, knows how dependent on each other she and Manuelzhino are. If he takes his hat off to her when he comes "sniffing and shivering" (*CP*, 97) begging for money, she takes her hat off to him in admiration at the end. She may be Lady Bountiful; he may be totally dependent on her. But he too is bountiful and she dependent.

Evidence of the tyranny against the poor, Manuelzhino is also a kind of magical creature. He may be the "worst gardener since Cain," but he produces "a mystic three-legged carrot" (*CP*, 96). A victim of the strangest things, he is also the witness of unusual insights, imagining his dead father not dead, for example. As generous as his mistress, Manuelzhino provides a bus for the "delighted mourners" at the funeral and "Electrical Baby Syrup" for his sick child, keeping his accounts in a dream book. Yet he appears also completely infantilized by his class and race, indulged by a woman whose generosity fetters as its supports him.

Written when she was herself living in the same household as Manuelzhino and enjoying, as he did, the affection of the same woman, Bishop would have little to condescend to in this portrait. If she is whimsical, it is only an imitation of Manuelzhino's whimsy. In contrast to the ambivalence of the earlier "Faustina, or Rock Roses" and the scorn of the later "Pink Dog," this poem sentimentalizes the bonds that tie this man to this woman. She dramatizes conflicts of race and class as a family farce rather than a social and political tragedy.

A quite different kind of conflict is evident in another early poem written in Brazil, "The Armadillo," which also expresses conflicted feelings toward the natives who honor St. John's Day each year by sending up dangerous fire balloons. But it introduces into what seems a purely descriptive scene the completely extraneous presence of Robert Lowell, to whom the poem is dedicated, who turns the poem in the direction of political commentary. The poem starts casually as one of Bishop's accounts of local Brazilian customs, noting, "This is the time of year / when almost every night / the frail, illegal fire balloons appear" (*CP*, 103). Moving toward the planets, Venus and Mars, love and war, these balloons seem, at first, merely splendid spectacles that "flush and fill with light" "like hearts," perfectly expressive of the launchers' devotion to St. John. But "turning dangerous," they fall to earth, burning the underside of the owls, their nest, turning the armadillo "rose-flecked," and burning off the baby rabbit's ear (103–4). This disastrous scene is detailed with such distance that the speaker herself seems capable of equal cruelty until her tone changes in the final stanza:

> *Too pretty, dreamlike mimicry!*
> *O falling fire and piercing cry*
> *and panic, and a weak mailed fist*
> *clenched ignorant against the sky!* (104)

This outburst, so long delayed, seems completely detached in its protest from the scene on which it comments. What is *"Too pretty"*—the fire balloons, the devotion to the saint, the speaker's own descriptive powers, the potential danger of the fire? Is this fire bombing reminiscent of the fire bombing of World War II? The poem's particularities seem to draw it away from any general reference, and yet the ending in italics has the power to unsettle the details. It is clear that, whatever is too pretty, the clenched fist will not overcome it. Physical force and "pretty" art that mimics the world are alike ineffectual, both inadequate to the panic that the falling fire brings.

Because this poem is dedicated to Lowell and titled "The Armadillo" instead of "The Owl's Nest," an earlier alternate title, the fist clenched against the sky calls up not just the armadillo's retreat from the fire, but all forms of retreat, "head down, tail down," such as Lowell's status as a conscientious objector during World War II as well as bouts of madness through which he retreated "weak" and "ignorant." Violence, the speaker seems to suggest, can never be countered by violence, folly by folly. In a world where fire balloons attract and appall us, where piety itself is pretty and dangerous, and—in a surprising turn toward the military—where clenched fists are weak and ignorant, the impulses to self-protection and self-destruction are fatally intertwined. If Lowell was inspired by "The

Armadillo" to write "Skunk Hour," which he dedicated to Bishop, he moved away from her mixed message toward an affirmation, however qualified, of the personal will to go on.[7] Bishop keeps free from Lowell's confessional "I," suggesting that that will is everywhere threatened, not just in the modern world but in its history where saints were honored and fists "mailed."

Bishop's wars may have been internal, but she figured them in ancient terms—the "insect-gladiator" of her nightmares in "Sleeping on the Ceiling," the "creaking armor" of the Christian conquerors of "Brazil, January 1, 1502," and the "mailed fist" clenched against the sky of "The Armadillo"—as if the quaintness of the reference might suggest something of her criticism of war itself. The images bear a certain burden of ridicule as the tiny insect diminishes the grandeur of the gladiator and the "tiny" Christians are further miniaturized by their "creaking armor," the fist rendered impotent by its ignorance. It is as if Bishop were engaging in her own "pretty" "mimicry" by capturing war in such literary and old-fashioned terms.

The relation between art and war, between efforts at commemoration and the acts of war, between poetry and politics—a recurring interest from her surrealistic Paris poems to her realistic Brazilian writing—finds its summary statement in "12 O'Clock News," a prose poem that juxtaposes the objects on the writer's desktop with an account of a reconnaissance flight in what might be the Vietnam War. According to Millier, this poem had been with Bishop in fragments of verse since her Vassar days (474); but, as it was completed, it depends on details of a war against an unknown "small, backward country, one of the most backward left in the world today," a "tiny principality" where "'industrialization' and its products" are "almost nonexistent" (*CP*, 174) that sounds like Vietnam.

As the poem plays details from the writer's desk against details of the war, an eerie connection between writing and war emerges. The writer's "gooseneck lamp" is matched with the full moon half the world over where "Visibility is poor"; the "typewriter" with the "elaborate terraces" of the enemy landscape; "pile of mss." and a "slight landslide"; "typed sheet" and a "'field'" that may be either "airstrip" or "cemetery"; "ink-bottle" and "some powerful and terrifying 'secret weapon'"; typewriter eraser and a dead native; and finally, in the most gruesome connection, "ashtray" and

> From our superior vantage point, we can clearly see into a sort of dugout, possibly a shell crater, a "nest" of soldiers. They lie heaped together, wearing the camouflage "battle dress" intended for "winter warfare." They are in hideously contorted positions, all dead. We can

make out at least eight bodies. These uniforms were designed to be used in guerrilla warfare on the country's one snow-covered mountain peak. The fact that these poor soldiers are wearing them *here*, on the plain, gives further proof, if proof were necessary, either of the childishness and hopeless impracticality of this inscrutable people, our opponents, or of the sad corruption of their leaders. (*CP*, 175)

All that destabilizes the clear connection between the writer's effort at her desk and war activity is the tone of the reporter on the 12 o'clock news, at every point exclaiming his/her "superior vantage point" while revealing his/her naïveté. Admitting ignorance ("The natural resources of the country being far from completely known to us"), s/he admits also the stupidity of her/his knowledge ("On the other hand, given what we *do* know, or have learned from our anthropologists and sociologists about this people") (*CP*, 175). As the news goes on, it becomes increasingly clear that the reporter can tell us very little about the other country and even less about the war itself; all s/he can really report is death and destruction. If the equation between writing and war is complete in this poem, then writing is destructive, not a memorializing of war but rather its apotheosis.

For a poet who had spent a lifetime writing about war, witnessing the conflicts not just of nations but of races and classes within the United States and Brazil, this final acknowledgment of the close collaboration between writing and war is, as James Merrill said, her "saddest poem" (quoted in Millier, 474). She had never liked "social-conscious conversation" or socially conscious poetry, and yet she returned again and again in her poetry to those points at which the world in which she lived and the world that she created could not avoid collision. The news reporter's language in "12 O'Clock News" is as inflated as the rhetoric of Felicia Hemans's poem of the Napoleonic Wars which the young Bishop had parodied, and the poet's deflation of it is as extreme; but, in the course of a long life of thinking about such matters, Bishop had come to fear that the poet's desk was not free from the world's corruption, her own creativity not unconnected to the subject of war from which she so often had recoiled.

In the dust jacket of *Geography III* where "12 O'Clock News" was published, John Ashbery is quoted as writing: "The extraordinary thing about Miss Bishop is that she is both a public and a private poet, or perhaps it is that her poetry by its very existence renders obsolete these two after all artificial distinctions (artificial insofar as poetry is concerned)" (MacMahon, 105). Strangely enough, in connecting the private and the public in her late poetry, Bishop came to understand the value of both, as she had learned their hazards. Perhaps the person who taught her most in this respect was Lowell, especially in his scandalous use of private letters from Elizabeth Hardwick in *The Dolphin*. In a long and tormented letter to Lowell, Bishop writes: "One can use one's life as material—one does, anyway—but these letters—aren't you violating a trust? IF you were given permission—IF you hadn't changed them . . . etc. But *art just isn't worth that much*. I keep remembering Hopkins's marvelous letter to Bridges about the idea of a 'gentleman' being the highest thing ever conceived— higher than a 'Christian,' even, certainly than a poet. It is not being 'gentle' to use personal, tragic, anguished letters that way—it's cruel" (*OA*, 562).

Given these views and Lowell's own willingness to make the most intimate details of his private life a matter of public record, it is certainly ironic that, when Bishop came to write an elegy for him, she memorializes his private moments—when he told her he had discovered "'girls'" one summer in Maine and "learned to kiss" (*CP*, 188)—but she concludes by noting—somewhat gratefully—that he can no longer change his art:

> You left North Haven, anchored in its rock,
> afloat in mystic blue . . . And now—you've left
> for good. You can't derange, or re-arrange,
> your poems again. (But the Sparrows can their song.)
> The words won't change again. Sad friend, you cannot change. (189)

The poet, who had started by considering the deadness of those un- changing monuments that surrounded her in Paris as a young woman, had come finally to rely on that permanence of public memorial, on words that will not change, on permanence as a stay against the folly of public de- rangement, even that of her good friend Lowell. Like Stein who wanted to write a play in which nothing happened, Bishop, too, came to appreci- ate that moment of stasis. She desired, at least for her troubled friend, the permanence of art.

6
Elizabeth Bishop's What Is a Map?

     Elizabeth Bishop was living in New York in 1935 when Gertrude Stein's article on "American States and Cities and How They Differ from Each Other" was published in the *New York Herald Tribune,* and she might very well have read Stein's statement, "and then we went west and then I began to begin to know what I now do know about the physical aspects of the land, the water is a part of the land, it is not land and water it is water in the land, that is what makes it American. And that is what makes it so real and so strange and so detailed and so there and so romantic."[1]

     Stein's ruminations on geography—especially her interest in the map of the United States with state lines that are straight until they hit the ocean—might have confirmed, if they did not inspire, Bishop's "The

Map," one of the first poems she published. "The Map," too, expresses an awareness of the water and the land; even more, it shares with Stein's article a sense of how "strange" details could be. It may be just an odd coincidence that Stein's article and Bishop's poem both appeared in 1935, although Bishop's letters attest to the fact that she was interested in Stein even if she found *Four Saints in Three Acts* baffling and "mostly unintelligible" (*OA*, 19). She attended Stein's lecture at Vassar and followed her American tour through Louise Crane, whose mother was involved in the arrangements (28), and so it seems more than likely that she would have read Stein's article and taken note of its accessible style and particular treatment of geography.[2]

Still, Bishop's interest in geography has never been associated with Stein's fanciful and abstract musing on the subject; rather, it is linked typically to that of her mentor Marianne Moore, and much is made of the connection.[3] Because the first poem in Bishop's first volume of poetry is titled "The Map," that first volume itself named *North & South* and later volumes *Questions of Travel* and *Geography III*, she has been read from the first as a poet of geography and, like Moore, a detailed observer of the visible world. Such an identification has endowed her with some of Moore's status as a minor poet of eccentric tastes as well as with an interest in just description or literal reality; although critics have sought both to question such an identity and revalue it, the judgment has had a remarkable tenacity.[4]

To approach Bishop through Stein will, of course, produce other restraints of interpretation; but it has the advantage of opening up the idea of geography, expanding its definition beyond description to imaginative speculation, beyond detailing the world to a consideration of what Stein indicates as "G stands for geographic and geographically" (*SR*, 469), or what Adrienne Rich calls "the geography closest in—the body" (*BBP*, 212). In the frontispiece of *Geography III*, her last volume, Bishop quotes *First Lessons in Geography* (1884): "*What is Geography?* / A description of the earth's surface" and "*Of what is the Earth's surface composed?* / Land and Water" (*CP*, 157). This reference recalls, as well, the first poem in Bishop's first volume of poetry, "The Map," as it goes on to quote Lesson X from *First Lessons*: "*What is a Map?*" / A picture of the whole, or a part, of the / Earth's surface" (157). And then she adds a flurry of questions, not so easily answered:

> In what direction is the Volcano? The
> Cape? The Bay? The Lake? The Strait?
> The Mountains? The Isthmus? (157)

These questions repeat what Bishop understood about geography from the start: it is a system of arrangements through which we read and understand the earth's surface—a system that often makes no sense, requires even as its discourages inquiry, promotes and retards imaginative reconsideration. And her interest in geography as a picture of surfaces was not limited to the outside world; it extended (or retracted) its focus to the surface of the body and, still closer in, to the systemic arrangement of the body of the poem or picture. Looking at all such arrangements, Bishop registered her uneasiness as well as her obsession with geographical systems. Her frequent use of strict, even archaic, poetic forms expressed both her interest in systems and her desire to enforce by concentration on the body of the poem an order that was nowhere else apparent. Her fascination with bodies—the world's, her own body, and the poem's—infiltrated everything she wrote.

Her first poems open with a view of the problematic "mapping" of the world and the body, systems intimately related to each other. Moving on from these forms to consider art itself as a map of the world, Bishop was first drawn to art's failure in "Large Bad Picture" only to reconsider her censorious judgment in "Over 2,000 Illustrations and a Complete Concordance." "The Map" introduces the general topic in a surrealistic treatment of mapping, "The Weed" interjects the image of the land or nature into the body, and "Over 2,000 Illustrations and a Complete Concordance" explores the way books and by extension poems arrange and disarrange any understanding of the world derived from direct experience or travels. Each of these poems questions maps and mapping as methods of representation.

Although Randall Jarrell claimed that all of Bishop's poems were written underneath the sign, "I have seen it" (235), in fact there is actually nothing visually verifiable in "The Map." The poem begins and ends in questions, its lines not connected by "and" and "and," as Bishop writes in "Over 2,000 Illustrations and a Complete Concordance," but rather by "or" and "or": "Shadows, or are they shallows," "Or does the land lean down to lift the sea," "Are they assigned, or can the countries pick their colors?" (CP, 3). The choices are varied; reading this map involves sorting through optical illusions, ambiguous relationships, and whimsical notions that often seem inconsequential. Yet the insistence here on such choices points to the limitations of maps. As Susan McCabe notes, the opening "Land lies in water" announces the map's duplicity as "lies" is both noun and verb (42). Moreover, the neatly rhymed opening stanzas are misleadingly simple as, for example, the "line" "where weeds hang to the simple blue from green" that cannibalizes its sense as it goes on. Can "hang to" be read as "cling to," or does it suggest something of the hazardous connections that a map simplifies? And how are weeds figured in a map? Mention of blue or "simple blue" turns the poem back to its opening line, which now appears, despite its simplicity, ambiguous: "Land lies in water: it is shadowed green"; but to what does the pronoun refer—land or water? (3)

The rigid poetic order of this opening stanza, where rhyming words repeat themselves, calls attention to its own organization even as it presents an image of disorder, optical illusion, constant lifting and tugging, instability. And the repetitive rhymes themselves—"green"/"green" and "under"/"under"—underscore the disordering of meaning as the same words change in context. Nor is the poem more firmly fixed in the second stanza where its reference to specific locations—Newfoundland, Labrador—which might tie the poem to geography gives way rather to the fanciful and figurative musings of "as ifs" and "like." Nothing "lies flat and still" in this poem, or rather everything remains duplicitous still (and duplicitously still) as the "bays" may be stroked "as if they were expected to blossom" or as peninsulas "take the water between thumb and finger / like women feeling for the smoothness of yard-goods." The impulse to stroke and feel or to see the parts of the map as feeling themselves is inspired by "emotion" that "too far exceeds its cause" (3), Bishop acknowledges, as if to apologize for her own figurative language that seems oddly unsuited to the map it describes.[5]

In the final stanza, Bishop returns to the rhyme scheme of the opening, and to the declaration that "Mapped waters are more quiet than the land is, / lending the land their waves' own conformation" (CP, 3). Reading this poem allegorically, Alfred Corn argues that here the poem or mapping makes the sea or unconscious smoother than the land or the conscious mind (27). But the whole direction of the poem has been toward disquieting any settled notion of land or sea, and Corn acknowledges that the paronomasia or pun of "Topography displays no favorites," rather than "plays" no favorites, allows both meanings to work—map making neither bets on sure things nor favors one country over another. It might be added that the line also suggests that such "displays" as maps favor neither the subconscious and fanciful nor the conscious and rational.

The concluding line—"More delicate than the historians' are the mapmakers' colors"—has been widely read as confirmation of Bishop's interest in geography, space, description; but for Sybil Estess, such an interest also embodies history, time, interpretation, as she claims, "A fragile, perhaps,

yet keen and subtle sense of discrimination—the 'map-makers' colors"—
are what amounts to his or her personal vision (712–13). The emphasis in
this line has been placed typically on the comparison between history and
geography when actually it should be on the "delicacy" or fragility and
vulnerability of both efforts to "map" the world.[6] "The Map" is about the
difficulties of reading and understanding a map that has already been
drawn up, about the impossibility of stabilizing an always turning and
apparently sensuous world, about the human desire to lift and stroke and
feel—and thus to change—the world, about any printer's or imprinter's
sentimental attachment to her own mapping. Intermixed with these difficulties of reading is the speaker's strange desire to "stroke" the "lovely"
bays or the impulse projected onto the peninsula to "take" the waters, as if
the whole enterprise of looking were erotically inspired. This poem was
written under the sign, "I have felt this," rather than "I have seen this" or
"I have a special way of seeing that always involves feeling." And what has
been felt but the body of the world, a body, someone's body?[7]

If the map of land and water is impossible to detail perhaps because it is
so erotically charged, more difficult to read is the map of the body, another
field of erotic possession, even when the speaker dreams in "The Weed"
that she is completely passive, "dead, and meditating" and "In the cold
heart, its final thought / stood frozen, drawn immense and clear, / stiff
and idle as I was there" (CP, 20). In this state of unnatural fixity, the
speaker is surprisingly disturbed by something completely extraneous to
the body, the natural weed growing in it: "Suddenly there was a motion /
as startling, there, to every sense / as an explosion" (20).

Bishop was reading Wordsworth's Prelude at the time she wrote this
poem (OA, 45), and she seems here to be reinterpreting for her own
time and gender the Romantic experience with nature. Not the calm
childhood scenes that recall Wordsworth to a youthful innocence and
wonder, Bishop's nature is wildly disruptive, "prodding me from desperate
sleep," pushing up through the heart and splitting it in two. Not flashing
on an inward eye to fill her with rapture as Wordsworth's nature, Bishop's
unbeautiful weed drops water in her eyes that provides no clear vision, but
rather confusion, as she admits, "so I could see— / (or, in that black place,
thought I saw)" "a light, / a small, illuminated scene; / the weed-deflected
stream was made / itself of racing images" (CP, 21). Although Bishop
could imagine herself jokingly as "a minor female Wordsworth" (OA, 222),
she seems intent on revising his still and beatific Romantic vision, replac-
ing it with the disquiet of a twentieth-century hallucination.

The surrealism of this poem where the weed infiltrates the body may have been inspired by what Bishop noted as the surrealism of George Herbert's "Love Unknown," on which she claims she modeled the poem ("An Interview," 295); but she took the violence of Herbert's imagery without any of its consolation.[8] More to the point is the influence of Max Ernst's frottage, which she claimed years later had been in her mind when she wrote "The Weed" (*OA*, 478). Frottage is the technique of creating a design by rubbing over an object placed underneath the paper. Art thus brings out that other art hidden in nature, in the grain of wood, for example, and, as such, paradoxically, it both copies nature and creates anew. If Ernst's frottage in *Histoire Naturelle* did inspire "The Weed," then the poem is a surrealistic image of the poem within the poet, detailing visually the quick growing or "racing images" that spring up from the poet's divided heart.

But the strange sensation of the weed's invasion of the body is given such detailed description that it cannot be so easily allegorized. If the poem is about creativity, its energies and its demands, it is also about the body that houses the creative spirit, about bodily changes and functions. Trying to map the geography of the body, the speaker defines a strange field of force. The adjectives in apposition—"stiff and idle" or "dead, and meditating"—cancel rather than reinforce each other, although together they are said to signify a repose "unchanged together / for a year, a minute, an hour" (*CP*, 20). A sudden motion that curiously drops to "cautious creeping" breaks into this bodily repose, and the weed's "green head" pushed up from the heart to grow or strangely not to grow but to appear "nodding on the breast." First one leaf, then another shoot out, "nervous roots" reach inward until the heart split apart "and from it broke a flood of water," and two rivers "glanced off from the sides" (20). (Interestingly enough, these two rivers will appear again and again throughout her career whenever Bishop writes about places real or imagined.)

The weed growing out of the body is a strange inversion of both Romantic tropes—the correspondence between man and nature and the identification of woman with nature. Rather than deriving inspiration from nature, the speaker in "The Weed" is flooded, divided, overwhelmed by a disturbing natural force growing in her own body; because she seems so curiously passive and unable to assert control over the weed, she might be recording her own bodily resignation to the elements in a literal death. But, in the weed's promise that it grows " 'but to divide your heart again,' " the speaker seems destined not to death but to the return again and again of a startling bodily invasion. The opening bed and "close-built bower," as well as the designation of the heart as the center of division, suggest that the weed is not just a life force but the force of love and sexuality as it invades the body and tears down the body's boundaries.[9] In the body, the weed is itself threatened—"almost swept away" by the floods it unleashes in the heart, struggling, dripping wet (*CP*, 21). Growing, changing, the body and the weed that invades it can never be "stiff and idle" or, the poem suggests, caught in the immobility of art (20). If woman is to be identified with nature, it is with a nature that is wildly disruptive and divisive, not with a nature that can be easily possessed. The geography of her body is like the geography of the map—divided but without clear boundaries of division, lifted as well as tugged by forces ranged against each other.

As Bishop moved away from surrealism and the dream world to write about the landscape she inhabited, she kept as a strategy the infiltration of the human and the natural, this time moving in the opposite direction by personifying nature rather than naturalizing the human body, and the effect is quite different. Whereas "The Weed" could rely on its bizarre image to render mysterious the human body, the insistent personification in "Florida" makes nature almost too familiar and too feminine. The "hysterical birds," "embarrassed" tanagers, clowning pelicans, "helpless" turtles, clattering palm trees, whimpering alligator, all combine to make the "state with the prettiest name" a refuge not of a strange and alien nature, but rather a world somehow too easily possessed by the poet, domesticated, mapped, dominated, and feminized. Although it "floats in brackish water" and seems strewn with skeletons, seashells, and refuse, Florida and its presiding spirit, the buried "Indian Princess," seem so humanly alive that their wilderness is lost. The state has lost the power of its Indian spirits and become, as Bishop notes, "the poorest / post-card of itself" (*CP*, 32–33).

Again in "Seascape," the personification of the "skeletal lighthouse" allows Bishop to invade the mystery of the sea by turning it into art, claiming it as "this cartoon by Raphael for a tapestry for a Pope: / it does look like heaven" (*CP*, 40). But the lighthouse "in black and white clerical dress" sees it differently, and he "knows better." "He thinks that hell rages below his iron feet," concludes that "heaven is not like this," and then turns on his conclusion to suggest that heaven itself "has something to do with blackness and a strong glare." Less willing to commit himself on this strange turn, the lighthouse ends by asserting that he "will remember something / strongly worded to say on the subject" (40). But for whom does this clerical, skeletal lighthouse speak—the government that set it there, the mapmaker, the poet? And for whom does the seascape look like heaven? The distinction here between the romanticist and the realist, the dreamer and the strong-worded observer, is perhaps too allegorical. "Florida" and "Seascape" are poems in which the human observer reads the landscape too clearly, confident that strong words will suffice.

It is as if Bishop had these poems in mind when she wrote "Over 2,000 Illustrations and a Complete Concordance," where she sets out the distinction between the book and the world, between the "serious, engravable" travels in the Bible or the book "tired / and a touch familiar" of the "Seven Wonders of the World" (*CP*, 57) and her actual experience. She draws the distinction, but only to collapse it in an ending that repeats what at first it seems to reverse. In the opening stanza, the book turns the world into a book so that "branches of the date-palms look like files" and the "cobbled courtyard" "is like a diagram" (57). It all appears to be governed by some guiding spirit, birds "suspended on invisible threads above the Site" or "the smoke rising solemnly, pulled by threads." And, although enigmatically the book seems itself to explode (as "God's spreading fingerprints" finally "ignite / in watery prismatic white-and-blue"), up to that end it maintains its power to reduce the world to images that can appropriate even when they might seem inappropriate.

"Thus should have been our travels," the poem opens with its conclusion. But the travels the poem details are, by contrast, neither "serious" nor "engravable." Rather, they are lusty as the goats' "touching bleat" (*CP*, 57) or the "little pockmarked prostitutes" "in the brothels of Marrakesh" who "flung themselves / naked and giggling against our knees" or "the fat old guide" who "made eyes" (58). The sights are lush and decaying as the "beautiful poppies" of "Volubilis" "splitting the mosaics," or the "rotting hulks" in the Dingle harbor that "held up their dripping plush" (58). But they also have a strange artistic deathliness about them, as the Collegians "crisscrossing the great square with black, like ants," or the "dead man" in Mexico, or "the dead volcanoes" that "glistened like Easter lilies," or the "holy grave" that frightened her most of all (58). Nonetheless, if the lines of the book ignite at the end, the travels end with the speaker's fear of what she observes, being itself observed by the Arab guide who "looked on amused" (58).

And this look turns back to the imperialist fear of "the squatting Arab" in the Bible, "plotting, probably, / against our Christian Empire, / while one apart, with outstretched arm and hand / points to the tomb, the Pit, the Sepulcher" (*CP*, 57). These are the very scenes the traveler has surveyed. And so her travels that seemed so different from (and unserious by contrast to) those recorded in the Bible have actually been a modern secular version of the same scenes, all under the guidance of the amused

Arab who patronizes the foreign tourist as he himself has been patronized by the biblical illustrations. This Arab guide looking at the tourist looking repeats the gesture of the Christian looking at the Arab world in Bishop's grandfather's Bible—both seemingly confident that their position is superior to that of the unholy invader.

As if to underscore this link, the final stanza opens, "Everything only connected by 'and' and 'and,'" as her travels are connected to the engravings of the Bible and her Arab guide connected to the Christian guide offered in the biblical illustrations, her view connected to the world. She turns back to the book, "Open the book," she orders and then repeats, "Open the heavy book." The book—now heavy with her own understanding of what it details and heavy too with her awareness that she has not departed from its engraved views—has a new meaning for her. "Why couldn't we have seen / this old Nativity while we were at it?" she asks, acknowledging in an offhand way the tourist's wish to see it all, having seen so much of what the Bible records. But in her desire, the vision of faith is strangely imaged as igniting the scene "with light, / an undisturbed, unbreathing flame" (*CP*, 58). Being undisturbed, this light might be eternal (then why the "*old* Nativity"?), but an unbreathing flame would be unable to inspire or give spirit to the faithful. Like the biblical illustrators, this tourist seems to have a rather dim sense of illustration.

The poem closes with the wish that we could have seen "this old Nativity" "—and looked and looked our infant sight away" (*CP*, 59). Eleanor Cook associates this infant sight with a pun on the Latin "*infans*" "unspeaking" and English infant. She comments:

> "Infant" first because of the Nativity scene that is seen and not seen. Bishop once saw it in the old Bible, but has not seen it in her actual travel in biblical lands. "Our infant sight": a sight of an infant, of the infant. But sight itself is also infant in the sense that sight is always "infans" or unspeaking. We translate it into words. Yet how can we look and look our infant sight away? In different senses. As when we look away to our heart's content (Bishop's repeated "look" works to prolong this moment of looking). Or "look away" in the sense of removing "infant sight," averting our eyes? . . . In this simply worded but intricate paronomasia, Bishop has laid out our possible responses to the Nativity scene. It's remembered from a book. It's not to be seen by travelling to the area where it happened. It's desired. It might fulfil desire and at the same time necessarily translate desire into something ordinary and familiar, so that we would be back where we started in one way if not another. (43)

But the line is more enigmatic still. The "infant sight" is also the view of the world determined in her childhood by the Bible with its 2,000 illustrations which all her travels and experience have not dislodged even if the faith that inspired that view has disappeared. So, fated to see the foreign world as it has been domesticated for her, she can never really see the world—either as it is, whatever that might be, or as it should be according to the Bible in which she can no longer believe. Maps of the world obscure as much as they illuminate, confound as much as they illustrate; but, Bishop seems to argue, so do actual travels.

Rereading the poem to see what the "infant sight" might have looked at, we discover that everything was not even then connected by "and" and "and." Rather, the Bible scenes are not so clearly defined despite the weighty lines the "burin" made, and the observer can only choose between possibilities of "or" and "or": "familiar" or "foreign," "the squatting Arab, / or group of Arabs," "plotting, probably," "history or theology," "camel or its faithful horse," "the specks of birds" "or the smoke rising solemnly," "Granted a page alone or a page made up," arranged in "rectangles / or circles." Suddenly the weightiness of the book gives way as the observer puzzles over its confusing images. And, by contrast, the weight of her own travels asserts itself, as she reads with assurance the foreign landscapes before her eyes, connecting everything with "and" and "and," until she realizes at the end that even this direct and seemingly random experience has been only an arranged tour, an illustration for the tourist. This poem with a title that points to over 2,000 illustrations is ultimately about the impossibility of escaping the already illustrated world.

Although Bishop was to try her hand at detailing the geography of sea and land both of the North in "Cape Breton" and the South in "The Bight" in her second volume of poetry, perhaps "Invitation to Miss Marianne Moore" most persuasively combines her interests in the geographies of North & South—those systems by which we map the world, the body, and the poem. Whether Moore's relationship to Bishop was maternal as Joanne Feit Diehl suggests or repressive as Betsy Erkkila argues, Moore herself dramatized for Bishop the close connections between the ways we conceive of the world, the body, and the poem. Moore, who dressed in the highly stylized costume of black cape, broad black brimmed hat, and pointed-toed black shoes, lived in an equally stylized world where "the grim museums will behave / like courteous male bower-birds" and the "mackerel sky" is white (CP, 82). For her, the world would become "the glittering grandstand of harbor-water" where "two rivers" (actual rivers and those ubiquitous waters of Bishop's imagination) are imagined "gracefully bearing / countless little pellucid jellies / in cut-glass epergnes," and waves "are running in verses." For her, the world is transformed: "Manhattan / is all awash with morals this fine morning," the lions on the step of the Public Library are "eager to rise and follow through the doors / up into the reading room." Dressing herself as a kind of witch or magician in Bishop's poem, Moore moves through a world equally stylized and dressed up. Moreover, both the poem that Bishop writes to Moore and Moore's own poems are highly wrought artifacts: products of "a musical inaudible abacus" and yet paradoxically "a soft uninvented music, fit for the musk deer," "with grammar that suddenly turns and shines / like flocks of sandpipers flying," "with a long unnebulous train of words" (82–83).

Underneath Bishop's insistence here on the extreme care with which Moore presented herself and structured the world in her poems is some hint of the fear she imagines may have prompted Moore's choice of such extreme and eccentric behavior. "The flight is safe; the weather is all arranged," she promises, repeatedly noting "this fine morning" in her invitation to Moore to leave the familiar haunts of Brooklyn for the "accidents," "malignant movies," "and injustices at large" of Manhattan. Although Bishop could poke affectionate fun at Moore's reserve and guardedness, she was aware of Moore's vulnerability, her delicacy, her need for care in such a dangerous world. Urging her out into that world with an invitation to come flying, Bishop is inviting her to share a world outside the "dynasties of negative constructions" that Moore has devised, a world not of joy and celebration, but one where "We can sit down and weep" or "we can bravely deplore" (*CP*, 83).

Bishop is not anxious to allay Moore's uneasiness about this world; rather, she wants the older poet to join her in a "game of constantly being wrong," perhaps morally or sexually. This invitation to "come flying" may be an invitation to "come," a brazen desire to see the other poet come out. And yet Bishop is not unlike the Moore she depicts here. She did not come out herself, and, although she was willing to travel to all kinds of foreign and perhaps unsafe places, she remained often ill at ease in such places. She, too, encased her body, if not in the peculiarity of costume that Moore chose, at least in the uniform of the middle-class matron that protected her from full disclosure of any departure from such a lifestyle. And her poetry, even this poem written with apologies to Pablo Neruda's "Alberto Rojas Jiminez Viene Volando," calls attention to its borrowed style in ways not unlike Moore's syllabic verse. In her essay on Moore, "Efforts of Affection," Bishop claims, "she looked like no one else; she talked like no one else; her poems showed a mind not much like anyone else's; and her notions of meter and rhyme were unlike all the conventional notions—so why not believe that the old English meters that still seem natural to most of us (or *seemed* to, at any rate) were not natural to her at all? That Marianne from birth, physically, had been set going to a different rhythm?" (*CPr*, 139–40). But the same might have been said of Elizabeth Bishop herself in 1948.

By 1952, when she stopped in Brazil on a trip to the Straits of Magellan, Bishop had not only a new geographical location to map, but a new bodily comfort and pleasure, and a newly relaxed attitude toward poetic form. But first, and not without its own significance, Bishop's entrance into Brazil was combined with a severe allergic reaction that caused her to swell up and break out with eczema as if a change of scenery would produce a changed body or, as the case was, a changed body enforce her stay in this foreign land. Once recovered, she wrote: "I like it so much that I keep thinking I have died and gone to heaven, completely undeservedly. My New England blood tells me that no, it isn't true. Escape does not work; if you really are happy you should just naturally go to pieces and never write a line—but apparently that—and most psychological theories on the subject, too—is all wrong" (*OA*, 249).

Excited about this new location, she wrote her editor: "I have moved to the other side of the Equator and have started a lot of quite different things, the work I am doing right now will be a new departure. . . . The last six months I've been working more than ever before in my life and I have many projects, including probably a book of pieces about Brazil" (*OA*, 253). She was delighted with the new productivity that Brazil inspired, admitting in a letter to Kit and Ilse Barker, "It is funny to come to Brazil to experience total recall about Nova Scotia—geography must be more mysterious than we realize, even" (249).

Bishop's focus in the three poems that open *Questions of Travel* is not on the mysterious power of geography, but on the tourist's own troubled reactions as she records her first impressions of Brazil's foreign geography. She is, as Bonnie Costello notes, a "tourist from a northern-industrial region, in search of paradisal innocence in the primitive south" (139), and, before she sees much, she is already disappointed or, rather, she comes with such need and "immodest demands for a different world, / and a better life, and complete comprehension / of both at last, and immediately" (*CP*, 89) that she is certain to be disappointed. And so, despite her effort at a minimal objective description ("Here is a coast; here is a harbor"), she notes a topography that soon seems to match her mood entirely: "self-pitying mountains, / sad and harsh beneath their frivolous greenery," "uncertain palms" (89). But traveling under the tourist's schedule, she must go on anyway, finish her breakfast, and get into the arriving tender, not, despite its name, a comforting vessel, but "a strange and ancient craft, flying a strange and brilliant rag" (89).

Despite its strangeness, the boat reminds the tourist that she is not in a "different world," but in one that has the same trappings of civilization (and colonization)—the flag, coins, and paper money—as the world from which she has departed in search of a "better life" (*CP*, 89). Although the descent into the tender has its hazards, particularly for six-feet-tall Miss Breen, eventually they "are settled," hoping in this strange land that they will have the accustomed "bourbon and cigarettes," and "customs officials" who will speak English. In short, even "driving to the interior" (90), the tourist does not want to leave behind the exterior comforts of home, and, thus armed, is she going to go too far or see too much?

"Questions of Travel," which Bishop had considered titling "A Strange Country" or "Another Country," takes up where "Arrival at Santos" leaves off as the tourist has a closer look at the country and at her own motives in traveling there. Unlike the port of Santos, which seemed "unassertive," not caring what impression it made, the "interior" here is too assertive, too lush, with "too many waterfalls" and "crowded streams" hurrying "too rapidly down to the sea (*CP*, 93). The "self-pitying mountains" of Santos give way in this poem to mountains more graphically described—the clouds on the mountaintops "spill over the sides in soft slow-motion, / turning to waterfalls under our very eyes"—but the impression here is one of plentitude, vitality, movement, where "streams and clouds" like the tourist herself are "travelling, travelling," turning the mountains into "hulls of capsized ships, / slime-hung and barnacled"(93).

Her complaint about the landscape immediately brings up doubts about her own motives, and the speaker thinks of "the long trip home," asking, "Is it right to be watching strangers in a play / in this strangest of theatres?" and, "What childishness is it" that makes us "rush / to see the sun the other way around?" But is it "childishness" that makes us travel or some uneasiness with our own adult world, some desire to find the home that the child never knew? For Bishop, home itself is always a long way off, and, thinking of home or of this strange place, the speaker is caught between them, turning unnecessarily censorious toward her desire to see new sights as if she were trying to cancel out the impressions she has just recorded. Travel as voyeurism or mere childish curiosity lingering on in adulthood offers only the most superficial views, "inexplicable and impenetrable," "instantly seen and always, always delightful." But, as the speaker eventually admits, home is not necessarily any less strange or inexplicable and impenetrable.

Watching and staring, the speaker here has nonetheless seen some sights "it would have been a pity / not to have seen." But, when she comes to draw up her list, it is strange and eclectic, composed more of sounds than sights: trees "really exaggerated in their beauty" (*CP*, 93), sounds of "the sad, two-noted, wooden tune / of disparate wooden clogs" or "the less primitive music of the fat brown bird / who sings above the broken gasoline pump / in a bamboo church of Jesuit baroque," the history in "the weak calligraphy of songbirds' cages," or the rain's "two hours of unrelenting oratory / and then a sudden golden silence" (94). It is not the splendid, overlush landscape that has attracted this tourist's notice, not the monumental architecture of its cities, or the range of the country's geographical diversity, not even the people of this strange land. What she has chosen to mention here as memorable are "sad" tunes, "primitive" music, "weak" calligraphy, sounds that seem to match her own mood. A stranger in a strange land, she has seen only her own strangeness. As she concludes, "'*the choice is never wide and never free.*'" And to the final question of travel, "'*Should we have stayed at home, / wherever that may be?*,'" the answer is, we are always at home, we are never at home (94).

As Bishop was settling herself into a place that was as close to home as she ever came, she turned to the question of where she belonged as if she had finally to decide. The Brazilian landscape was beautiful, but it was strange and different. To succumb to its lure seemed childish, and yet she seemed fated to this choice. Here, she might find a location that would keep her, one to which she could become habituated; but it was a landscape that was foreign, not familiar.

By the time she wrote "Brazil, January 1, 1502" in 1960 (some eight years after she dated "Arrival at Santos" "January, 1952"), Bishop had deepened her understanding of the predatory nature of tourism, associating it now with the colonial conquest; she had also become disillusioned with contemporary Brazil. Moreover, having written out the first burst of creativity that Brazil inspired and having passed through a year of struggling to write, she had found a new voice and tone in which to describe and comment, according to Millier (300). Still, in her interchange with Robert Lowell over this poem that he praised as one of her most beautiful, although he seems to have missed her attack on the Christian colonizers, she does not acknowledge directly the newly critical tone she was to take, admitting only that the poem is a "bit artificial but I finally had to do something with the cliché about the landscape looking like a tapestry."[10]

Quoting from Sir Kenneth Clark's *Landscape into Art* ". . . embroidered nature . . . tapestried landscape," Bishop draws on Clark's view that conceiving landscape as a tapestry is a medieval construction of nature as symbolic. If the Portuguese colonizers were heirs to this view of nature ("already out of style when they left home"), Bishop herself presents not a symbolic nature but rather a scene of "determined empiricism," as Parker suggests (89). Opening with the acknowledgment that "Januaries, Nature greets our eyes / exactly as she must have greeted theirs" (*CP*, 91), Bishop clearly depicts a nature that only her eyes could have picked up. Multicolored, oversized, undersized, exotic vegetation greets her eyes. Here is nature perceived as a woman by a woman who celebrates its fecundity, its variety, its undersides, its sexually predatory female lizards "red as a red-hot wire." Not so the Christians "tiny as nails" in this new world. They found this nature imaged as a woman "not unfamiliar" because "corresponding" "to an old dream of wealth and luxury," not unfamiliar because they can only see what they came to see, "wealth, plus a brand new pleasure" that is much like the old pleasure of sexual plunder and possession.

In *Brazil*, the *Time-Life* book that Bishop was writing at about the same time that she wrote this poem, she quotes the scribe on the boat of the first Portuguese explorer on the beauty of the Brazilian women and notes that "the Portuguese had always been romantically drawn to women of darker races; they had long taken Moorish wives and Negro concubines, and there were already many Negro slaves in Portugal. In Brazil it was only natural for them to become eager miscegenationists almost immediately" (*B*, 27–28). Her poem is much more accusatory. The Christians "ripped away into the hanging fabric, / each out to catch an Indian for himself— / those maddening little women who kept calling, / calling to each other" (*CP*, 92).

"Brazil, January 1, 1502" is not a poem of clear-cut distinctions between past and present, symbolic and representational views of nature, male and female observers. After all, they saw what we see—"Nature greets our eyes / exactly as she must have greeted theirs"—and we see as they saw nature as a painting, "just finished / and taken off the frame (*CP*, 91). As "Arrival at Santos" indicates, the modern tourist has come to Brazil with needs as great as the Portuguese colonizers, and, in the second stanza of "Brazil, January 1, 1502," the speaker blurs the distinction between past and present by calling the realistic description of "A blue-white sky" "a simple web," as if to emphasize the artistry of her own natural detail, placing there evidence of the older "embroidered nature" with "the big symbolic birds" "each showing only half his puffed and padded, / pure-colored or spotted breast." "Still in the foreground there is Sin," the speaker notes, as if the first colonizers' view of nature had permanently planted sin on the landscape along with or as their flag. But, without further comment, the speaker moves back to a more detailed view of nature that is again a nature heavily symbolized as if it were itself not just violated but fraught with violence: as rocks are "threatened from underneath," "attacked above / by scaling-ladder vines" and the animals engage in a "wicked" battle of the sexes where the females are the predators. "Just so the Christians," the next stanza opens, comparing the colonizers to the animals and, in a reversal of sexes, the male Christians to the female lizards (91–92).

But, we might consider, just so Bishop herself, who came and found Brazil "a brand-new pleasure." This poem, read often for its political insights into colonization, may also indicate how thoroughly Bishop herself had colonized Brazil, ransacked the landscape for her poetry, found pleasure in her sexual encounters there. Writing to Lowell, she expresses her concern about using Brazil: "but I worry a great deal about what to do with all this accumulation of exotic or picturesque or charming detail, and I don't want to become a poet who can only write about South America. It is one of my greatest worries now—how to use everything and keep on living here, most of the time, probably—and yet be a New Englander herring-choker bluenoser at the same time" (*OA*, 383–84).

The accumulation of details that Bishop cites here came from a trip down the Amazon in 1960 made with her Brazilian friend Rosinha Leõ and her sixteen-year-old nephew Manoel, and these details were to stay in her mind for years. She wanted to go back immediately, she told Lowell, and she dreamed about the Amazon every night (*OA*, 383); although she did not actually go back, she was to return to the trip years later as the subject of "Santarém."

This trip even figures in the *Time-Life* book that Bishop wrote in 1961 where she recounts the story told her aboard ship of a young woman doctor arriving at a small village on the Rio Tapajós. There, on her first night a group of wild men asked her to make out the death certificate of a fellow villager whose body they claimed they had found in the river. On examining the body, she discovered that the man had been stabbed, and, figuring that one of the men who brought it to her had killed him, she decided nonetheless not to sign a death certificate but to require someone to go for the nearest police, half a day's trip by motor boat. She managed to get it done (*B*, 116). Bishop comments: "small, animated and dark, probably with Indian blood, this doctor was a 'modern' Brazilian woman.

There are not many like her, but there are a few and the numbers are increasing" (116). Then, she proceeds to argue, "Brazil is a man's country."

In Bishop's imagination, it was also very much a woman's country. "Song for the Rainy Season," one of the few poems that she located specifically (*"Sítio da Alcobaçinha / Fazenda Samambaia / Petrópolis"*), explores her sense of comfort in the protective company of a home, a woman's place. In this poem about the most intimate place, "the house we live in," Bishop locates a place that is both "hidden" and "open," where "vapor / climbs up" and "effortlessly, turns back, holding them both, / house and rock, / in a private cloud" (*CP*, 101). This privacy is not exclusive but "open" "to the white dew / and the milk-white sunrise" and open, too, to an assortment of natural intruders—silver fish, mouse book worms, moths (102). Nature here is imagined as a maternal presence guarding her human intruders as well as her own creatures. But nature is also erotically charged, as the "fat frogs" "shrilling for love, / clamber and mount" (101).

This erotic nature takes over as the speaker designates the house itself as "darkened and tarnished," but "by the warm touch / of the warm breath, / maculate, cherished," as if nature took it in her embrace. More than holding house and rock, preserving this privacy of place, nature here seems intimately drawn to the house, and suddenly nature and human nature, the outside and the inside of the house, the weather and the people, all seem to mingle together in the celebratory exclamation, "rejoice!" But this exclamation, tacked onto the long two-stanza sentence, is almost hidden away and, once enunciated, taken back in the warning— "For a later / era will differ." Bishop goes on:

(O difference that kills,
or intimidates, much
of all our small shadowy
life!) (*CP*, 102)

This awareness of impending doom seems out of place in this "song for the rainy season," this celebration of love and protection. It is not that a later era will differ, bring death or the end of love; it is rather that their difference from the world, a difference that requires the hiding that the house ensures, is what threatens these lovers, this house, their bower of bliss. And so the song of rejoicing is shadowed by a fear of celebrating too loudly or of identifying the hidden place where the two lovers live. Situating the poem, Bishop relies on the foreign Portuguese to hide the exact location. This fear of celebrating her love by identifying its place, the fear of time itself as sure to destroy love, the anxiety that nature will not preserve the place, all seem so unique to Bishop with her sense of restraint that it is surprising to discover them again in Rich's "Twenty-One Love Poems," as she too expresses her sense of the fragility of love in a world ranged against it.

Certainly one of the most moving experiences of Bishop's life was the trip she made down the Amazon in 1960. Almost twenty years later, acknowledging in "Santarém" that "Of course I may be remembering it all wrong," she revisits "that conflux of two great rivers, Tapajós, Amazon," claiming, "I liked the place; I liked the idea of the place. / Two rivers." Here she returns to that image of two rivers that she has used obsessively since she wrote "The Weed," and she revises that early image, declaring:

> Even if one were tempted
> to literary interpretations
> such as: life/death, right/wrong, male/female
> —such notions would have resolved, dissolved, straight off
> in that watery, dazzling dialectic. (*CP*, 185)

Acknowledging temptations that she has felt and expressed throughout her poetry—the right and wrong of colonization, the male conquest of the female land—and writing from Boston where she might have been too aware of "literary temptations," she finally allows the landscape to dominate its interpreter and not to be "littered with old correspondences" as she wrote much earlier in "The Bight." There the harbor's "untidy activity" had been "awful but cheerful" (61); in this late rendition, the river is full of traffic, "everything bright, cheerful, casual—or so it looked" (185).

Finally, nature itself has taken back the landscape, prevailing against the encroachment of civilization—"stubby palms" overlook "buildings one story high," "one house faced with *azulejos*," the street "deep in dark-gold river sand" (*CP*, 185). Although the Christians remain, they are now not "tiny" men, but "A dozen or so young nuns, white-habited," "—off to their mission, days and days away / up God knows what lost tributary" (186). The foreign invasion is represented now by the "occasional blue eyes, English names, / and *oars*" left by the Southern families that came after the Civil War because they could still own slaves in Brazil (186). Their heritage has been reduced to the fact that settlers of this place, alone along the Amazon, use oars not paddles.

Nature even seems to be advancing on the Church or "(Cathedral, rather!)," Bishop reminds herself, which the week before had been struck by lightning so that one tower had "a widening zigzag crack all the way down" (*CP*, 186). And the priest's house next door had been struck so that his brass bed was galvanized black—a suggestion perhaps that, if one were tempted to literary interpretation, might be read prophetically. From this "golden evening," the speaker takes as a souvenir an empty wasp's nest that she saw in the pharmacy, admired, and was given. Returning to the ship to her fellow passenger, Mr. Swan, "really a very nice old man, / who wanted to see the Amazon before he died," the speaker is greeted with his question, "What's that ugly thing?" (187). What is it indeed but the empty husk of a nest, a home no longer in use, "small, exquisite," and not at all like the teeming and foreign river life the speaker has just visited (186). Yet it stands in the poet's memory for a place that she had much admired, a geography that she had never been able to detail without projecting herself into it, not able to regard without the fear that she was appropriating it and perhaps, she suspected, not able to appreciate any better than Mr. Snow did.

It is interesting that "Santarém" is one of Bishop's most detailed renderings of Brazilian geography, and it came years after she had been forced out of Brazil first by her lover's suicide and then by the difficulties of her presence there without the protection of that native friend. She saw it most clearly in her mind's eye only after she had lost it, a loss significant enough to place it in the accelerating losses of her villanelle just before the loss of her new lover:

> I lost two cities, lovely ones. And, vaster,
> some realms I owned, two rivers, a continent.
> I miss them, but it wasn't a disaster. (*CP*, 178)

There are the two rivers that have flowed through her imagination from the very beginning, places she never lost. The geography of her imagination was marked by them even before she actually saw the conflux of the Amazon and Tapajós.

From "The Map" to "Santarém," Bishop's interest in geography has always been an interest in representation. She is more often engaged in commenting on how a landscape is conceived than in looking at it directly herself. Rather than "I have seen it," Bishop writes under the sign, "I have seen others looking at it." The mapmakers, the travelers, the tourists, the colonizers, memory itself, all have looked and been looked on. Writing so often not about her native land but about a foreign, if familiar, land, Bishop was from the start extremely self-conscious about the view she might take. She was always an outsider, one of many and not the worst, as she seems to suggest in "Brazil, January 1, 1502." And yet, she was always concerned about any effort—her own and those of others—at literary interpretations that would distinguish between the real world and the one described. For her, there was no original, but only copies—maps of geographical locations, descriptions of places. Moving toward the authentic or the original, the speaker of her poems finds herself going toward a world that, like the Indian women in "Brazil, January 1, 1502," retreats before her.

Bishop worked to keep open the question, "What is a Map?" Even the delicacy of the mapmaker's colors was not subtle enough to detail the world through which she traveled. As a tourist, she was always at a disadvantage—misled by native guides into seeing only the tourist view, misinterpreting as well as resisting what she heard, constantly dislocated and self-doubting, still more at home away than close by. Unlike Stein who saw "G" as "geographical" and longed for an iconic identification of state and self, Bishop could find no public place in which to situate herself. Rather, entertaining even in her dreams a two-pronged river as the landscape to which she obsessively returned, she identified only with a strangeness that was forever shifting.

7

Adrienne Rich
Whatever Happens
with Us

In a 1977 interview about a course she was teaching, Adrienne Rich said, "I was talking about encoded feelings in women's poetry, and feelings that are censored even before they get to the page, poems that are censored by editors, the Emily Dickinson phenomenon, and so on. If we have come to a point where it begins to be possible for women to write out of their feelings for other women in a freer way and be published, and for that work to be available to other women, this is a kind of milestone, a literary phenomenon" (Bulkin, "Interview," 1:57–58).

Here, Rich notes two different restraints: the self-censorship that women poets have practiced and the external censorship that they have suffered. The two have a complicated and historically variable relationship, despite Rich's conflation of the two in women's persistent encoding of their feelings. Although she is more direct than Stein was or Bishop wanted to be, Rich seems to understand the problem as they did. Stein's refusal to use the name of a thing and Bishop's restraint were both forms of self-censorship responding to editorial or social restraints. Although neither Stein nor Bishop spoke so openly about their need for an encoded language, they both employed it, as we have seen, in response to cultures in which, as Frank Bidart discussing Bishop suggests, "in both social and literary terms, *not* to be in the closet was to be ghettoized; people might know or suspect that one was gay, but to talk about it openly in straight society was generally considered out-of-control or stupid."[1] Thus, censorship and coding have been intertwined. It would appear that censorship—both external and internal—would repress expression whereas coding develops from a desire to open expression. And yet, in the works of these poets, censorship was a powerful motivation to find a means of expression, and the codes they created served to keep secret as well as to reveal their meanings.

Coding has been an important strategy for women, as this study suggests; but it is a more complicated practice than Rich imagines it to be. First, it is not limited to women writers. Writing in code is a widespread practice of both women and men, both the accomplished and the apprentice poet—those who know a particular code such as that of courtly love, for example, and those who have yet to develop a vocabulary for themselves and must adopt the available codes, as Rich did in her very early poetry. Even in Rich's own career, the coding and decoding of her experience are more mixed experiments than she sometimes allows.

To a certain extent, poetry is always coded, as Rich herself seems to acknowledge in another interview where she admits that for her, from the very beginning, "poems were a way of talking about what I couldn't talk about any other way" (Montenegro, 14). She goes on: "I think the fact that it was poetry rather than, say, fiction or some other kind of prose was important because I learned while very young that you could be fairly encoded in poems, and get away with it. Then I began to want to do away with the encoding, or to break the given codes and maybe find another code. But it was a place of a certain degree of control, in which to explore things, in which to start testing the waters" (14). Or, again, in talking about meeting Robert Duncan in 1960, Rich writes, "I too was using my poetic language as protection in those years, as a woman, angry, feeling herself evil, other" (*WIFT*, 167).

When asked if she would write a poem rather than prose in order to deal with "certain unnameable sensations or experiences," Rich replies, "for the kind of exploration we've been talking about, I want to be working in poetry more. I feel there are a lot of places that I still need to go— I'm just getting the outlines of certain things" (Montenegro, 14). Admitting then that it was the coded possibilities of poetry that allowed her to express herself freely and to continue to explore so-called unnameable sensations, Rich appears again "split at the root," divided between the recognition that women must be free from the necessity to write in code and the acknowledgment that coded expression did allow her, as it had Stein and Bishop, the freedom to write her own experience.

Rich's remarks remind us that coding and decoding are not just experiences of the poet writing; they also involve her audience reading. Coded expression might allow the poet some freedom, but it also constricts her to a coterie audience, those select few who have access to the code, and sometimes even those will need some additional information in order to read the code, as, for example, Rich herself needed when she read Elizabeth Bishop. Rich admits that she had felt drawn to Bishop, but also repelled by her early poetry, unable to connect the themes of outsiderhood and marginality that she saw in the poetry with a lesbian identity (*BBP*, 125). Her experience is not uncommon. For example, Elly Bulkin admits reading Muriel Rukeyser's poetry without being alerted to the possibility of her lesbianism, and, like Rich rereading Bishop with new appreciation, Bulkin, once aware of Rukeyser's lesbianism, went back to see the opening poems in Rukeyser's *The Speed of Darkness* (1971) as coming out poems ("'Kissing / Against the Light,'" 35). If coding is a safeguard against a hostile audience, its protective power may be so strong that it excludes a more receptive audience. Moreover, something of the limited reception of Stein and the appreciation of only the restrained Bishop may be attributed to audiences that did not comprehend the code or that were looking for another code.

Even the poet herself may be afforded multiple readings and new understandings of her own work and its codes as a result of her coming out. For example, Rich comments on a poem she wrote in 1962, "To Judith, Taking Leave": "When I wrote that, I didn't think of it as a lesbian poem. This is what I have to keep reminding myself—that at that time I did not recognize, I did not name the intensity of those feelings as I would name them today, *we* did not name them" (Bulkin, "Interview," 1:64).

Rich also has identified "Stepping Backward," a poem from her first volume, as a poem dealing with a relationship with another woman, commenting, "It is very intellectualized, but it's really the first poem in which I was striving to come to terms with feelings for women" (Bulkin, "Interview," 1:64). Thus, the decoding process goes on and on, even for the coder herself.

Still, Rich continues to comment on women's coded writing, arguing in an interview in 1993: "By the time I came out in my work, which would have been impossible for me not to do, there was no question of my being able to suppress that . . . because one of the things I had come to understand was so many of the women poets of the earlier part of the 20th and the 19th century had written their lives in code, whether it was as lesbians or just women. I didn't think that had been wonderful for poetry, in spite of Dickinson, who was just a very original and unique kind of genius and who might have written her life in code wherever she'd been, whenever she'd been" (Kastor, 4).

Rich seems to be dismissing a wealth of women's poetry in an effort to champion freer expression, as if free expression were itself the one requisite of "wonderful" poetry. But is it? Coming out in her poetry was without doubt an important political act for Rich, and, as a poet who has admitted struggling all her life against the idea that poetry and life are not profoundly connected (Kastor, 4), she would have to find such an act important for her poetry as well. But has it been? What has writing in code meant to Rich? And what fuller expression has she been allowed by coming out? Only a close attention to the poetry itself can provide answers to these questions; yet, surprisingly, despite her prominence, Willard Spiegelman is right in claiming that Rich's poetry has seldom received the "*literary* criticism she most deserves" (Spiegelman's italics, *The Didactic Muse*, 147). Read, appreciated, and attacked for her political positions, Rich herself would be the first to resist a literary criticism that divests the poetry of this political life even when the politics haunts the poetry so that it is read chiefly for its polemical statements. Yet there is more to the poetry than the politics or, rather, the poetry reveals an emotional vulnerability and turmoil that appears to be hidden in Rich's political assurance.

As a political gesture, Rich's coming out has provided powerful support for lesbian poetry, inspiring women writers to celebrate the generative love of women for women; but in her own poetry it has opened up reserves of uncertainty and pain, suppressed perhaps or coded in the political certainties of her middle poetry and the technical skill of her early work. Unlike most of her critics, Spiegelman detects this coding, commenting, "One sign of the relative unease in so many of the early poems is, ironically, the unalleviated quality of the sureness . . . the poems are *all* conclusion, with little tentativeness, exploration, or emotional variety" (Spiegel-man's italics, *The Didactic Muse*, 180). Rich has matured into tentativeness as she has acknowledged an emotional variety in her poetry, and, in crucial ways, her poetry is a much more complex statement than her political prose.

In her prose and in interviews, Rich continues to assert the importance of freeing herself and all women writers from the necessity of coding their emotions, as if her case were every woman's. But not everyone has felt the need to write her life in code; in fact, women are often accused of being too emotional, sentimental, and personal in their poetry. They have chosen to write their lives in many different modes, ranging from the openly confessional and lengthily autobiographical to the gnomic and the riddling.

Rich follows a pattern familiar to women writers, such as Sylvia Plath, who were so successful in restraining emotion or sentiment in their early verse. Maturing as a poet, Rich has come into the fuller expression she now feels she enjoys; but, in some sense, the freedom and richness of Rich's late poetry are the fruits of her long life in poetry. Coming out has been one moment rather than the single act in a long development that released her from coded writing, if, in fact, she has enjoyed such a release.[2] It might be argued that coming out has ensnared her in other codes and in polemical arguments quite ancillary to her creative work.[3]

Rich's expression of her lesbian identity has had a long and shadowy history. So it is no surprise that the poetic identities she has created are quite distinct from the politically committed lesbian she has become (and, of course, even that public persona has had more than one identity). The speakers she has created in her poetry are less easily fixed than Rich's political identity as a lesbian activist; the poetic identities are figures more like Terry Castle's "apparitional lesbian," the figure that the culture and, it seems, the poet herself have "ghosted." In creating this term, Castle is concerned with public figures, both real and fictional, such as Greta Garbo, Henry James's Olive Chancellor, and Brigitte Fassbaender, who have been defined as ghostly in order to drain their lesbianism of any moral or sensual authority. Rich would not appear to fit into this list because she is a poet rather than a fictional character or a public figure, and, as a poet, she is anxious to assert the creative power of women's love for women. And yet, apart from her public statements and polemical positions, her poetry reveals the extent to which the lesbian in her is in the margins, hidden even as she is evoked, still not quite present either as speaker or as lover.

The lesbian in Rich's poetry is often departing, dead, or mutilated. For example, the lesbian lovers in Rich's most sensational coming-out sequence, "Twenty-One Love Poems," are parting, and their affair is ending. An earlier poem, "Transcendental Etude," in which two women meet "eye to eye," would appear to be a more direct confrontation, but here also retreat and solitude are the result, and the poem ends on a note of uncertainty "as if a woman quietly walked away / from the argument and jargon in a room" (*FofD*, 268). The speaker forswears the "mere will to mastery," acknowledging "only care for the many-lived, unending / forms in which she finds herself" (269).[4] What Rich celebrates is the woman alone, the "forms" in which *she* finds *herself* not in union or communion with someone else.

Poem after poem in *The Dream of a Common Language* (1978) concentrates on what Castle calls the cultural "ghosting" not just of the lesbian but of all women (4–8). Death is one of the volume's most persistent themes: Marie Curie, Elvira Shatayev, Paula Becker, "A Woman Dead in Her Forties," all dead. Silence is another theme, announced in "Cartographies of Silence" and emanating through other poems. Perhaps Rich is simply surveying the field, detailing women's lives as they have been lived. Perhaps the common language she would find remains only a haunting dream. Betsy Erkkila has argued that throughout the volume "lesbian love is mythologized and, in effect, universalized as a return to a primal bond between mothers and daughters and a primal identity shared by all women" (174); but actually, in most of the poems in this volume, the bond is not only never permanently formed but often dissolving, and the situation for both women and women's poetry remains hazardous.[5]

These hazards are what Rich discusses in an early interview: "One thing I was trying to do in *Twenty-One Love Poems* was constantly to relate the lovers to a larger world. You're never just in bed together in a private space; you can't be, there is a hostile and envious world out there, acutely threatened by women's love for each other. Women who are lovers have to recognize that—in the sense that I was trying to express in 'From An Old House in America': 'I cannot not now lie down / . . . with a lover who imagines / we are not in danger.' And that danger and threat is also internalized within ourselves. So many of these things enter in when two women are together: joy like none other, vulnerability like none other, the breaking of the core prohibition at the heart of patriarchy" (Bulkin, "Interview," 2:57).

Internalizing danger, the speaker in "Twenty-One Love Poems" is often engaged in "self-ghosting," claiming to come out but always hiding.

In the beginning, she seems to want to locate her love life in the real world, "inseparable / from those rancid dreams." But the real world is really a dream world, however "rancid," and, in some ways, ghostly as "screens flicker / with pornography, with science-fiction vampires" (*FofD*, 236). A private life inseparable from such a public world will share its flickerings, its vampires. Trying another strategy by associating herself with nature rather than civilization at the end of the first poem, she writes, "We want to live like trees," but again the trees are in danger in a poisonous world: "sycamores blazing through the sulfuric air," "exuberantly budding" but only into death (236).

In the second poem, the speaker is dreaming, and, although kissed to awaken, she identifies her lover as a dream poem: "*I dreamed you were a poem, /* I say, *a poem I wanted to show someone . . .*" (*FofD*, 237). She is dreaming of coming out, of writing the poem she is actually writing, and yet she is turning the human and emotional world into language, spiritualizing it, dematerializing it, making a person a poem. Dreaming a lover into a poem may be a treacherous evasion, as in VII, where the speaker asks, "am I simply using you, like a river or a war?" "to escape writing of the worst thing of all" (239). And what is the "worst thing of all"? In naming it, Rich's language turns oblique. It is "not the crimes of others, not even our own death, / but the failure to want our freedom passionately enough / so that blighted elms, sick rivers, massacres would seem / mere emblems of that desecration of ourselves?" (239–40).

What does it mean? To want freedom to see the devastation of nature as the devastation of self, to accept the age-old male-inspired association of woman with nature? To want freedom enough to free the environment itself from disease? To want freedom enough to render oneself ghostly, a mere emblem rather than a person? The grammar weakens here as the poetry turns on both its figurative possibilities, calling even "emblems" "mere," and its literal possibilities so that the sentence cannot be parsed.

In poem VIII, the speaker suggests that worst of all in the woman's love of suffering is the failure to love. The speaker announces, "The woman who cherished / her suffering is dead" and claims a new start, "I want to go on from here with you / fighting the temptation to make a career of pain" (*FofD*, 240).

Loving rather than either suffering or writing may be this speaker's choice, as she wonders, in Jamesian terms, if she is a "kind of beast" for turning her life into words. But the unwritten life has its failures as well. In V, in an apartment full of books by men, the speaker remembers "the ghosts—their hands clasped for centuries— / of artists dying in childbirth, wise-women charred at the stake, / centuries of books unwritten piled behind these shelves" (*FofD*, 239). In all this musing, the poet is alone, her lover silent, and she enters into another ghostly awareness: "Your silence today is a pond where drowned things live"; "I fear this silence, / this inarticulate life" (240). Even when they touch in sleep and know they are not alone, the speaker acknowledges that "the dream-ghosts of two worlds / walking their ghost-towns, almost address each other" (241). In XIII, "out in a country that has no language," the lovers are again in danger of hallucinating: "driving through the desert / wondering if the water will hold out / the hallucinations turn to simple villages" (242).

The ghostly is not absent from "(The Floating Poem, Unnumbered)," the only erotic moment in the sequence, which is announced as a haunting of the body, imagined as memory as soon as it is concluded—"whatever happens, this is" (*FofD*, 243). Here the words seem more than super-fluous, destroying the moment in favor of some announced future posses-sion of it. The repetition of "whatever happens" underscores a peculiar hollowing out of the present happening, an obsessive attachment to the future, a denial of the present or perhaps an eagerness to haunt the present moment with the future. In XVII, these lovers' experience becomes again ghostly: "Merely a notion that the tape-recorder / should have caught some ghost of us," not only for her own remembrance but also to "instruct those after us" (244). Even as the love affair comes to an end the speaker remains in a midregion between cold reality and the dream world, asking in XIX, "Am I speaking coldly when I tell you in a dream / or in this poem, *There are no miracles?*" (245).

The final image of the beloved is of a woman "drowning in secrets, fear wound round her throat / and choking her like hair" (*FofD*, 246). And in the last poem, the speaker acknowledges herself, if not as a ghost, then as a figure shimmering in both the light and the darkness.

Rich's obsessive transformation of the body into the ghost, of the real world into dreams, of experience into haunting memory, would appear to express a wish to dismiss the love announced by the title of the sequence, and yet it also argues for that love's strange vitality. As Terry Castle, commenting on the ghosting of lesbians, has suggested, "Only something very palpable—at a deeper level—has the capacity to 'haunt' us so thor-oughly" (7). And, Castle continues, "within the very imagery of negativity lies the possibility of recovery—a way of conjuring up, or bringing back into view, that which has been denied" (7–8).

The haunting in "Twenty-One Love Poems" as well as the haunting *of* it bespeaks the tradition of silence in which, Rich believes, women poets have belonged. It suggests, too, that when the woman whose erotic feelings have been silenced by heterosexuality escapes from its strictures, she discovers that she is not only haunted by that history, but also haunted by a ghostliness that that history can neither contain nor suppress. She speaks in the silences of her own voice.

Commenting on "Twenty-One Love Poems," Joanne Feit Diehl has argued: "Helpful as sexual truth-telling may be, however, it does not resolve the problem these poems so starkly articulate: the difficulty of reinventing names for experience, of placing the female self at the center of the mimetic process" (*Women Poets*, 148). Feit Diehl goes on to interrogate Rich's program: "can language survive if we divest it of its appropriative power over the world of things?" (153). But it would appear that Rich's strategies are more subversive than Feit Diehl's model. The woman speaker, without presuming to take on appropriative power, possesses the world nonetheless by haunting it, by being herself haunted. She possesses, and she is possessed: "Whatever happens with us, your body / will haunt mine" is her first ominous utterance (*FofD*, 243).

Perhaps Rich has neither reinvented the names nor placed herself at the center, but rather hollowed out the old names and rendered ghostly both center and circumference in this poem. For example, in "(The Floating Poem, Unnumbered)," she claims, she has come, and she has "come." But how has she "come"? Or, rather, who has "come"? What are thighs that are "traveled, generous"? (*FofD*, 243). Like "innocence and wisdom," these words are awkwardly abstract as they are reworked in this context to express passion.

Later, Rich appears to be acknowledging an appropriative gesture when she writes, "your touch on me." But, if it is, as described, "firm, protective, searching," how is it different from its heterosexual version? Has Rich rendered ghostly the "firm, protective, searching" male in appropriating his role? Who is touching, who is being touched? The language is borrowed, not new, and it blurs the distinction between same-sex sex and different-sex sex in a way that Rich disclaims in commenting on her lesbian poetry. She has herself admitted being affronted by having her love poetry universalized, stripped of its meaning, "integrated" into heterosexual romance (Bulkin, "Interview," 2:58). She sees it as the denial of who she really is. But, we might ask, who is she as she uses this particular language?

Helena Michie suggests that for many lesbian poets and activists working today, "one can only make the simple, powerful, and highly painful gesture of a choice between the different and the same." She comments:

"The private and privatized vision that 'Twenty-One Love Poems' ends with posits a safe space for the self within the image of the circle; the very word 'circle,' however, reminds us, indeed compels us, to go back to the beginning of the poem, to read circularly. If we read linearly we can only choose an erotics of the same, where otherness is systematically exiled. If instead we read the poem as an invitation to reread, that exile is never permanent, and we are embroiled in an erotics of difference horrifyingly similar to and exhilaratingly different from the pornographics invoked by the opening poem" (130).

In the power of her articulation of this difference, this similarity, Rich haunts the culture. She has become a public figure, championed and vilified for her poetry and the polemical prose she feels impelled to write to accompany the poetry. Indeed, her own polemical positions haunt her poetry so that, despite the ambiguity and complexity of "Twenty-One Love Poems," the sequence is read through the lens of her political commitments. Lines are abstracted from it without much exploration of the sequence's full meaning and quoted universally in discussions of her poetry, of lesbian poetry, of erotic poetry. Without a mention of the poem's equivocations, Erkkila, for example, reads it as a direct transcript of political action: "a sonnet sequence in which Rich names her personal love relationship with another woman as the source of new creation and the base of political action and power in the world" (174). Approaching Rich with "disbelieving wonder" at her desire to write an entirely new poetry based on two women's limitless desire, Catharine Stimpson restricts her comments of "Twenty-One Love Poems" to identifying the most explicitly erotic lyric in the sequence as "(The Floating Poem, Unnumbered)" "as if physical passion drifts and runs like a deep current through the seas of the connection between 'I' and 'you' in the sequence" ("Rich and Lesbian/Feminist Poetry," 255). Again, Caroline Halliday fits Rich's poem into her study of contemporary lesbian erotic poetry by acknowledging that only one poem is erotic and claiming nonetheless that "The implication of this, for me, is that the poet does not tell of the joy of physical loving often because of the necessity of understanding the web of daily meeting, working, reading the papers, making it all knit in with her lover and her self" (85).

Clearly, in all these cases and others like them, critics find it more important to cite Rich's poem than to read it carefully because, curiously, the sequence has a larger and more ghostly life as political statement than as poetry. The poem that announces that Adrienne Rich, a major figure even in establishment poetry, has come out has itself not come out of the shadow of its own notoriety. Read carefully, however, the poetry reveals itself at odds with the prose even when it appears to support Rich's statements. For example, in the context of her influential essay, "Compulsory Heterosexuality and Lesbian Existence," "Twenty-One Love Poems" appears to be an effort to make up for the loss that Rich describes in that essay: "The denial of reality and visibility to women's passion for women, women's choice of women as allies, life companions, and community, the forcing of such relationships into dissimulation and their disintegration under intense pressure have meant an incalculable loss to the power of all women *to change the social relations of the sexes, to liberate ourselves and each other*" (Rich's italics, *BBP*, 63).

Certainly, by writing "Twenty-One Love Poems," Rich has succeeded in making public and asserting the reality of her passion for a woman. Paradoxically, she has done so in the poem itself not by making such a passion visible, but rather by expressing the power of its very invisibility and silence. The ghostliness of the sequence, its dreams and hallucinations and retreats, are the ways in which her imagination gains back its power of expression over her social consciousness. The denial of visibility, the ghosting of women's passion for women, has one meaning in the cultural criticism of Rich's prose; it has almost the opposite meaning in her poetry where ghosting is a way of possession, a new understanding of what it means to possess. But the ghosting of women's passion for women also calls up the melancholy that is at the base of women's longing for the woman's body. Not the site of generativity, the body desired by the speaker in Rich's poems is often mutilated and in pain.

Denying the visibility of women's lives takes many forms in Rich's poetry. In a curious image that makes harrowingly visible the invisible "breasts / sliced-off" in "A Woman Dead in Her Forties," Rich's speaker takes up again the whole question of visibility, this time acknowledging the woman's own complicity in the denial (*FofD*, 250). The present/absent breasts focus the speaker's attention, and she claims, "I want to touch my fingers / to where your breasts had been / but we never did such things" (251). Once again, in Rich's poetry, the body has been diminished, mutilated, rendered ghostly, as the woman speaker declares her love for another woman. She is not just the childhood friend, but, the speaker says, "You are every woman I ever loved / and disavowed" (253). And, rendering her an actual ghost, the speaker goes on, "Of all my dead it's you / who come to me unfinished" (254).

The poem is dense with potential meanings: the cultural mutilation of women's bodies in the effort to cure, cancer itself as a culturally induced disease, the friend's pain and suffering. Rich mentions them all: noting "your scarred, deleted torso," "the gynecologist touched your breast / and found a palpable hardness," "you rise / reproachful // once from a wheel-chair pushed by your father / across a lethal expressway," "You played heroic, necessary / games with death" (*FofD*, 251, 253–54). But the central meaning of this woman's death for the speaker here is the speaker's own treachery and loss to which she returns again and again. Even as children, these friends were unable to express their love, resorting to jokes and silent support. Still, they "cleaved to each other," Rich claims, using that strange term that connotes union and separation (253). Asking the question that recurs in her love poetry, "How am I true to you?" (254), Rich seeks now a more direct expression of pain.

In this obsessive return to what is lost and mute as well as visible and invisible, the speaker seems to be speaking a simple and direct language; but it is full of word play, a complicated way of making audible the unspoken. Self-silenced, the perfect child of a culture that taught her never to speak her passion, the speaker in this poem now feels impelled to use the richest, most variable language to include all that she wants to say. The double meanings of "cleaved" or "keening" suggest not just the duplicity of words but their incorporation of self-canceling alternatives—of joining and separating, of cutting and lamenting—so that to voice one meaning is not to exclude its opposite. Nor do the words stop reverberating there: cleaved calls up cleavage, the space or invisibility that made the breasts, now invisible, once visible; keening reminds us of the sharpness of the cut as well as both the wordless and the loudest lament.

Among its multiple meanings, "A Woman Dead in Her Forties" includes necrophilia. What the speaker desires here is not only a dead woman, but that sexual contact with that part of her that is dead, her sliced-off breast. Necrophilia in this woman is part of her melancholy, of her nostalgia for all the dead and maimed women she might have loved, of her separation from the womanly body she was denied. Necrophilia is a way of repossessing all that she would have cleaved to. It associates the woman's desire with what is transgressive in desire and unassuageable.

Rich writes here a love elegy for the modern age. Ringing changes on the motifs of the Latin love elegy—the transitoriness of life, the fragility of beauty—the speaker mourns for the chances she had to express her love now lost, for her friend's "scarred, deleted torso" that she never touched. Erotic melancholy is a dominant mood in Rich's love poetry, where love's loss or the regret that love's expression has been but a "mute loyalty" in life is linked to Rich's own awareness of how much she herself has silenced and repressed in her own emotional experience. The passage of time, conventionally a source of sorrow but inevitable in the elegy, figures in Rich's love elegies as a judgment on her own limitations. Rich's speaker laments time past by asking, how could I have lost the experience of such love that my past cast up to me?

Expressing her desire for the living and unmutilated body in "Contradictions: Tracking Poems" 3, the speaker is less poignant: "My mouth hovers across your breasts . . . your fingers / exact   my tongue exact at the same moment" (YNYL, 85). Set aside "A Woman Dead in Her Forties" where the breasts and fingers are not exact at all, "Tracking Poem" 3 appears somehow forced; the experience of tongue on breast counterpointed with exact fingers reduces physical pleasure to a mathematical equation. Much more ardent is the elegiac "A Woman Dead in Her Forties" where breasts and fingers, missed and missing each other, conjure up the frenzy rather than the cool exactness of desire.

Even here in "Tracking Poem" 3, the joy is set in winter, not the conventional season of love, and delimited even as it is experienced. Rich's speakers always hear time's winged chariot not at their backs encouraging them to capture the moment, but rather out in front carrying off the moment even as it is experienced.

Melancholy is never far from Rich's imaginative grasp even of this gray winter afternoon's amazing sex which is one of the pleasures of winter, as the speaker assures herself. Rich's lesbian love poetry has all been written as one of those pleasures that come late in the cycle of life when the night is falling. The pleasures of winter are not those of the springtime. The body, even in its capacity for joy, plays within a more limited range of possibilities. Pain is one of its constituents, as Rich writes in a letter to herself in 7 of the "Tracking Poems," claiming "nothing is predictable with pain" (YNYL, 89). "Signified by pain," Rich's speaker would appear to have the meaning the poet has long been seeking in language; yet, no sooner is she "signified" (both made significant and given a sign), than she realizes that even the most harrowing signs predict nothing.

The body in pain is the body most passionately understood by Rich. Yet even this body, like the body in "Twenty-One Love Poems," signifies most fully for Rich when it signifies something other than itself, when it can reduce its pain to the world's pain. Because the existing vocabulary for pain is so limited, we pass quickly into "as if" structures in describing pain, as Elaine Scarry has reminded us (15). Rich's speaker turns the "as if" structure around, refusing to admit that she feels, for example, as if a hammer were coming through her spine; rather, she writes that the pain she feels is indistinguishable from the pain that she sees around her. In her, the personal is rendered ghostly by being politicized out of existence. Yet, all that we know about physical pain convinces us that it is not communal, and the speaker's assertion that it is diminishes both the pain in the body and in the world. Again in 11 of the "Tracking Poems," she tracks the connection between her body and the world's body, "not knowing how to tell / my adhesions   the lingering infections / from the pain on the streets" (*YNYL*, 93).

Not knowing how to describe her pain and separate it from the pain of others is also another form of self-ghosting, of removing the body from its material identity, of making it not real. Scarry states: "the failure to express pain—whether the failure to objectify its attributes or instead the failure, once those attributes are objectified, to refer them to their original site in the human body—will always work to allow its appropriation and conflation with debased forms of power; conversely, the successful expression of pain will always work to expose and make impossible that appropriation and conflation" (14).

Rich does not leave her pain where she has located it in poem 11. Pain is not in the world's body, but in her body, the speaker claims in poem 13, and, playing on Emily Dickinson's "Pain—has an Element of Blank—," she longs to be rid of it, claiming, "Trapped in one idea, you can't have your feelings" (*YNYL*, 95). Rather, she will suffer the weight of pain, "drive and cry and come home" "and slowly even at winter's edge / the feelings come back." In 17, she tracks pain back to her self, this time connecting it to her heart. She is traveling the backroads "to places / like the hospital where night pain / is never tended enough," and she claims "I know / all of those roads by heart" (99). Suddenly, in one of those reversals of language, knowing by heart means not just the dull monotony of chronic pain but the anguish of knowing what pain excludes. The pain that is never tended and the heart that would tend grate against each other. Knowing pain by "heart" is a way of unknowing the heart's other moments.

In the poem just before this one, 16, the speaker takes up the subject of loss, recalling Elizabeth Bishop's poem "One Art," even as she disagrees with it, acknowledging "no art to this but anger." The speaker here is doubly bereft: both living through losing and self-divided so that she claims to be "watching myself in the act of loss." For her, it is no art but "acts of the heart forced to question / its presumptions in this world," "acts of the body forced to measure / all instincts against pain" (*YNYL*, 98).

Perhaps because the body is forced in this way, the speaker in 18 projects outward her own methods of denial, claiming that she lives "in a world where pain is meant to be gagged / uncured un-grieved-over" (*YNYL*, 100). Yet it is not in the world that pain is gagged, but in the speaker herself when she casts the moment "hot with joy" in a winter afternoon, or announces that she is "signified" by a pain that makes everything unpredictable, failing to distinguish her pain from the pain on the streets. The silencing of her pain is a minor theme running throughout the sequence of the "Tracking Poems." Even in this poem, she feels "The problem is / to connect, without hysteria, the pain / of any one's body with the pain of the body's world." "The best world is the body's world," she argues. It is "our raft among the abstract worlds" (100). But anyone's body and the body's world can only be connected by denying someone's body or abstracting it in favor of the world. Anyone's body makes the speaker's body anonymous. Whereas earlier in "From an Old House in America," Rich had written that "Any woman's death diminishes me" (*FofD*, 222), in this later poem the empathy for any one's pain appears to be a denial of her own.

In the next poem, she voices her fear, admitting: "If we're in danger of mistaking / our personal trouble for the pain on the streets / don't listen to us" (*YNYL*, 101). She advises her audience to "take off on your racing skis," adding that "Trapped in one idea, you can't have feelings / Without feelings perhaps you can feel like a god." The speaker, by contrast, is "grounded," afraid she might sound embittered, when actually it is she who is frightened by her own fury, she who cannot listen to her own feelings (101). Later, in poem 22, the speaker takes up that possibility, again projecting it onto a woman walking in a radioactive desert and asking if we should accuse her of self-denial. Over and over again, Rich expresses consciously or unconsciously this denial of the self.

In the final "Tracking Poem," 29, she advises herself and her lover, "cut it short cut loose from my words," as if the cut could be made, even when she knows it cannot. Love and pain are joined here in the writing that they both inspire. Writing for that "You," who might be both lover as other and her own body as other, the "You who think I find words for everything," the poet acknowledges the wordlessness she feels before both love and pain (*YNYL*, 111).

She is writing out of the pain that keeps her awake in the night hours, the pain that follows a familiar arthritic track from shoulder to elbow to wrist bone, and that has been noted before in her poetry. But what was once described as the clear "thread of pain" has degenerated into "the insect of detritus," the cartilage "sifting" rather than "shifting" around bones that have become strangely "mystical" (*YNYL*, 111). The language of the speaker blurs here even as she makes the distinction between "the body's pain and the pain on the street." The bones lose their connective power literally, and figuratively the "jointure of the bones" turns ghostly as it becomes mystical. But the opposition between mystical and bone is no greater than that between mystical and jointure, a settlement on the wife of a freehold estate for her lifetime. The jointure is not the joint; the connections are not of body or of spirit but of the law.

The night hours are both those of pain and of love, of the "wrecked" and the "jointure," a private moment when the jointure of the bones connects the pain and a communal moment when the bones of lover and beloved are joined. The final address to the lover is to remember the message that has not been in the poem, that contrary to what has been written and lived, the public and the private are not the same, although— and here the speaker assumes an enabling humility—"you can learn / from the edges that blur" (*YNYL*, 111).

Recently, Rich has taken as an example of the connection between poetry and politics Elizabeth Bishop's poem, "Chemin de Fer," a ballad where the speaker is walking on the railroad track by the "little pond where the dirty hermit lives." In the final two stanzas, Bishop writes:

> The hermit shot off his shot-gun
>   and the tree by his cabin shook.
> Over the pond went a ripple.
>   The pet hen went chook-chook.
>
> "Love should be put into action!"
>   screamed the old hermit.
> Across the pond an echo
>   tried and tried to confirm it. (*CP*, 8)

Rich comments: "The gun in this poem, like a real gun, might be fired out of despair at love's inaction, passivity, inertness, abuses, neglect. It's a 'dirty hermit' who fires the shotgun at nothing in particular. . . . Someone long isolate, outside community, who like the pond has been 'holding onto [his] injuries / *lucidly* year after year.' And who is the other character in the poem, the narrator of all this? . . . A someone who is legion across the globe. For whom the hermit's scream, the shout of the shot-gun, might be relief in a scene of enormous, unnameable tension and impoverishment. But there is nothing more lonelier-sounding or more futile than an echo, and the poem ends with this" (*WIFT*, 56).

To this paragraph, Rich appends the following footnote: "James Merrill comments that 'to anyone who has known love the merest hint of ties grown unmanageable will suffice.' I agree" (*WIFT*, 56). Although Rich uses this passage to introduce a series of reflections on women's responses to violence in politics as well as in poetry, she saw in Bishop's poem, as her footnote suggests, also an expression of love—the hermit's scream as a relief for all those who have held onto their injuries, felt the impoverishment, and then responded in one outburst and returned to their injuries. Such a response might have been Rich's own. But, as much as she understood the old hermit and his listener, the single shot has not been her way of expressing injuries she has held onto year after year—bodily injuries as well as those of the imagination and the emotions.

In "Chemin de Fer," Bishop's speaker is walking alone on the railroad track "with pounding heart. / The ties were too close together / or maybe too far apart." Merrill took the hint of meaning in the "ties" that Bishop encodes here to express her speaker's despair about love that turns the hermit's pond into "an old tear" and yet her hope to see the hermit's exclamation confirmed. Bishop's way was the hermit's; she chose the same isolation and single action that, like the hermit's, could be witnessed as either extravagant or pointless. Rich's way has been quite different.

She has chosen not to isolate herself but to put her love into action by coming out, by engaging in polemical arguments on behalf of lesbian feminism, by writing discursive prose, by involving herself in politics. In expressing herself, in writing about the love that she has held onto year after year until she could find the language that would give it its lucidity, she has not chosen the single shot. Rather, she has tried again and again to find what she wanted to say and the words that would express it. That attempt, that freeing of herself from the necessity of writing in code, opened for her a wide range and variety of emotions, allowing her to express her love for women as it has haunted her life and that of the culture, as it has possessed her body and mind even through pain.

8

*Adrienne Rich
and War*

It would seem that only a poet could claim that "War comes at the end of the twentieth century as absolute failure of imagination, scientific and political. That a war can be represented as helping a people to 'feel good' about themselves, their country, is a measure of that failure" (*WIFT*, 16). Writing about the Persian Gulf War in January 1991, actually Rich makes the point that politicians as well as poets have made about the Gulf War: Americans fought there for any number of political and economic reasons but chiefly to erase the ineradicable defeat of Vietnam with a military victory. The nuclear revolution that appeared to destroy permanently the Homeric myth of war had simply to be put aside as Americans took up conventional, if technically advanced, weapons to win again. The

Gulf War was an anachronism as it was fought in this age of postmodern-ist wars, as Miriam Cooke describes it: "Whereas wars previously codified the binary structure of the world . . . , today's wars are represented as doing the opposite. Postmodern wars highlight and then parody those very binaries—war/peace, good/evil, front/home front, combatant/noncom-batant, friend/foe, victory/defeat, patriotism/pacifism—which war had originally inspired. . . . Postmodern wars participate in undermining a system of meanings that had been in place until the outbreak of the nuclear revolution (182).

By exalting in the Gulf War victory, Americans failed to imagine the future, preferring instead that old system of meanings where the enemy is always bad, the victory always decisive, and good always triumphs. But none of these meanings is quite accurate applied to this war. Saddam Hussein himself, considered as both bad and good in America's recent political maneuverings, also claimed victory for that war, quickly reestab-lished his control over his country, and resumed nuclear production. He too felt it his right to celebrate victory.

The American public simply lacked the self-awareness, one form of the critical imagination, to see this war as a parody; it failed to interpret the media's own interpretation of the war scene in its deep-seated and regres-sive desire for the old meanings. Instead, Americans have colluded in parodying themselves, turning their feelings about the war into instant commodities, as Rich discovered when she found for sale *A Gulf War Feelings Workbook for Children* (*WIFT*, 16) in the San Francisco airport in March 1991.

Against the mass despair of the nation and its consequent vulnerability to manipulation by the media and to self-parody, Rich herself refuses to become cynical; but, in trying to arise above despair, she has had to look once again to the very binary oppositions she has also fought to overcome, seeing the despair, like the war, as evil, "the fruit of massive national denial, of historic national realities" (*WIFT*, 17). The idea that a nation that forgets its history will be doomed to repeat it is an old diagnosis of national fates, but Rich gives it here a kind of modern psychoanalytic turn as if a nation, like a person, could rise out of despair by uncovering its repressed memory. The analogy does not work. A nation is not a person who can be called into account easily and forced to take responsibility for its misdeeds. A nation is not composed only of the powerful and the victimizers. It includes the powerless and the victims as well. What role would they have in such a national soul-searching?

Rich's analysis seems hardly adequate for the situation of the world at the end of the twentieth century where it is no longer a question of them and us, of winners and losers. Addressed to a nation of victims, Rich's message could unleash its own war. Moreover, in an age of violent nationalisms throughout the world, Rich's advice to her own nation seems blindly chauvinistic. Counseling Americans to look to their own national history, there to face up to the inequities of race, class, and gender that have been from the start an intricate part of their dream, Rich seems to be addressing only a white middle-class male audience. What would an audience of African Americans, Native Americans, or Japanese Americans do if they faced up to the inequities of American history? What could they do but revolt?

As a poet, Rich has cast about for a role in such a nation, trying to find the relationship between poetry and politics. The scourge of the nation, Rich herself occupies an awkward position in the postmodernist war era. In a world where war has collapsed the old binary oppositions, there is no standing room for the moralist. Good and evil, victory and defeat, victim and victimizer are difficult to locate or separate, and the poet can neither place herself outside that blurring of boundaries nor distinguish one from the other. Moreover, no matter how hard she resists it, this poet—honored by the establishment, winner of prizes, middle-class, white, educated—is complicit in the system. She is not an innocent bystander to a war she watched on television along with the rest of the nation because, insofar as she understands war as spectacle, theatrical and competitive, she must also understand that she is one of the spectators. How is the poet to stand outside this theater of war?

Rich is not the first poet to confront this question of what a poet can write in wartime, and she searches for answers no less desperately despite her awareness that the war she must write through puts unusual pressures on the imagination. Her only strategy is persistence, to keep on writing despite her awareness that "all our work has suffered from the destabilizing national fantasy, the rupture of imagination implicit in our history," because, she claims, even in such a situation "poetry becomes more necessary than ever: it keeps the underground aquifers flowing; it is the liquid voice that can wear through stone" (*WIFT*, 122).

Water against stone, these are ancient oppositions, and, throughout her essays, she uses and draws back from such binary oppositions as those unequal adversaries, poetry and politics. In her prose, Rich is haunted by voices whispering that poetry is a marginal activity, "having as little to do with common emergency, as fly-fishing" (*WIFT*, 18). This self-doubt appears so persistent that it becomes a self-indulgent strategy used to put off her audience by agreeing with its most adversarial claim. Acknowledging that she herself suspects, along with them, that she could be, perhaps should be, more actively engaged for the political good, still Rich continues to write because she wants to write poetry, and she wants to find the relationship between poetry and politics in a culture hostile to political poetry. And so, even as she makes the case for its improbabilities, Rich wants to claim a public role for poetry, arguing that "we have rarely, if ever, known what it is to tremble with fear, to lament, to rage, to praise, to solemnize, to say *We have done this, to our sorrow*; to say *Enough*, to say *We will*, to say *We will not*. To lay claim to poetry" (Rich's italics, 20).

Once again, Rich entangles herself in oppositions. The poetry to which she would lay claim here is public poetry, poetry for the nation "*as a people*," poetry that is a public confession and cleansing, poetry that sounds like a prayer of contrition. It is poetry for a people who have trembled with fear, lamented, raged, in short, poetry for a people unlike the very Americans Rich is describing. The poetry to which America might lay claim, in Rich's view, is the poetry of public lament. It is ancient poetry for a people who can acknowledge and accept blame, who can distinguish good from evil, saying "*We will*" and "*We will not*." It is a poetry hardly workable in the postmodernist war era.

Yet, the lament is perhaps Rich's true voice, and it has many expressions in her poetry. In the lament of her love poetry, she speaks her erotic melancholy, her regret that for so much of her life she has silenced her desire, her sense that even as she experiences sexual pleasure it is passing. Her poetry of place, as we shall see, is often a lament for lost landscapes, for lost regions of the country, for lost homesteads. Here, as she turns to politics, Rich expresses her longing for the ancient poetry of public lament not just for herself, not just for the poet, but for the country she would unite in addressing.

Rich seems to acknowledge the futility of her longing for this poetry, and at the same time she cannot give it up, persisting in her wish that Americans will recover all that they have lost to advanced technology and capitalism even when she admits that "our lives are terrible and little, without continuity, buyable and salable at any moment, mere blips on a screen" (*WIFT*, 20). She persists, trying one way and then another, using her imagination "to voice public pain, speak memory, set words in a countering order, call up images that were in danger of being forgotten or unconceived" (18). She has not been banned or tortured for her poetic activity; perhaps worse than that, she has simply been overlooked. Poetry in America is today under house arrest, she argues, "precisely *because* of its recognitive and recollective powers, precisely because in this nation, created in the search for wealth, it eludes capitalist marketing, commoditizing, price-fixing, poetry has simply been set aside, depreciated, denied public space" (Rich's italics, 18).

Rich's task in her latest collection of prose, *What Is Found There: Notebooks on Poetry and Politics* (1993), as before in her writing, is to keep open the possibility for poetry, trying one space then another, and always working to keep alive poetry's recollective powers for an age without memory or imagination, to find a public space for poetry or, as she puts it, to "*bear witness to a reality from which the public—and maybe part of the poet—wants, or is persuaded it wants, to turn away*" (Rich's italics, *WIFT*, 115).

In this undertaking, she calls upon the revolutionary artist who "in opposition to a technocratic society's hatred of multiformity, hatred of the natural world, hatred of the body, hatred of darkness and women, hatred of disobedience" "loves people, rivers, other creatures, stones, trees inseparably from art, is not ashamed of any of these loves, and for them conjures a language that is public, intimate, inviting, terrifying, and beloved" (*WIFT*, 250).

But this is Rich's most advanced position. She realizes, as she admits, a revolutionary poem will be written only out of one individual's confrontation with her longings, including all she is expected to deny, in the belief that her readers deserve "an art as complex, as open to contradictions as themselves" (*WIFT*, 241). Her own longings may be political and encompass the possibility that 1992 will be a watershed year in which the histories of the Americas will begin to be told and listened to not as the conqueror's narrative, but as the multiplicity of real stories, a year too in which Americans will examine the conditions on which this country was founded and admit the lies about the country's past they have been told and told their children. But Rich's poetry is more complex, taking up quite different issues, turning her politics inward and trying to do for herself what she has urged for her country.

The poetry written in the years immediately before the Gulf War, and indeed in the year of the war, devotes most of its energy not to a cleansing and reinvigoration of the national imagination, but rather to probing a deep recess in her personal imagination where the nation hardly counts. Identifying with the international crisis of the Holocaust and turning to an older war in which she, as a Jewish girl who happened fortunately to be an American, escaped the suffering and death meted out to Jews of other nations, Rich seems to retreat entirely from the political reality of the end of the century and the postmodernist wars that mark it. Moreover, she speaks in a language that is far from the "public, intimate, inviting, terrifying, and beloved" language that she claims her revolutionary artist can conjure. Here, hardly the loving poet she heralds in her essay, she seems to seek a time and a war in which she can live out another part of her imaginative grasp of politics—her role as guilt-ridden survivor. Surviving so many personal losses—her father's death, her husband's suicide—Rich turns from them to trespass on ground to which she may have little claim as an American—ground that is public, not private, international not national, and far from the present moment. World War II is a safe place for the moralist of the postmodern war; it is a war where, at this remove, we might imagine that good and evil could be separated, a war that any postmodernist war poet would long for, a war that allows Rich to try out a completely different possibility for the relationship between poetry and politics. Perhaps most important of all, it is a war that the poet experienced as a child, protected and unaware and not accountable.

Before considering her retreat to childhood and World War II, I want to look at the poem about the Gulf War, Section XI of the title poem of her 1991 collection, "An Atlas of the Difficult World," where she appears again much less adamant than in her essays because it is here that she reveals most clearly why she has gone back to an earlier war to write war poetry. In this section, her tone is one of melancholy and nostalgia, a sad corrective, rather than an outraged protest, and, as such, the Gulf War is on a continuum with her World War II poems. Denying the new language of this most postmodernist of wars in Section XI of a long poem that concerns itself with many kinds of battles, Rich seems to want to turn back time and restore language to its former meaning. She writes, "A patriot is not a weapon.   A patriot is one who wrestles for the /   soul of her country," "A patriot is a citizen," trying to recover her innocence from a century of wars (*ADW*, 23).

Compare this passage of poetry to Rich's comments on the Gulf War in her essay, "The hermit's scream":

It revealed the invasions of Grenada in 1983, of Panama in 1989, as rehearsals, war games, dressed in a rhetorical language of rescue and the deposition of a monster. Manipulative images—a crusade against a new monster, a "butcher" (recently our client in the arms trade)—were used to camouflage in 1991 the fact that the invention, manufacture, and sale, not of nuclear arms but of the most dazzlingly refined "conventional" weapons, have become the lifeblood of global capitalism. . . . Arsenal building for profit, legal and illegal, plays off old and new nationalisms and ideologies, while a more and more sophisticated weaponry allows both for the closing down of old military bases and the reduction of nuclear arms. (*WIFT*, 59–60)

The voice of the poet, unlike that of the essayist, is elegiac. It may want to speak the nightmare of race in American war as in peace; it may want to name the "burnt-out dream of innocence" of the founding fathers in which America would be both "a city on the hill" and the new Eden; it may want to translate Whitman's description of the grass—"the flag of my disposition, out of hopeful green stuff woven"—into a different kind of flag—"every flag that flies today is a cry of pain" (*ADW*, 23); but, within each of these efforts, the voice of the poet also searches for terms to negotiate with that older system of values where a patriot is a citizen. Yet, while Rich is raising her voice against the violence of the twentieth century, she is simultaneously recalling dreams of innocence that were also imperialistic and poetic voices that were both appropriatively hopeful and a cry of pain.

In the Gulf War, a patriot *was* a weapon, and to turn the noun toward its earlier meaning of citizen is to retreat from both the reality and the consequences of that war, but not in fear and anger. It is rather to take a word back from what Rich has called the misprision of history in her essay, "'A clearing in the imagination'" (*WIFT*, 107–8). In taking back the word "patriot," Rich is also trying, as she writes, quoting John Haines, to "provide 'a space in which creation can take place, a clearing in the imagination'" (110). Releasing the word, patriot, from its misprision, Rich seeks to reveal the severe loss of memory the public imagination has suffered when it fails to acknowledge the gap in meaning between citizen and weapon, the immense distinction between patriotism and killing, that the American public simply overlooked as it watched the war avidly each night on television. Like Ezra Pound in another war, Rich would advise, "get a dictionary / and learn the meaning of words" (*The Cantos*, XCVIII), realizing, as perhaps only a poet can, that a misprision of language leads inevitably to a misprision of power.

What does it mean to be a patriot wrestling for the soul of her country when, as Rich reports in an essay, the commander in chief of the Persian Gulf War resigns his command and sells his memoirs for five million dollars (*WIFT*, 102)? Will his words suffice? What does it mean to be a poet-patriot in such times? It means, Rich writes, that such a patriot, like the nurse in the poem lifting the war-wounded, must blow "with her every skill on the spirit's embers still burning by their own laws in the bed of death" (*ADW*, 23). It means that such a patriot will write poetry that, unlike war, will not be used by America's "free" enterprise system for profit. It means that at least one citizen among many will set herself apart from those who want to memorialize dead heroes and revive the spirit of war mongering, that at least one citizen will learn rather to think about questions of power and powerlessness.

Rich is aware of this war as a postmodernist phenomenon, although she sees its theatricality not as unique, but rather as part of the history of war. In her essay, "The hermit's scream," she notes that twentieth-century citizens are not the only ones who have passively taken in war; in the nineteenth century people attended military battles as spectators, watching live war through telescopes and field glasses as we watch it on television. Amateur historians have reenacted battles of the Revolutionary and Civil Wars annually—and in full military costume. Such theatrics, she admits, might distract from or be a consolation for "the knowledge that at the end of the twentieth century there is no demilitarized zone, no line dividing war from peace, that the ghettos and barrios of peacetime live under paramilitary occupation, that prisoners are taken and incarcerated at an accelerating rate, that the purchase of guns has become an overwhelming civilian response to perceived fractures in the social compact" (*WIFT*, 64).

Here, curiously, Rich joins Stein and Bishop in her understanding of war as theater, as spectacle, from which the lyric poet retreats. The system of command that Stein parodied in her war poems, the military monuments that Bishop derided in her poems about Paris and Washington, like Rich's scornful account of the Gulf War, all are efforts to reduce the posturing and histrionics of war and expose its diminishment of human life and values.

Strangely enough, although she can clearly identify the blurred boundaries of this postmodernist war in her essay, in her poem Rich places herself in the tradition of male war poets, going back to rewrite, as she echoes, Ezra Pound's "Hugh Selwyn Mauberley" where the poet, expressing his disillusion with a war fought under the old system of values, is himself recasting Horace in ironic terms. Of World War I, Pound writes:

These fought in any case,
and some believing,
　　　　pro domo, in any case . . .

Some quick to arm,
some for adventure,
some from fear of weakness,
some from fear of censure,

some for love of slaughter, in imagination,
learning later . . .
some in fear, learning love of slaughter;
Died some, pro patria,
        non "dulce" non "et decor" . . .
walked eye-deep in hell
believing in old men's lies, then unbelieving
came home, home to a lie[1]

Rich recasts Pound's lines, writing not about those who fought, but instead about those who witnessed the war: "some busy constructing enclosures," "some trying to revive dead statues," "some who try to teach," "some who preach," "some who aggrandize," "some who diminish," "some for whom war is new," "some marching for peace," "some for whom peace is a white man's word and a white man's privilege" (*ADW*, 22–23).

Rich is a skilled list maker in her poetry, but here, in comparison with Pound, her list appears flaccid, tired, pointless. Even the internal rhymes ("teach"/"preach") hardly do the work of Pound's "adventure"/"censure" with their double thrust at the excitement mixed with the fear of war. It is not that Pound takes a stronger position. After all, his antiwar sentiment was ready-made for him by the war poets who surrounded him and by the tenor of the times. It is rather that he writes more clearly and wittily. His contribution is stylistic: he has found a way to blame and praise at the same time, to castigate the warmongers and eulogize the innocent war-dead. He can set the ready-made antiwar sentiment against Horace's standard in a model of brevity that slashes into the decorum of patriotism and, at the same time, provides a litany that will honor the patriotic dead, however wrongheaded their leaders.

Like Pound, Rich too took her antiwar position from the air. But her language is slack, her oppositions are predictable. She has looked past Pound to take Whitman's long line as a model, not to express his largeness of vision that enclosed multitudes, but rather to state her disgust with the evasions of her fellow citizens. Such a line cannot rely on Whitman's catalogs to carry the sharpness of her criticism nor can it fully express the task she has set herself, as she claims she is bent on "fathoming what it means to love my country" (*ADW*, 22).

In this, Rich has taken on a more difficult position than Pound. Patriot that he was, Pound never made such an effort or rather thought that he could scold, vilify, and manipulate his country into a place he could love. It is not that Rich has not tried some of his tactics herself; but, in her most recent collection of poems, even when she places herself in the line of war poets to which Pound belonged, she has not found her voice among them. She descends below the plain style to a level of banality that threatens to implicate the poet in the imaginative weakness she seems anxious to deplore.

In this mode, her interest in turning "patriot" from its Gulf War meaning of a technologically sophisticated weapon toward its earlier meaning may seem like a retreat to an earlier era. Although her "patriot" is one who wrestles for the soul of her country, not one who loves and serves its authority, Rich's lines lack the vigor to make that distinction clear; in fact, it is not a distinction that she wants to pursue, as she states her intent to fathom "what it means to love my country" (*ADW*, 22).

Rich's seems to be a regressive dream, and yet, as she entertains it here to move beyond the death-ridden century in which she lives, beyond the Gulf War, beyond the national despair, she wants to turn it toward the future. Poet that she is, she wants to escape the politics of the present where the flags of nationalism are blooming in a deadly drought.

Turning into an exile like Pound is not a way to learn love of country. Nor is the separation of herself as a poet from the politics that she resists such a way, as she acknowledges, "the internal emigrant is the most home-sick of all women and of all men." The only way is to identify with her country, "wrestle" for its soul as Jacob wrestled for his country, and, like Jacob, return through memory to a world uncorrupted by time. Where Pound wrote, "remember that I have remembered," calling into his "tale of the tribe" the voices of history, Rich seeks to "remember her true country, remember his suffering land" by re-membering, finding again the parts of the true country to which she belongs (*ADW*, 23).

Moving away from the Gulf War in other sections of this long poem, "An Atlas of the Difficult World," Rich has discovered that to remember her "true" country she must search through the density of her own memories, where even the most idyllic moments have been streaked with pain and loss and violence. She calls her long poem an atlas—that mixed genre of maps, illustrations, charts, and text—and it serves as a repository for Rich's wide-ranging and open-ended reflections on her country, its history, her own history. Although related, an atlas is different from a history, as Elizabeth Bishop explains in "The Map": "More delicate than the historians' are the map-makers' colors" (*CP*, 3). And Rich's "An Atlas of the Difficult World" is keen to catch that delicacy of color (racial, natural, geographical), opening with the attentive woman, perhaps the poet herself who, bending her head to read or pray, is "listening for something," and closing in the final section with the attentive reader in whom the poet places her desperate faith (*ADW*, 3).

The woman listening, the reader listening, open and close a long poem that designates itself "an atlas," (not *the* atlas, but one among many, as if everyone could draw her own atlas). These listeners for something read the maps of this particular country, and they see a land strewn with battlefields—not just personal battlefields between husband and wife, but a landscape of battlefields, memorializing a nineteenth-century war or existing in modern urban settings such as Centralia or Detroit, or the whole range of locations where civil rights have been contested from Appomattox to Selma and Saigon. These listeners read of the stalking and killing of two lesbians along the Appalachian Trail and other random violence (*ADW*, 15). The list is random, potentially endless, varied, international. Whatever figures in this map have been touched in some way by war and loss; even Rich's homage to beauty and to her beautiful partner notes "the blueprints of resistance and mercy / drawn up in childhood," which is "already acquainted with mourning" (24).

But in this atlas, there is one place that seems to focus the poet's loss, and there Rich's eye bores down on the delicate colors of the map to read a history, her own, her family's, her friends', her "true" country's. It is a place where Rich is least likely to find her true country—Vermont—small-town rural northeastern poor Vermont, full, as she wrote in *Sources* (1983) of "Protestant separatists, Jew-baiters" (*YNYL*, 5). It is a location that haunts her poetry, not a place for a Southerner, with "the shortest growing season / south of Quebec" (*ADW*, 8), not a place she can understand with its "difficult unknowable / incommensurable barn" (7). And yet, it is the place that stirs up the longest memories in her and turns her toward home.

Opening this section of "An Atlas of the Difficult World" with images of two five-pointed, star-shaped glass candleholders, Rich would appear to move straight to her subject: her Jewish ancestors, her Jewish husband, their suffering and her own as a guilty survivor, her connection with a history far beyond her own country. But, despite the simplicity of the language, Rich has placed at the start of the poem an image of memories inextricable from, however much they might appear unconnected to, the map of Vermont, that map itself intricately connected to the map of Europe. The Star of David fixed in these candleholders is almost canceled out by the descriptive phrase that follows, "bought at the Ben Franklin, Barton, twenty-three years ago" (*ADW*, 7). The candleholders, like so much in this poem, come out of no particular heritage—here, the five-and-ten-cents store in small-town rural Vermont yet named for that quintessential American—and Rich does not come back to their hinted significance until she has meandered through a landscape that seems idyllically remote from the wars and suffering. It is a location that calls up her children, picnics in a world that seems little because it is so pure and innocent, where she read Gaskell's *Life of Charlotte Brontë*. But, read again, the idyll gives way and Vermont becomes a "place of sheer unpretentious hardship," Brontë a "genius / unfurled in the shortlit days, the meagre means of that house," the speaker herself not thinking of lives around her "extinguished in the remote back-country I had come to love," "the landscape / of the rural working poor" (*ADW*, 8).

The darkness for which these memories have prepared comes into the poem as the world outside darkens from storm or nightfall. Turning into the house, the speaker seems to turn from the darkness, surveying instead, in what appears to be a random glance around, the furnishings of the house which call up a particular history. It is at once the usual clutter of a summer house and the particular mementos of an unusual life: her grandmother's Chinese teapot, another given by a German Jew, "a refugee who killed herself," her father's bookplace with its motto *"Without labor, no sweetness,"* a "little handwrought iron candlestick, given by another German woman / who hidden survived the Russian soldiers," "odd glasses for wine or brandy, from an ignorant, passionate time" with someone she identifies not as her husband but as "the father of the children who dug for old medicine bottles." She remembers that they spent afternoons discussing such works as Karl Shapiro's *Poems of a Jew* and Auden's "In Sickness and in Health" (*ADW*, 9). The eye of the poet seems simply to scan the room, and yet, of course, *as* the eye of the poet, it can never move simply by chance; it will find even the "unused" "useful." These are not meaningful oppositions in the poem and, we discover, not meaningful in the life that is recorded either.

Chance/choice, Christian/Jew, labor/sweetness, marriage/separation, sickness/health, living breath/dead husband, Brooklyn/Harvard Yard, the scene is made up of oppositions that in the end do not oppose. The Christian grandmother Mary "travelled little, loved the far and strange" (*ADW*, 8); the suicidal German Jew "instructed" the poet to use her teapot for "'flowers'" for life; the speaker learns in "grief and rebellion"; the speaker and her husband read poems of a Jew and a Christian, of sickness and of health, living in a time of ignorance and of passion. For this poet, who has seemed so often "split at the root" and here identifies her father's bookplate as "cleft tree-trunk," the recognition that oppositions are not differences might appear to be a healing wisdom (9).

Yet, the memories that sweep over this speaker are not comforting; rather, they remind her of a time past that produced hardship instead of ease, labor without sweetness, death, bare if miraculous survival. They are memories of wars, some far and strange, some close to home, of Germans and Russians, all churned up in the wind in this remote backcountry of Vermont. And the wind itself, which "has a voice in the house," for this postromantic poet, is not a force of nature, destroyer and preserver, offering consolation. It is not even a wind that conjures up ghosts from the past. It is instead the "unwinding wind" that releases the voices of the house, ghostly but not speaking plainly (*ADW*, 9). Rich does not specify their subject. At the heart of this section of "An Atlas of the Difficult World" is an unwillingness to name the difficulties of her world, to locate in all the locations she evokes the actual place of her uneasiness.

In the end, Rich deflects an ending by turning to nature again, and to another image laden with a literary history, the spider who in the opening image had been working between the five-pointed, star-shaped candles. By asking the question, "But how do I know what she needs?" Rich both opens her poem and assumes control of the spider image she has so boldly stolen from Whitman. Like his noiseless, patient spider, Rich's spider is the admirable and winning worker, who "will use everything, nothing comes without labor" although "not all labor ends in sweetness." What does she need? Rich asks as she concludes, "Maybe simply / to spin herself a house within a house, on her own terms / in cold, in silence" (*ADW*, 10).

Here is the woman's spider, the domestic spinner, not Whitman's spider with its soul's gossamer thread, but a creator, like Rich herself, who "Maybe" simply wants to spin a house within a house, a place of safety in the difficult world. "Maybe" she works so hard because she wants to show that even a house, a woman's place, is no longer safe from the memories of war and hardship, that even women must find a house within a house. But, as Rich writes, "how do I know what she needs?" The spider works, after all, "in silence."

In Rich's understanding of the woman's need for a safe house within her house, she has been inspired by the work of women poets, especially those with whom she has associated as a Jewish American writer and as a lesbian. Perhaps it is the work of writers such as Irena Klepfisz, Muriel Rukeyser, and Minnie Bruce Pratt that has been the greatest education to Rich in her efforts both to fathom what it means to love her country and, at the same time, to acknowledge its terrors no less than its weaknesses. Each one of these poets has occupied a more advanced position of Rich's own politics, and it might be that the work of each of them has forced Rich into new ranges of her imagination which, taken out of this context, might have seemed to be merely retreats—into memories, childhood, an age of innocence. But, in the context of these poets' work, Rich's own seems less a retreat than a rethinking of experience, the meaning of which she herself had missed.

In Pratt, the lesbian mother, nature lover, Christian Southerner, Rich has seen a younger and more daring model of the subject she herself claimed as her own in *Of Women Born* (1976). As a lesbian mother, Pratt has helped Rich realize and perhaps address the subject of secrets—"what can be told in the face of fear and shame, what can get heard, if told: the secret spoken yet unreceived because it is dissonant with the harmonies we like to hear" (*WIFT*, 147). And, in her, Rich has found a political message. She writes: "but the energy of Pratt's erotic poetry derives not only from a female sensuality only now beginning to find its way into poetry, but from the inseparability of sensuality from politics. To act on a criminalized sexuality demands, in this poet's experience, many kinds of decriminalization—not only of sexual acts, but of poverty, skin, difference" (150).

In the slightly older Muriel Rukeyser, Rich has come to know the work of a woman, also a mother, who also writes affirming her sexuality and her desire, and who refuses to be easily categorized despite her political identity with the causes of the left in the 1930s and 1940s. The "poet of inseparables," Rukeyser writes "as a sexual woman and as a Jew—unapologetically" (*WIFT*, 100), encouraging Rich to meet her at the "crossroads" of her own interests in poetry, politics, sexuality (101).

Perhaps, of these poets, it is Irena Klepfisz's example that has most forcefully pushed Rich back to her own childhood there to consider World War II. Klepfisz is, for Rich, a paradigm of cultural re-creation, and she serves as a model for a poet bent on fathoming what it means to love her country even though Klepfisz has no country. Born in 1941 in the Warsaw Ghetto, Klepfisz begins with almost total loss of family, culture, country, language, and, from that loss, she has taken up the task of learning to articulate that destruction and to re-create herself as a Jew, a woman, a writer. Her way has not been to leave behind the Holocaust, but rather to search "through her poetry, for what is possible in a world where *this* was possible" (Rich's italics, *WIFT*, 131).

The question of what it means to be a Holocaust survivor has haunted Jewish life worldwide, and it has been answered variously with silence, denial, amnesia, and mythologizing. For Klepfisz, it is not just a question of present memory, but "of lost, irreplaceable resources, cultural and emotional riches destroyed or scattered before she could know them" (*WIFT*, 132). She has been forced to ask herself what it means to grow up as a Jew in the United States after the Holocaust or, as Klepfisz writes in Yiddish, *der khurbin,* to become a Jewish woman, single, childless, lesbian, from a community of survivors who see their greatest hope for meaning in a new generation of Jewish children.

Klepfisz's life goes on in a United States where, Rich writes, echoing language she has used to describe her own purpose, she tries to "fathom her place as a Jew in the larger American gentile world" where the black ghettos surrounding an elite American university appear to her like the blasted Jewish ghetto of postwar Europe (*WIFT*, 138). Klepfisz is not trying to assimilate, to find the better life promised immigrants in America; rather, she wants to understand her life as she lives it in the borders between two great continents. Rich calls Klepfisz's poem *Bashert* "one of the great 'borderland' poems—poems that emerge from the consciousness of being of no one geography, time zone, or culture, of moving inwardly as well as outwardly between continents, landmasses, eras of history" (139). Strangely enough, it is from this poet writing without a country that Rich might have learned how to fathom the ways to love her country.

In white North America where poetry has been set apart from political meaning, Klepfisz, "inheriting an entwined European-Jewish-Socialist-Bundist political tradition and a Yiddish cultural tradition," has refused to segregate art from daily life (*WIFT*, 141). In this, she has shown Rich another model of accountability, of poetry's ancient role in keeping memory and spiritual community alive. Most important, Klepfisz has taught Rich the lesson she is most apt to learn—that survivorhood is not a stasis, the survivor not an artifact. Klepfisz feels, acts, and writes in living time, moving to respond to new crises, as Jewish history changes and shifts. Identifying with the Palestinians under Israeli occupation, for example, Klepfisz writes of her pain and sorrow, acknowledging that to forget these new victims would be to forget her own past.

The work of all these women poets—not just Klepfisz, but Pratt, Rukeyser, as well—has played into Rich's most recent poetry, teaching her, as the "masters" of her youth never could, what it means to be a political poet.[2] Their examples may explain, too, why Rich has turned back to write about her own safety as a Jewish American girl in World War II. It seems an odd choice since, in that period of her life, Rich was not clearly identified as a Jew. She notes that her Jewish father, calling himself a Deist, and her Protestant-born mother, secular by default, sent her nonetheless to the Episcopal Church for several years "as a kind of social validation, mainly as protection against anti-Semitism" (*WIFT*, 194).

There seems to be in her own background the same kind of massive denial of history that Rich diagnoses in the country's need to feel good about itself in the Gulf War. In her recent war poems, she seems bent on acknowledging her own denial, opening herself to it, to see what it will render. Still, much is suppressed in that autobiographical fragment, and we might ask, why in a city with a strong Jewish community would Rich's father feel the necessity of identifying himself as a Deist? Why would he feel the need to protect his daughter against anti-Semitism? Rich does not explain, although she seems to be acknowledging here her own affinity with Klepfisz's loss of cultural heritage, with Pratt's double alienation from and attachment to her white Southern Christian culture, with the outsider stand of Rukeyser. If Rich does not share the extremes of their experience, she has learned from them how to open up parts of her life that have remained unspoken and to consider again her uneasy, if comfortable, childhood in World War II America.

Almost a third of the sections of *Sources* focuses on Rich in World War II. But in that long poem where she speaks forthrightly for the first time about and to her dead husband and her dead father, she creates a strangely nuanced voice in which to write of the war. She seems to be both inside and outside of history, both unaware of what was going on around her and superbly aware, both the child living in the war and the adult far distant from it. And, in her memories, the war, her Jewish heritage, her family's part in a segregated South, all are inextricably intertwined. The war seems fought on many levels, its history repressed on many levels.

Even as a young American girl during World War II, she felt she had a special destiny. Here, she draws on both the idea of America as a nation with a special destiny and the belief in the destiny of the Jewish survivor of the Holocaust. Writing well after that war, Rich casts onto its speaker an awareness that few American children of her generation would have felt: the sense that there was some reason she had been spared the life and death of the European Jews. The speaker of this poem is hard to fix in time since her imagination works both backward and forward, acknowledging that she knew nothing of the Holocaust in her childhood and yet felt she had a special destiny to fulfill as a result of being spared. Both as victim and victimizer (her kin were "the Jews of Vicksburg or Birmingham"), moving through a complex personal history of racial and religious violence, the speaker can find no place for herself.

Seeking her "sources" in this history, the speaker of *Sources* has to confront the special destiny of her kin, *"a chosen people"* but actually only shopkeepers who developed strategies by which they could live, which could serve their needs. They were proud of their long stay in America, prejudiced against newer immigrants, the latecomers (*YNYL*, 8). But these are not the ancestors she wants, and, by contrast, Rich writes, the Jews she felt "rooted among" were those who died in the Holocaust (18). Denying her heritage, no less than her father, the "Deist," who dying nonetheless followed the Six Day War, she has become, as he advised her, "a citizen of the world," herself responding to crises in the Middle East as if it were her own country (18). Citizen of the world, that advice spoken with the evasion that fatherly concern appropriated and repeated sneeringly in the daughter's poem, is advice she must turn on herself as she is compelled to repeat her father's suffering.

Writing about wars that are far distant in time or in place unlike her treatment of the Gulf War, Rich does move war poetry away from the oppositions that war has always engendered: us/them, peace/war, victory/defeat, men fighting/women waiting. These are wars that never end, and although as a child, an American, a girl, Rich appears in these poems partially shielded from blame, still, as an adult poet, she cannot remove herself from their shame, acknowledging that she shares the sufferings of every family that has been beaten in a pogrom and swathed in bandages.

The death camps, she writes, are where "history was meant to stop"; but they have become rather both "terrible" and "familiar," both arresting and "on-going" (*YNYL*, 20). Rich's double voice allows her to name "YERUSHALAYIM" as "*a city on a hill*" and the promised land that is also the site of broken promises (24). Thus the speaker can call into her poem the separate strands of her life—Zion, America, women's unity. Religion, nation, gender have all been broken promises to her; yet as the pattern gives way and becomes a different but still terrible pattern, Rich herself keeps up her ongoing and multivalenced search for the promised land.

In "Eastern War Time" from *An Atlas of the Difficult World*, Rich turns again to World War II and to her girlhood. "Memory lifts her smoky mirror: 1943," on a child being schooled in Latin ("*Latin for Americans*," Rich writes, as if Americans needed special training in the classical language of war and poetry). She joins uniformed girls singing the Christian hymn not of prayer for victory or of help in battle, but the totally irrelevant plea: "Eternal Father, strong to save. . . . O hear us when we cry to thee" "*For those in peril on the sea*" (Rich's italics, *ADW*, 35). Singing under the artificial memorials of past heroic moments, plaster casts of "chariots horses draperies certitudes," well cared for with donations the children have provided from their lunch money, the girl here is deprived of her true heritage in a time when her nation's government is being informed that "AT ONE BLOW EXTERMINATED TO RESOLVE / ONCE

AND FOR ALL JEWISH QUESTION IN EUROPE" (36). The speaker asks the question she cannot even finish, wondering, "what is that girl," "what's an American girl" who knew neither that she was Jewish nor what was happening to the Jews in war-torn Europe, what was that girl trying to learn about the world through books (36)?

Such a girl is not going to go to war, not going to understand war, not going to read the telegram sent through the American legation in Bern, Switzerland, on August 11, 1942, to the State Department in Washington warning of the extermination of the Jews. Then, what is that girl? Ignorant perhaps, but not saved from history by that ignorance, as the speaker contends "what the grown-ups can't teach   children must learn" (*ADW*, 38), not just about the war in Europe but about anti-Semitism closer to home, in the South, for example, the lynching of Leo Frank in Atlanta, Georgia, in 1915.

Moreover, what she has had to learn is that her "true" country is with other girls like herself. That American girl with "her permed friz of hair" (*ADW*, 36) can blur into another girl "having her hair done   its pale friz / clipped and shaped," thinking her beauty would save her from death by gas but dying instead in the Nazi experiments in the operating room (39). Or that American girl is like still another girl described whose best marks are in history and geometry and who wanders with a boy into the woods near Vilna, "a romantic walk," to escape persecution by the Soviets (40). That girl has perhaps turned into "A woman of sixty," living in a century that may be a mere blink in geological time "though heavy to those who had to wear it" (41). In her dreams, she sees the long history of war and violence and racial and religious persecution both here and abroad, both in the American South and in the Northern ghettos, both among the Palestinians and the Israelis in the Middle East.

Rich writes of "A woman wired in memories" who has witnessed the suffering and resistance of her own family, and the speaker of her poem wonders to whom this woman will be able to let down enough to tell her story. Who? "Who must hear her to the end / but the woman   forbidden to forget" (*ADW*, 42). And so, Rich reclaims for women the role of the witness to history, the teller of the tale, and the listener to that telling. But the woman is no mere passive witness. Memory speaks for herself in this poem: "I'm nothing if I'm just a roll of film" "left for another generation's / restoration and framing." Memory goes on: "unkillable though killed" (43).

The final poem of the series, "Eastern War Time," connects the war of Rich's childhood Baltimore and the Persian Gulf War of her adulthood, as memory speaks again, asking "Want to do right? Don't count on me." Memory continues, identifying herself as "a mass grave," "a table set with room for the Stranger," a woman in mourning standing on the streets of Haifa, Tel Aviv, Jerusalem, "a woman standing in line for gasmasks" in the Gulf War. Finally, she is the woman in the poem, "standing here in your poem   unsatisfied / lifting my smoky mirror" (*ADW*, 44).

It might appear that Rich has taken women's war poetry out of the woman's everyday domestic life during wartime that Stein chronicled and, beyond that, into a more intimate acknowledgment of public events than Bishop made. Yet, for all her public position, in her poetry Rich writes about women, maintaining her allegiance to their private domestic world where, dressed in black, they mourn the war dead. Like Stein, she identifies in her poetry with women going about the daily tasks of life in a war zone, standing in line for gas masks. Like Bishop, too, she has worried over the connection between war and writing, between the poetry of war and war itself. But she differs from both Stein and Bishop in her moral outrage, her willingness to take sides and divide the world between the good and the evil. In insisting on speaking out, assuming the authority to address the nation, calling Americans to account for their violence, Rich has taken on a public role that neither Stein nor Bishop assumed. In her poetry, too, she has moved beyond their positions. Stein's silence on the Holocaust is a marked contrast to Rich's anguished willingness to engage the subject, and, although Bishop's sensitivity to issues of race and class has come to Rich much later in her life, she has treated it in her poetry with a greater political force than Bishop.

Still, especially in her more recent work, Rich has moved away from the troubles of her own time to probe the memories of the Holocaust, of racial conflicts in the South, of far distant wars, as if the real experience of war for her had to do with memory rather than battlefields, with psychic rather than physical wounds, with passive suffering rather than action on the battlefield. In this sense, then, her war poetry is not so immediate as Stein's reporting from the battlefield or from occupied France nor so immediately reflective as Bishop in "Roosters," detailing the military life she witnessed in Key West during World War II. What Rich has contributed to this tradition of war poetry is an awareness that a patriot is a citizen and a citizen is a woman too.

9

Adrienne Rich
A Politics of Location

"Notes toward a Politics of Location" is the title of a talk Rich gave at a conference on Women, Feminist Identity, and Society in the 1980s in Utrecht, Holland, on June 1, 1984, in which she acknowledges "the marks of a struggle to keep moving, a struggle for accountability" (*BBP*, 211). Then she confesses, "It can be difficult to be generous to earlier selves, and keeping faith with the continuity of our journeys is especially hard in the United States, where identities and loyalties have been shed and replaced without a tremor, all in the name of becoming 'American'" (223).

At first, this candor appears unnecessary. Surely, among poets, it is Adrienne Rich who has remained accountable and can be most clearly located in the political issues of her times: an outspoken opponent of the Vietnam War, an advocate for feminist positions in most of the movement's phases, an important public voice for lesbian and gay rights. She does not appear to have been disloyal to her commitments or to lack a political location. And yet, in this talk to a European audience, acknowledging an uneasiness that the titles of her recent collections also indicate, Rich suggests the extent to which, in moving quickly through a long career, she has come to feel the need to identify her location. Citing the difficulties of the task, she excuses herself by turning to the most incontrovertible justification of all, that ultimate "politics of location"—her identity as an "American."

This identity, which seems so simple, has been, according to Rich, the complex result of a series of relocations. Growing up in Baltimore, Maryland, she claims to have known one kind of politics of location: on her mother's side, gentile and "white southern Protestant" with "southern talk of family" "as heritage, the guarantee of 'good breeding'" (*BBP*, 102). Only when, as a college student, she moved to another part of the country, to Cambridge, Massachusetts, did she come into a partial awareness of the other branch of her heritage—her father's family of Ashkenazic and Sephardic Jewish descent, again with Southern roots. But once more this understanding was filtered through a location—Radcliffe College of the 1940s—that provided its own particular political interpretation of that identity, as Rich writes of the contemporaries with whom she came to explore her background: "For these young Jewish women, students in the late 1940s, it was acceptable, perhaps even necessary, to strive to look as gentile as possible; but they stuck proudly to being Jewish, expected to marry a Jew, have children, keep the holidays, carry on the culture" (108).

This complicated new identity was blended with and not separate from a location: the New England of Rich's imagination. Leaving what she calls "the backward, enervating South for the intellectual, vital North," Rich moved to a location that, she writes, "had for me some vibration of higher moral rectitude, of moral passion even, with its seventeenth-century Puritan self-scrutiny, its nineteenth-century literary 'flowering,' its abolitionist righteousness" (*BBP*, 108). Thus, even in discovering her Jewish identity, she was doing so against a version of the social world of her childhood that was "christian" "genteel, white, middle-class" (103).

Then, in marrying a Brooklyn-born "Jew of the 'wrong kind' from an Orthodox eastern European background," as she describes him, Rich claims to have discovered another location and its politics (*BBP*, 114). She reports that she was "moved and gratefully amazed by the affection and kindliness [of her] husband's parents" and enjoyed gatherings at their home on Eastern Parkway in Brooklyn, seeing "it all as quintessentially and authentically Jewish" (115–16). But, even here, authenticity was not simple or pure, as she was to understand eventually, noting "how in my own family, and in the very different family of my in-laws, there were degrees and hierarchies of assimilation which looked askance upon each other—and also geographic lines of difference, as between southern Jews and New York Jews, whose manners and customs varied along class as well as regional lines" (117).

Another shift in Rich's "politics of location" came when she moved to New York in the 1960s and became involved in the debate over community control of public schools in which African American and Jewish teachers and parents were often on opposite sides. She writes: "I didn't understand then that I was living between two strains of Jewish social identity: the Jew as radical visionary and activist who understands oppression firsthand, and the Jew as part of America's devouring plan in which the persecuted, called to assimilation, learn that the price is to engage in persecution" (*BBP*, 120).

Finally, in the 1970s connecting with the Women's Liberation movement, Rich began to realize that, as a woman, she stood in "a particular and unexamined relationship to the Jewish family and to Jewish culture" (*BBP*, 116). Moreover, participating in the feminist movement in New York, Rich was attuned to its radical politics and to the movement-within-the-movement of lesbian activism and visibility. In this location, releasing what she would come to feel as the suppressed lesbian within herself, Rich began to see also that her identity as a feminist, like her identity as a Jew, was with a movement that had yet to acknowledge "its own racial, class, and ethnic perspectives or its fears of the differences among women" (122).

As she describes them, the political positions of her life have been tied to the many locations in which she has lived or, rather, they have been tied to coming out of particular locations. She has had to come out of the South, out of Cambridge, out of New York, in order to see the differences within herself and to work at "enlarging the range of accountability" in her life (*BBP*, 123). Starting from what might have seemed the archetypal middle-class American childhood, Rich has taken a lifetime finally to "come out" as an American with links to a varied politics of location: Southern Christianity and racism, Northern liberalism as well as a Jewish identity, the New York feminist movement in general and its marginalized lesbian community, and, most recently, California and its ethnic variety.

Central to all these identities has been her decision to come out as a lesbian and, as a curious result, to move politically away from a feminist separatism toward a new willingness, as she says, to "speak from, and of, and to, my country" (*YNYL*, back cover). Learning to begin, as she announced in her talk at Utrecht, "not with a continent or a country or a house, but with the geography closest in—the body" (*BBP*, 212), Rich has picked up "the long struggle against lofty and privileged abstraction" (213), no longer willing to write, "Women have always" because "'always' blots out what we really need to know: When, where, and under what conditions has the statement been true?" (214). Rich's interest in the material circumstances of her country has led her to examine the particular details of her own life, its locations as well as its history.

Of course, the story she tells of her life is not without its own abstraction. Going back over the material conditions of her own life, Rich makes a good story, but it is always the same story. A Jew in a Christian household, a Southerner in a Northern school, a Sephardic and Ashkenazic Jew in a marriage with an Eastern European Jew, a Jewish liberal among Jewish bigots, a lesbian among feminists. There is a long strain of righteousness in these arrangements. No matter where she finds herself, she manages always to locate herself outside the dominant culture, doing battle for the good cause, always learning that she must be accountable for more and more difficult problems.

Because her own world is always growing and expanding, she can allow herself to be fairly censorious of those on the other side, whom she leaves behind even when they have helped her realize her own potential. For example, she feels no reservations about revealing the limitations of her Jewish acquaintances at Radcliffe with whom she must have shared some adolescent growing pains, nor does she restrain herself from caricaturing the Puritans whom she has conjured up to serve her own purposes.

Hers is indeed the archetypal American story of moving on, shedding identities, assuming new identities in the next new town, and always moving. Estranged from her family of origin, eventually estranged, too, from her husband, Rich has kept going by going on. She has been protected from her own anti-Semitism by identifying herself as a Jew, protected from her own bigotry by taking up the cause of the victim, protected from her own white middle-class allegiances by sympathies for the African American and the poor, protected from her own sentimentality about motherhood by her identity as a lesbian. She is the conscience among American poets, and yet, by her own admission, she speaks from no permanent ground. Then, we must ask, what is a conscience without a firm foundation?

Perhaps it is only in her most recent work that she has found that foundation in her own body. In *Sources*, forswearing her usual way and announcing finally, "I refuse to become a seeker for cures," the speaker acknowledges, "Everything that has ever / helped me has come through what already / lay stored in me" (*YNYL*, 4). Yet, relying on these stores and practicing a politics of location that starts in the body and in the coming out of the lesbian poet, Rich has found no peace, but, rather, a new kind of danger and, strangely enough, a new community with younger poets, such as Minnie Bruce Pratt. Writing about this Southern Christian poet, Rich can identify with her. She writes: "Is this lesbian poetry? Yes—and most potently—because it is grounded in and insistent to grasp the poet's own white southern Christian culture with its segregated history and legacy of contradictions, the beauty and sorrow of its landscape, its sexual codes and nightmares" (*WIFT*, 149).

Mired in the material of her own location in a much less restrained way than Rich's earliest work, Pratt's poetry is also explicitly erotic. But, Rich observes, "What has received less attention, perhaps, is that the sexual women in these poems are activists whose bedroom is never far removed from what happens in the streets. It should go without saying, but probably doesn't, that no lesbian or gay bedroom—in whatever gentrified neighborhood or tent pitched off the Appalachian trail—is a safe harbor from bigotry (and for some, not only bigotry, but lethal violence)" (*WIFT*, 150). Coming out of the safe haven of middle-class Baltimore into the threatened world of even the white lesbian community, Rich has traveled through a wide and varying landscape that has allowed her to come into her own experience and to connect it with those less privileged than herself who have suffered from a quite different politics of location.

Her biographical journey has been matched by a poetic one. The titles of her recent collections—*The Fact of a Doorframe* (1984), *Your Native Land, Your Life* (1986), *An Atlas of the Difficult World* (1991), *What Is Found There* (1993)—all point to what might appear to be Rich's new interest in describing both the geography and the politics of the world in which she lives, although actually this interest is simply a return to her earliest fascination with location. Willard Spiegelman suggests that Rich's 1974 "From an Old House in America" is the "beginning of what might be called her Elizabeth Bishop phase" (*The Didactic Muse*, 155), but her first volume was entitled *A Change of World*, and it is full of poems of location: "The Kursaal at Interlaken," "Purely Local," "A View of the Terrace," "By

No Means Native," "For the Felling of an Elm in the Harvard Yard," "A Clock in the Square," "Eastport to Block Island," "Five O'Clock, Beacon Hill," "Itinerary," "A Revivalist in Boston," "Walden 1950." Although these poems are less eccentric than Bishop's (one does not find Bishop writing about Vassar College even in her apprenticeship, for example), they evince the same concern with geographical details and the value they communicate.

From "Storm Warnings," the first poem in her first volume of poetry, to her most recent work, Rich has chosen to write about people "Who live in troubled regions" (*CEP*, 3). In this very early poem, the speaker, drawing the curtains against a storm and lighting a candle, announces in a melodramatic way that "This is our sole defense against the season; / These are the things that we have learned to do." In maturing Rich has learned other defenses and at the same time the need to open up her defenses as her speakers have emerged into the storm, there to do battle with "Weather abroad / And weather in the heart" (3). Weather in these early poems is thus both physical and psychological or political. It stands for a land and an attitude toward that land in which Rich seems to be using weather as a name for something she could not express more directly or fully.

Not knowing how to state what the weather represents to her, the speaker here is still aware that she needs a defense against it, in part, at least, because she is "by no means native" to the New England landscape in which she locates her speakers in these early poems. Long before she became a feminist or could announce that she herself was "split at the root," she writes from an awareness of oppositions between natives and non-natives, between "us" and "them." In the early poem, "By No Means Native," the speaker offers a candid view of the displaced person, describing a man who, despite efforts at assimilating, "felt there lay a bridgeless space / Between himself and natives of the place" (*CEP*, 13). Very much like the father whom Rich was to describe in her late essay, "Split at the Root: An Essay on Jewish Identity," and to some extent like herself, still the man in this poem appears to be distanced from the speaker, who describes him in the third person, although, as this speaker slips into the second person in the penultimate stanza, she reveals her ambivalent identity with the man she both judges and understands.

The man, foretelling Rich's own history of dislocation, is doomed to feel self-divided. But, unlike Rich, he is an immigrant, an exile whether he remains in his new country or returns home. The final four lines of the poem reflect the ambivalence, even confusion, of the speaker. They do not make literal sense or, rather, grammatically they state the opposite of what they would appear to mean: the non-native *is* enamored of being held and owned by the ground not only because he is not so held but also because only a non-native American would wish to have such an attachment to the land. His is not an American but rather a European view of the ground. By contrast, Americans, pioneers and movers from the start, view the ground as something to leave behind, as opportunity rather than as ancestral territory. And so the speaker in this poem, who seems to be judging the immigrant from the vantage point of a native, actually expresses the immigrant's own bias and reflects his reactionary politics. Like the immigrant's speech, more correct than the native's, the speaker's sense of the native's pride in "local ground" belies her own adopted chauvinism.

In her early poems, the location is frequently New England, a landscape that Rich adopted and, along with it, the attitudes of its poets.[1] But when the young poet tries out the views of native poets such as Emily Dickinson or Robert Frost, she does not quite capture their tone. Her speaker is too wary in "Purely Local," for example, where she writes, "No matter how the almanacs have said / Hold back, distrust a purely local May, / When did we ever learn to be afraid?" (*CEP*, 11). This poem echoes both Dickinson's "These are the days when Birds come back" and Frost's "Reluctance":

> Ah, when to the heart of man
>   Was it ever less than a treason
> To go with the drift of things,
>   To yield with a grace to reason,
> And bow and accept the end
>   Of a love or a season? (29–30)

But Dickinson and Frost are writing about fall, not spring, and they express a reluctance to accede to the season rather than a distrust. Or, again, in "Eastport to Block Island," the speaker seems more bleak in her preparations than a native might be as her speaker is set to "prepare / As usual in these parts for foul, not fair" (20). Hers is not only a sadder note than those of Dickinson and Frost; it is also a more frightened one. In "The Return of the Evening Grosbeaks," she comments, "No matter what we try to make them mean / Their coming lends no answer to our scene" (37). The world is diminished here, as it is in Frost's "The Oven Bird," but without Frost's tight-lipped consolations. More stark than the stark native poets, Rich also lacks a precise grasp of the New Englander's language. For example, in "Walden 1950," concluding, "any Yankee son with lonesome notions / Would find life harder in the town today" (43), she reflects accurately the descent into commercialism of Walden Pond; but she misses the New England nuance of the term "Yankee," using it here in its Southern and more negative valuation.

The politics of these early locations in this poetry is the politics of acceptance and, for Rich, of assimilation into an imagined Puritan forbearance that she was to call "some vibration of higher moral rectitude, of moral passion" (*BBP*, 108). The characters are termed "Yankees," but they are Puritans as a Southerner might understand them, more like H. L. Mencken's Puritans than the real thing. Their battles are with seasons that, for Rich, appear unbearably difficult and not at all like the winter in Dickinson's "The Robin's My Criterion for Tune" or Frost's "Stopping by Woods on a Snowy Evening." Again, Rich's judgment about the weather is Southern, and, as the weather comes to stand for something else, her attitude reveals her own dislocation and uneasiness.

Moreover, the New England characters in Rich's early poems are really caricatures. For instance, drinking "auburn sherry" with Curtis in "Five O'Clock, Beacon Hill," the speaker draws a portrait that is as self-consciously mannered as the language with its dislocated syntax and strained rhymes: "I, between yew and lily, in resignation / Watch lime-green shade across his left cheek spatter" (*CEP*, 26). In the feminine rhymes of this stanza ("madder" and "spatter," "negation" and "resignation"), the speaker expresses the humor of this portrait, but the speaker's judgments appear all too serious when, for example, she looks at Curtis's nose, "Intelligent Puritan feature, grave, discreet," and wonders "What rebel breathes beneath his mask, indeed? / Avant-garde in tradition's lineaments!" (26). Her exclamation mark undercuts her humor and belies her naïveté. From Puritan to avant-garde, from nose to tradition, the speaker thinks in stereotypes, generalizing about class and gender. The poet behind these speakers may be more knowledgeable; but, if so, her frequent return to places like Harvard Yard and Beacon Hill suggests that she is restricting herself deliberately and pointlessly to a very limited social and political scene.

The speakers in poems such as "A View of the Terrace" or "For the Felling of an Elm in the Harvard Yard" or "A Clock in the Square" look out on an artificial or literary world. They may present themselves as "furtive exiles," but, like the "potted exile shrubs" in Curtis's Beacon Hill garden, they appear to be as artificial as their unreal settings (*CEP*, 12, 26). Quick to categorize the people they see, they divide them neatly into the pragmatists, those who admire the "clean dispatch" with which the felled elm came down, and the allegorists, those who "turn the symbol to their own" (16). The judgments dare very little and reveal only their speaker's equivocal position.

In her second volume, *The Diamond Cutters and Other Poems* (1952), Rich moves to another location, writing often about her experience as a tourist in Europe. Dropping the New England landscape which she had assumed as her home territory, she frees her speakers from ambivalence only to release them into simpler judgments. This tourist's landscapes are all too often a postcard image, picturesque, overly civilized, artificial. In "The Wild Sky," England "Comes softened in a water-colour light / By Constable," whereas America is "My country, where the blue is miles too high / For minds of men to graze the leaning sky" (*CEP*, 78). Or, again in "At Hertford House," she writes, "Perfection now is tended and observed, / Not used" (77). "Versailles" is "Merely the landscape of a vanished whim" (67). Although she admits, "There is a mystery that floats between / The tourist and the town," the speaker also claims, "To work and suffer is to be at home. / All else is scenery: the Rathaus fountain, / The skaters in the sunset on the lake / At Salzburg" (71, 72).

Much in these poems is scenery of a very serene, familiar, if foreign, nature. Although there is a beggar here or a murderer there, in general the poems are of scenes without human troubles. Yet, prophetically again, as if the young poet were aware of how much she was leaving out and would have to return to reconsider, she notes in "The Middle-Aged" the reticence within the calm of the older generation. She was eventually to consider how much was left unsaid in her own background and perhaps even by herself. But, again in "The Strayed Village," a man achieves peace by denying what he cannot accommodate and by leaving his childhood town. The speaker seems to speak for Rich herself when she describes the man whose life could be written in terms of places he had to leave "Because their meaning, passing that of persons, / Became too much for him" (*CEP*, 101). The poem has its oddities; the childhood hometown that the man seeks has not disappeared, rather it has "strayed," one day there and the next gone, and gone, the man surmises, "'lest I should come.'" It is "The last of losses" (102). Again, Rich opens up a subject to which she will return in her later poetry, but here she masks its darker revelations in whimsy. Writing about a man rather than a woman, another person rather than herself, she is nonetheless acknowledging a sense of homelessness that has sent her on her own long journey for a place that might be a home where the meaning would not be too much for her.

The locations of Rich's poems shift abruptly in the 1960s away from these serene landscapes to places that are at the opposite extreme, locations of violence. In "Jerusalem," she discloses, "In my dream, children / are stoning other children" "and I wake up in tears / and hear the sirens screaming / and the carob-tree is bare" (*FofD*, 85, 86). Or, in "On Edges," when the speaker does look at simpler scenes, it is not with her customary calm; rather, seeing ice on the pond or even waterlily leaves, she claims, "the word *drowning* flows through me" (96). The speaker seems to seek these visions, preferring them to conventional wisdom.

Gradually, willing to see danger even in the simplest scenes, Rich begins to look at different scenes and in a different way. The speaker in "From the Prison House" "sees / the violence / embedded in silence"; she sees "the fingers of the policewoman / searching the cunt of the young prostitute" (*FofD*, 158). Rich has dropped the decorum of her early language; yet even here, in this new plain speaking, she writes as an outsider, seeing the "world of pain" from the outside, a tourist again but in another country (158).

Moving closer into this country in "From an Old House in America," Rich identifies with the heritage of suffering that the location of America has brought to a variety of women. Still, even in acknowledging, "I am an American woman," Rich is locating herself in general terms rather than in the particulars of her own life (*FofD*, 215). In choosing America as the location in which to find herself and her identity with all women, the speaker in this poem is naming a particular politics of location: the sacrifice and trials of women that have marked American history in all areas of the country from Puritan New England to the slaveholding South to the Western pioneers. But this is a history far removed in place and time from the speaker, who reads history and uses geography now for her own political purposes.

Rich has had to come into another location from this generalized America, and, moving rapidly, she has acknowledged: "There are words I cannot choose again: / *humanism   androgyny*" (*FofD*, 262–63). It has been a long journey to the "fibers of [her] actual life." Although she has always written about the places that she inhabited and even written about those who have felt estranged from the places they inhabited, she has finally stopped trying to feel at home, realizing, as she writes in "History stops for no one":

And yet, as the poetry of this continent has become increasingly a poetry written by the displaced, by American Indians moving between the cities and the reservations, by African-Americans, Caribbean-Americans, by the children of the internment camps for Japanese-

Americans in World War II, by the children of Angel Island and the Chinese Revolution, by Mexican-Americans and Chicanos with roots on both sides of the border, by political exiles from Latin American, "*Bashert*" [Yiddish for "fated" and the title of a poem by Irena Klepfisz] takes its place (as does Klepfisz's poetry as a whole) in a multicultural literature of discontinuity, migration, and difference. Much of this new literary flowering is also lesbian or gay, feminist, and working class. (*WIFT*, 139–40)

And so, locating herself within this new literary flowering, Rich has been able to turn to her own multicultural sources as a subject of poetry.

Although this turning in Rich's poetry in *Your Native Land, Your Life* would appear to be inspired by her "coming out" as an American as that term is conceived in the 1990s, in fact, as we have seen, Rich returns here to her earliest preoccupations. The mood has shifted from certainty to tentativeness, and the mode has moved from satire to autobiographical inquiry; but the "politics of location" in this late work remains remarkably similar—the dislocation of the Southerner in the Northeast, the immigrant in America among the native born, the Jew among Christians—and it provides a new understanding of what it means to assimilate. Rich now conceives of these politics of location in more complicated terms. Gone are the stereotypes of the Puritan, the caricatures of New Englanders as well as Northern Jews, as Rich studies other aspects of the northeastern Vermont she has inhabited—the dislocations of the Indians and of the French Canadians, for example—and, in her own life, her safety as an American Jewish child in World War II.

Writing about *your* native land, *your* life, Rich is actually inquiring into her own native land, her own life, and this connection between land and self, America and the poet, conjures up immediately the vision of Walt Whitman. Yet, Joanne Feit Diehl does not appear to be entirely accurate when she argues: "The audacity of Rich's 1986 book commences with its title, for in naming this collection *Your Native Land, Your Life*, Rich asserts an authority over the reader's experience as she invents a patriotism that locates its origins in Whitman's audacious claims for the poet as not merely representative, but also himself the embodiment of America in all its diversity and difference" (*Women Poets*, 155).

The gusto of Whitman's outsetting bard claiming, "And what I assume you shall assume," is nowhere evident in Rich's late and considered arrival at an identity with the discontinuity, difference, and dislocation of Americans. Whitman started from a sense of himself as representative; Rich has worked toward that self not so much to claim her identity with her readers as to find it for herself. Certainly her patriotism is a public performance, but it is, even more, a private owning up. And within this privacy, paradoxically, Rich has moved more freely and publicly than Whitman, who did not enjoy the permissive sexual politics she has partly encountered and partly created.

In *Your Native Land, Your Life*, Rich uses the second person singular as she had used it in "By No Means Native" as a slip of the tongue, addressing herself as the other and her own native land as someone else's. This sense of difference and dislocation is at the heart of her understanding of her life in *Sources*, where she returns to New England, there to contemplate her own attachment to such a non-native place. She wonders why her imagination has stayed in the Northeast, "hooked into" New Englanders who have gone on, "believing their Biblical language / their harping on righteousness?" (*YNYL*, 11). As in her earliest poems, she finds the New England climate hostile, and she wonders again about "this unlikely growing season // after each winter so mean, so mean / the tying-down of the spirit" (11).

In writing *Sources*, Rich is not going all the way home. Rather, she returns to Vermont after the brief interval of sixteen years, recalling the vixen she met at twilight, "an omen / to me, surviving, herding her cubs / in the silvery bend of the road / in nineteen sixty-five" (*YNYL*, 3). Although she appreciates this omen and notes the wild plant's "Multifoliate heal-all," this landscape is no haven for her. Here a cold voice confronts her, asking, "*From where does your strength come, you Southern Jew? / split at the root, raised in a castle of air?*" (5). And she answers, with the old hostility edged now in bitter knowledge, "(not from these, surely, / Protestant separatists, Jew-baiters, nightriders // who fired in Irasburg in nineteen-sixty-eight / on a black family newly settled in these hills" (5). She is writing here about Vermont towns with populations sometimes of no more than one hundred as if they could be connected in her sense of history with the more famous locations of bigotry and hatred where her "kin / the Jews of Vicksburg or Birmingham" lived. Condemning the Vermonters, she is slightly more forgiving of her kin, whose "lives must have been strategies no less / than the vixen's on Route 5" (7). Theirs was "a way of life / that had its own uses for them" (8).

Living themselves in the heart of the Ku Klux Klan country, these kin considered themselves "*a chosen people*" who remained nonetheless "proud of their length of sojourn in America" (*YNYL*, 8). Implicated in the politics of their chosen location, these patriarchal kin built "a castle of air, the floating world of the assimilated who know and deny they will always be aliens" (9). She herself is not immune from this confusion, she acknowledges. In her conflicted relations with her father, Rich confesses that she has joined a lineage of denial, of assimilation, of insensitivity to the suffering of others.

She starts again, going over the same ground, in the second third of *Sources*. Heading north again in VIII, she claims, "I thought I was following a track of freedom / and for awhile it was" (*YNYL*, 10), until she begins to realize that Northerners are not free: for all their "rectitude," they were "invaders," their villages "built on stolen ground" (12). The unexpected "passion" that she finds there "beyond the numb of poverty / christian hypocrisy, isolation" (13) may come, she thinks, perhaps from "Mohawk or Wampanoag," "people who kept their promises / as a way of life" (14). And once again, Rich moves from this history of oppression to her own history in "that dangerous place / the family home" (15). There, again, she confronts the "oldfashioned" and "outrageous" belief in a "'destiny'" that is also part of the heritage of prejudice and suffering, "of being a connective link / in a long, continuous way // of ordering hunger, weather, death, desire / and the nearness of chaos" (17). Despite her own more privileged and American background, Rich insists that the Jews she felt "rooted among" are those victims of the Holocaust (18). Wearing the Star of David on a thin chain at her breastbone and admitting that she is following the wars in the Middle East, Rich finally relinquishes her bitter distance from her father, seeing herself now repeating her father's own deathbed "desperate attention" to the Six Day War. The politics of location have placed both father and daughter in peculiar positions to this suffering where again they are outsiders in worlds to which they feel nonetheless intimately attached.

The final third of the sequence is devoted to her husband, addressed curiously through the father as "The one I left you for. The one both like and unlike you" (*YNYL*, 19). Living also in the world of the assimilated, Rich's husband had a different formula of acceptance: "*There's nothing left now but the food and the humor*" (19). Addressing him finally directly, Rich asserts, "You knew there was more left than food and humor" (25). But he did not know or could not find his own place in the world, as she writes: "There must be those among whom we can sit down and weep, and still be counted as warriors. . . . I think you thought there was no such place for you, and perhaps there was none then, and perhaps there is none now; but we will have to make it, we who want an end to suffering, who want to change the laws of history, if we are not to *give ourselves away*" (25).

The sequence ends with Rich's acknowledgment that, sixteen years ago reading Gilbert White's *Natural History of Selborne*, she was thinking, "I can never know this land I walk upon / as that English priest knew his," and a voice answers that she will not know the land because she has chosen something else (*YNYL*, 26). In the final prose passage of this sequence, Rich admits that what she has been seeking is a knowledge of the world:

> When I speak of an end to suffering I don't mean anesthesia. I mean knowing the world, and my place in it, not in order to stare with bitterness or detachment, but as a powerful and womanly series of choices: and here I write the words, in their fullness: powerful;   womanly. (*YNYL*, 27)

Almost a decade after *Sources*, in *An Atlas of the Difficult World* (1991), Rich locates herself again in that geography closest in, the body, claiming, "We write from the marrow of our bones," but now it is a location that has been intimately connected in this collection with the larger world (*ADW*, 51). Rich's notes to the volume indicate her sources: among them, Muriel Rukeyser's *U.S.1*, a report of the murder of a lesbian in *Gay Community News*, *Anne Sullivan Macy: The Story behind Helen Keller* by Nella Braddy, "The Irish and Afro-Americans in U.S. History" by Frank Murray from *Freedomways: A Quarterly Review of the Freedom Movement*, *Soledad Brother: The Prison Letters of George Jackson*, *The Abandonment of the Jews* by David S. Wyman, *Back to the Sources: Reading the Classic Jewish Texts* edited by Barry W. Holtz, and *Waiting for God* by Simone Weil. This is a world far removed from the sources of her earlier work: the poetry of Emily Dickinson and Wallace Stevens, the young tourist's picturesque Europe, even the primers of American history in which she sought evidence of women's suffering.

In the title sequence of *An Atlas of the Difficult World*, Rich announces her new location, California, but she does not fail to include maps of all her landscapes in her atlas. She writes "an atlas" and she is an Atlas who bears the heavy burden of her country's history written into its land. The world this Atlas bears is the varied one of Rich's poetry seen now from the vantage point of her new location in "THE SALAD BOWL OF THE WORLD" (*ADW*, 3), where agribusiness empires have produced pollution and death. Nonetheless, it is a landscape she has come to love and to evoke lovingly in a way that no other landscape has attracted her. Addressing someone, perhaps her former husband or perhaps her longtime reader, Rich admits that "This is no place you ever knew me" (4), and yet, she claims, "it would not surprise you / to find me here" (5).

How different is her response to this new landscape from the old Vermont landscape newly visited in this poem which has, she repeats, "the shortest growing season / south of Quebec" (*ADW*, 8). From the shortest growing season to the longest, Rich has moved westward, the direction that Americans have always taken—out of New York, "the dream-site / the lost city the city of dreadful light" (16), past "Centralia Detroit," "the forests primeval the copper the silver lodes," "the suburbs of acquiescence" (6), to the Pacific where she might have imagined "there would be a limit" and it would stop her. Instead, she encounters the ocean: "no teacher, only its violent / self" (17).

Yet, California is the right landscape for Rich's "politics of location." There she can locate herself in the earthquake and drought, among the Mexican Americans and the African Americans, the permanently deracinated, the state with few natives, and there claim, "I am bent on fathoming what it means to love my country" (*ADW*, 22). It is here that she can draw her loved ones around her, remembering both the way she and her husband read aloud Karl Shapiro's *Poems of a Jew* and W. H. Auden's "In Sickness and in Health," "using the poems to talk to each other" (9), and the beauty of her female lover of which she writes, "What homage will be paid to beauty / that insists on speaking truth, knows the two are not always the same, / beauty that won't deny, is itself an eye, will not rest under contemplation?" (24). The homage that she pays is to speak of the lover's beauty, as the two had spoken of the landscape's beauty, commenting: "eyes drinking the spaces / of crimson, indigo, Indian distance, Indian presence" (24).

Rich has learned to people her landscape, but, more than that, she has learned to write the landscape into her people, now seeing her lover's "providing sensate hands, your hands of oak and silk, of blackberry juice and drums." Connecting the beauty of the "low long clouds" in New Mexico with the beauty of her lover, linking the woman's hands with the blackberries she handles, Rich is repeating the patriarchal association of woman and nature; but she is setting both woman and nature against the world of abstraction and death. She has reamed out the conventional meaning of the gaze, of women's beauty as something to be gazed upon, arguing rather that beauty "is itself an eye, will not rest under contemplation," and that the woman's "spirit's gaze" informs her body (*ADW*, 24).

In these late poems, Rich has indeed found a "politics of location" in the body. She is not at home; she is not even at ease; she remains impatient. Living, as she does now, at the very rim of the country she would like to come to love, Rich has had to divest herself of any number of other locations and their political purposes. Like the reader she addresses in the final poem of the sequence, "An Atlas of the Difficult World," Rich can say of herself: "there is nothing else left to read / there where you have landed, stripped as you are" (*ADW*, 26). She herself has landed in California, which might be, for once, the right place for her.

Although this study has been divided by subject, it has been about poems. Its interest has been in how these three poets created a lesbian public lyric voice out of their private passions and needs. Because they realized that their love poetry would cause a public sensation, these women put immense pressure on the word and the form of the lyric in order variously to deflect such a response, to play with it, and to confront it directly. They perfected their art in response to a potentially hostile audience that turned them intensely inward and, at the same time, curiously opened them more fully to the public. The immense range of styles—from the coded expression of Stein's experimental verse to the layered language of Bishop's formalism and finally to Rich's plain style—attests to the variety, tenacity, and originality of these women poets who persisted in writing against a legally sanctioned censorship, a reading public ill-prepared to read their work, and even their own self-doubts and guilt. In their work, the poem triumphs over polemics, art dominates politics, and social taboos succumb to the creative imagination.

The development from Stein to Rich might appear to be in the direction of simplicity, and yet Rich too has had her elaboration of language, using words newly coined as in "agribusiness empires / THE SALAD BOWL OF THE WORLD" (*ADW*, 3), or words out of a new decorum or a new politics as in "Rape," where "a cop" is "both prowler and father," and "you have to turn to him, / the maniac's sperm still greasing your thighs" (*FofD*, 172), or words chosen deliberately to speak the heretofore silenced and repressed as Rich's insistent celebration of "the live, insatiate dance of your nipples in my mouth" (243). At the other end, Stein valued simple, if not straight, talk. She made her experiments with common words, disrupted sense and syntax in order to simplify. As she said in a late interview, "I like a thing simple, but it must be simple through complication" (*GofM*, 515–16).

More clearly, the change of style that marks the distance between Rich and Stein has been in the accelerating directness with which the words have been delivered. Stein, we will recall, wanted to make a thing be a thing that could be named without using the names; Rich wants to use the names. Stein, witnessing World War II in occupied France, expressed her grief by her silence about the Holocaust. Rich, an American child far removed from the terrors of the death camps, cannot stop writing about them, identifying "with other women dressed in black / on the streets of Haifa, Tel Aviv, Jerusalem" (*ADW*, 44).

Moreover, this change in the words and their use evident in the course of the century is there in each poet's career as well. Stein moved from the coded celebration of her love in *Tender Buttons* (1914) to its open declaration in *The Autobiography of Alice B. Toklas* (1933), from the brief lyrics of her World War I experience to the journalistic *Wars I Have Seen* (1945), from the experimental *Geography and Plays* (1922) to the tribute to France *Paris France* (1940). The surrealism of Bishop's early work gave way to the quasi-realism of such later poems as "In the Waiting Room," for example, or to the crafted admission of private pain in "One Art." In the course of her long career, Rich's work has developed into sincerity and a public acceptance of her own accountability. Commenting on "Aunt Jennifer's Tigers," a poem that she wrote as a student, she claimed, "In those years formalism was part of the strategy—like asbestos gloves, it allowed me to handle materials I couldn't pick up barehanded" (*OLSS*, 40–41). Rich has learned, as she writes in "North American Time" (1983), that "Words are found responsible / all you can do is choose them / or choose / to remain silent" (*FofD*, 325).

And yet the development of the lesbian public lyric voice in individual careers and in the course of the century has not moved unvaryingly toward an open style and an enlarged vocabulary. Sometimes, as in the case of Stein, the poet has discovered that she could not speak her entire mind in a public voice, and so she composed the hermetic *Stanzas in Meditation* at the same time that she wrote the more accessible *The Autobiography*, for example, to detail the complexity of her relationship with Alice B. Toklas. At other points, the poets have retreated to earlier modes, as Bishop turned back from the more openly autobiographical writing of her middle years to her earliest interests at the end of her career, reworking "Large Bad Picture" more forgivingly into "Poem" or recasting her earlier imagery in "Sonnet." Moreover, the open style has revealed its own mysteries and murkiness even for Rich, who has certainly learned political lessons from it. After a lifetime of protests against the government, she now has the speaker of "An Atlas of the Difficult World" admit that she is "bent on fathoming what it means to love my country" (*ADW*, 22). Part of Rich's new and broader political awareness rises from a more thorough excavation of her inmost feelings, an acknowledgment of the difficulties in understanding what it has meant to her to love the people closest to her, not just her lover but her father and her husband as well.

It is perhaps more accurate to assert that the public lyric voice in these women's poetry, as it has been articulated in the course of the century from Stein to Rich, has come out, but also into a new directness that each poet has found problematic, useful for a time but not for all occasions. Rich has been able to be the most direct, concerned with "making it 'as clear as possible,'" as she claims of the "nonassimilationist" poets whom she now admires (*WIFT*, 227). But in her poetry and outside her political pronouncements she has been much less sure of what that clarity consists. In a poem entitled "Final Notations" from one of her most recent collections, she writes, "it will not be simple, it will not be long" (*ADW*, 57). She has had to make an effort to win back from the public some of her privacy, a desire—expressed chiefly in her poetry—to return to what has been suppressed or denied or written in code, not to bring it out into the open, but rather to do justice to its recalcitrance. Her most recent poetry has grown out of an appreciation for those mysteries in her own life that she cannot fully fathom.

The same coming out and going back may be witnessed in Stein's career. She courted a public more flagrantly than Rich, but, when she had it, she found that she could not write for it and for herself, too. She had to write for herself and strangers, as she admitted, for people to whom she could still be strange, not fully accessible, not easily accommodated. More than that, she prized herself as an original, and for her as for Picasso anyone who created a new thing had to make it ugly. In a late lecture, Stein said: "you always have in your writing the resistance outside of you and inside of you, a shadow upon you, and the thing which you must express. In the beginning of your writing, this struggle is so tremendous that the result is ugly; and that is the reason why the followers are always accepted before the person who made the revolution. . . . But the essence of that ugliness is the thing which will always make it beautiful. I myself think it is much more interesting when it seems ugly, because in it you see the element of the fight" (*GofM*, 490–91).

To make her point in this late lecture, Stein uses examples from her earliest work, *The Making of Americans* or her portraits; but later, in works such as *Ida* or *The Mother of Us All*, she returns to the struggle. She never gave up her experimentation, acknowledging in the late *Doctor Faustus Lights the Lights*: "I have sold my soul to make a light and the light is bright but not interesting in my sight and I would oh yes I would I would rather go to hell be I with all my might" (*SR*, 621).

The movement in Bishop's career has never been out so far nor in so near as Stein's wavering between publicity and secrecy, and yet she too came out and back, countering poems of biographical revelation with those of elaborate artifice throughout her career. Although she freed her voice of its early arch and precious tone and gradually came into what might be mistaken for a conversational style, Bishop never relaxed her vigilance on words. In the narratives of *Geography III*, she may appear to open herself more fully to revelation; but for someone who could praise "the absolute naturalness of tone" in George Herbert ("An Interview," 294), the natural would always be somewhat artificial. She was adamant in her condemnation of Lowell's direct use of Elizabeth Hardwick's letters in *The Dolphin* (*OA*, 561–62), as I have noted, and about confessional poetry she declared, "You just wish they'd keep some of these things to themselves" ("An Interview," 303). Jane Shore recounts Bishop's response to Rich's openness: "Elizabeth said, '*My God*, I've been a feminist since *way* back. I don't feel that you have to write about sex that way.' She liked Adrienne Rich, felt that she was a very intelligent woman, but said, 'I could never use [sexuality] as a subject or write about things as baldly as Rich does."[1] If late poems, such as "The Moose" or "Santarém," seem to be more open confrontations with the places that have held Bishop's imagination from the beginning, they are also layered with the long history of their composition, some twenty-six years for "The Moose" and many drafts for "Santarém." Bishop came slowly even to exact recall.

Still, as these poets have enlarged their range and perfected their style, they have moved lesbian poetry from avant-garde and private publishing houses to the popular press, from coterie audiences to public followings, from hermetic experimentation to common language, from coded erotic expression to open declaration, from political acquiescence to dissent. What was silenced or suppressed in Stein's time is now perhaps not easily but at least more freely avowed. Where Stein was, if lionized, also frequently ridiculed, Bishop became a consultant to the Library of Congress and a winner of important poetry prizes, and Rich has taken on a major public role not just in the women's movement, the Gay and Lesbian Rights movement, but in the antiwar movement as well.

The generating power behind this flowering, this coming out of a nineteenth-century feminized culture, out of the domestic and sentimental and into the political and public world, has been the desire of these poets to express their desire, a desire that fit neither into any known or acknowledged nineteenth-century literary legacy nor into the cult of the domestic or sentimental. Unlike the Emily Dickinson of Rich's " 'I Am in Danger—Sir—,' " who in her "half-cracked way" "chose / silence for entertainment" (*FofD*, 71) in order to have it out on her own premises, these women poets have chosen to speak and so to have it out at last on their premises, knowing that the expression of their most intimate desire would give them a public and polemical prominence that even the eloquence of poetry could neither hide nor escape, but knowing too that this prominence would save them from ever being merely a "woman poet." In choosing to write at all, they knew that theirs was inevitably the choice of a political persona.

In an open letter to Arturo Islas, Rich writes: "Arturo—would you agree?—we're unable to write love, as we so much wish to do, without writing politics. You, as a Chicano/Mexican, gay, not a 'man' in your culture's terms. I, as a woman, lesbian, Jew, in my sixties. Like you, I've been a problem within a problem: 'the Jewish Question,' 'the Woman Question'—who is the questioner? who is supposed to answer?" (*WIFT*, 23). Rich was, of course, a poet long before she began writing the politics of love, and she was a political poet before she began writing lesbian love poems. But even she has gone back to read her career in terms of the desire suppressed in her early work. In an interview, as I have noted, she comments that she eventually realized the early poem "To Judith, Taking Leave" was a lesbian poem, although she did not recognize it as such when she wrote it. She says, "In 1962 there was precious little around to support the notion of the centrality of a relationship between two women. I was amazed when I went back to look for those poems and found them again—the kinds of truth they told" (Bulkin, 1:64). Although Rich can claim of her early career that "women like me were totally in the closet to ourselves and I blame that silence very much" (65), her power as a poet derives from the creative explosion that that silence eventually created.

More immediately than Rich, Stein's desire to write came from her desire. She began her writing career with her efforts to write out and thus understand her unrequited love for May Bookstaver and later to write the "portrait" of her new love, Alice B. Toklas. This need to express her desire was intimately connected, Ulla Dydo claims, with her need for an audience and so, by extension, for a public. Dydo comments on Stein's portrait of Toklas, *Ada*: "storytelling is about the intimate interaction between Toklas and Stein. Endless telling and listening to stories is the perfect writer's situation and the perfect lovers' situation, each enabling the other. *Ada* is in a sense about audience—finding a you who listens to me. It is about speaking and hearing, writing and reading, making love in words and making words of love" (*SR*, 101). With Toklas as an audience, Stein fulfilled a need essential to her creativity; she also found a collaborator, one whose household ministrations privately enabled Stein to write and whose presence as a muse inspired Stein's confidence in a public audience.[2]

In Bishop's case, the connection between her desire and the desire to write is more occluded, although many of her early works circle around questions of love and sexuality. For example, the early story "The Thumb" expresses the strange attraction of mysteriously marked sexuality. "Three Sonnets for the Eyes" record the secret recognition of lovers guarded from the blind eyes of the public, and "Three Valentines" acknowledges that the speaker is "Sure of my love, and Love; uncertain of identity" (*CP*, 226). Writing at first under the eagle eye of Marianne Moore, Bishop seemed to restrain her expressions of desire, although, as I have argued earlier, she encodes such expressions in the early packed "A Miracle for Breakfast" or the strange "Casabianca" or the surrealistic "The Weed" and "The Imaginary Iceberg." Her periods of greatest productivity coincided with her moments of greatest emotional intensity and companionship in Key West, in Brazil, in Boston. She came into her public audience not by coming out as a lesbian in Rich's style, but by honing her craft so that she could express without revealing her desire. Her sense of herself as "uncertain of identity" gave her, in Rich's terms, the eye of the outsider, "the experience of outsiderhood, closely—though not exclusively—linked with the essential outsiderhood of a lesbian identity" (*BBP*, 127). But she needed at least one other person with whom to share that state, with whom she could be an insider and more certain of identity, in order to write most productively.

Deciding to speak their love has not been the same as coming out for these women poets, and Bishop's career is a good argument against those feminist critics (including Rich herself) who have acknowledged the poet's coming out as a necessary condition for the full expression of experience, essential not just for women poets but for the community as well.[3] As we have seen in the poetry of Stein, who either never came out or was always out, speaking her love was synonymous with writing. For Bishop, on the other hand, closets were a requirement of writing. Even in Rich's own most recent work, coming out has freed her from some constraints only to introduce her to new complexities of expression.

The first generation of self-consciously lesbian poets, including Stein, did not take up the political cause of sexual freedom; if they did not remain exactly closeted, they often left unpublished their more overtly lesbian erotic writing. Yet they wrote frequently and, it would appear, fully of their experience. A generation later, Bishop, wanting only closets in which to preserve her private identity, made secrecy the source of her creative energy. Even Rich's development has not been keyed exclusively to her coming out; she began to free her poetry from its early formalism long before she identified her sexual politics, and she has moved on from the imaginative inspiration of coming out to embrace worlds of suffering and victimization that have a political resonance for her quite apart from gender.

Still, Rich's coming out in *The Dream of a Common Language* (1978) has been important to readers of lesbian poetry. Diana Collecott claims that Rich "made statements that were 'hardly syllabled yet' in our conscious minds" (100); Catharine R. Stimpson asserts that she created "'a whole new poetry' that was to begin in two women's 'limitless desire'" ("Rich and Lesbian/Feminist Poetry," 249). Rich encouraged a general, popular, and political interest in lesbian poetry that may have inspired the burgeoning interest in women's poetry in general, and, in particular, in the critical attention to Bishop's work as well as the recovery of Stein's.

These developments have drawn attention to women poets and to particular aspects of their careers. For example, the recent reissuing of Stein's work in response to this new audience has created an entirely new understanding of her importance. Stein's earliest readers approached her through her biography rather than her more hermetic erotic work. Although they were merciless in their attacks on her writing, they maintained a certain reticence about her relationship with Alice B. Toklas. "It was enough that Alice should be described as a dedicated friend, companion, and secretary for forty years, leaving the reader to infer the nature of the relationship," James Mellow notes in his biography (130). Stein was known chiefly as the author of *Three Lives* and *The Autobiography of Alice B. Toklas*, the writer of realistic, if slightly whimsical, fiction. Although *Tender Buttons* was included in Carl Van Vechten's *Selected Writings of Gertrude Stein* in 1964, "Lifting Belly" and "Patriarchal Poetry" were not easily accessible until the publication of *The Yale Gertrude Stein* (1980) and "Pink Melon Joy" not until Cyrena Pondrom's reissue of *Geography and Plays* in 1993 and Ulla Dydo's *A Stein Reader* also in 1993. So Stein's emergence as a writer of lesbian erotic poetry is fairly recent; she is still not identified as a war poet since her poetry of World War I remains hidden away in the Yale edition of her works. And her poems about geography are only beginning to appear in the new editions of Pondrom and Dydo. Even her first feminist critics read her just as she wanted to be read, through her own obfuscating and theorizing late lectures as a poet engaged in abstract experimentation with words. A writer of *master*pieces, as she would want to have been known, this Stein fit into the early desires of feminist theorists, anxious to identify the experimental, theoretical, and subversive range of women's writing. They could identify the *jouissance*, but they missed the erotic play along with Stein's wit.

Even more than Stein's, Bishop's most recent readers have extended our knowledge of her range and style. Pioneering books like Robert Parker's and Thomas Travisano's concentrated on her poems of travel, history, geography, not emphasizing those aspects of her life and work—her lesbianism and alcoholism—that more recent critics have studied. Even Lorrie Goldensohn, who tracked down an unpublished erotic poem, "It is marvellous [*sic*] to wake up together," and made it the centerpiece of her 1992 study, notes of the poems, "There are really only a handful that talk about love" (29). The publication of Brett C. Millier's biography and Bishop's letters make more explicit the concerns of her life and their expression in her work. It was not until Susan Schweik's study of women poets and World War II in 1991 that Bishop's war poetry became an object of study and a few years later before cultural critics penetrated her artfulness to identify her politics. Focusing on "One Art" or "Sonnet" rather than the much anthologized "The Fish," critics now can claim Bishop for a lesbian tradition that even Rich missed in her first reading of the work.

Rich's prominence has had quite a different impact on her audience. Although one of the founders of feminist criticism, she has taken on a variety of positions in the movement and, as a result, has attracted a changing and changeable readership. Critics have frequently riveted their attention to her work at one of the many positions she has occupied, failing to follow her as she has moved and changed and reconsidered her views. Phrases such as "the lesbian continuum" or "compulsory heterosexuality" have been lifted from her essays and applied without much subtlety to her work. Ironically, whereas Stein and Bishop have actually gained an audience in the rise of a feminist community of readers, Rich herself, who has done so much to create and encourage such an audience, has often been the target of its censure as well as its acclaim. Stein's sense that first the poet creates her audience and then the audience creates the poet is painfully true of Rich. She has created audiences for poetry she no longer writes.

Her political commitments have moved her far from Stein's experimental poetry to try out other ranges of voice. Arguing with Paul Goodman's view that, as a style, the avant-garde "is an hypothesis that something is very wrong in society," Rich writes: "what is its significance in a society of immigrants and survivors of genocide, the meeting place of many colonized cultures, whose emerging artists, far from being disgusted with their peoples' traditions and styles, are trying to repossess and revalue them?" (*WIFT*, 227).

She finds that the poetry of emerging groups ("women, people of color, working-class radicals, lesbians, and gay men") cannot afford to upset their audience as Goodman's avant-garde does; rather, they are concerned to make their art as clear as possible "because too much already has been buried, mystified, or written of necessity in code" (*WIFT*, 227). Sympathizing with their needs, she has returned to her own people's tradition and styles, examining what it has meant for her to be a survivor in that tradition. But, as we have seen, her willingness to be "as clear as possible" has brought her into places with which she is not clearly aligned and into a language and experience that she must co-opt. Moreover, identifying with these emerging groups, she has underestimated the interest that an experimental writer like Stein had in upsetting her audience.

In her attack on the avant-garde, Rich displays a sobriety that has infiltrated her poetry as well. One result of her attachment to the political is that she has lost touch almost entirely with the element of play that so enlarged the work of Stein and Bishop. She is the living example of Paul Goodman's sense that "in a confused society, *avant garde* does not flourish very well" (*WIFT*, 226). She lives in that confusion of politics that is so inimical to art. In her own life, she has moved through that society, first railing against its repressions in the conclusion of "Disloyal to Civilization: Feminism, Racism, Gynephobia" (1978), arguing: "as I thrust my hand deeper into the swirl of this stream—history, nightmare, accountability—I feel the current angrier and more multiform than the surface shows: There is fury here, and terror, but there is also power, power not to be had without the terror and the fury. We need to go beyond rhetoric or evasion into that place in ourselves, to feel the force of all we have been trying—without success—to skim across" (*OLSS*, 310).

More recently, she has described another role for the artist as a "revolutionary poet" who conjures for her audience "a language that is public, intimate, inviting, terrifying, and beloved" (*WIFT* 250). Claiming that "forms, colors, sensuous relationships, rhythms, textures, tones, transmutations of energy, all belong to the natural world" (250), Rich has moved in her art closer and closer toward that natural connection, farther and farther from the resources of art.

From this perspective, looking back on a century of women's poetry, Stein's career seems utterly artificial, and yet Stein's experimental writing may not be so far removed from Rich's willed naturalness. Stein too wanted to "conjure" for her world a language that was both public and intimate, inviting and terrifying. She claimed that "poetry is essentially the discovery, the love, the passion for the name of anything" (*LA*, 235); but in order to make that discovery, she perceived that she had first to rid herself of a dead language. Acknowledging Whitman as the pioneer in changing the form of poetry because "we who had known the names for so long did not get a thrill from just knowing them," she states, "what was there to do. This that I have just described, the creating it without naming it, was what broke the rigid form of the noun the simple noun poetry which now was broken" (237).

Although Stein belonged to an avant-garde that put her beyond the reach of the popular audiences that Rich seems to need to court, she had a public as well as a private mission. In one sense, like every poet, her concern was to return to the public a passion for words. In another sense, she wanted to find words for her own passion, to create without naming it.

In writing poetry that was "nothing but using losing refusing and pleasing and betraying and caressing nouns" (*LA*, 231), Stein found that excess and repetition were successful strategies for refusing referential meaning and still caressing the noun. This kind of language play freed words for new uses; it also freed the speaker of such words from the rigid identity she might have been assigned as a writer of lesbian love poetry at the turn of the century. Moreover, in a generation of poets frightened by what T. S. Eliot called the dissociation of sensibility, Stein reveled in such dissociation, as Elizabeth Meese suggests in distinguishing between her and Djuna Barnes: "where Barnes focuses in *Nightwood* on the horror of loss through fracturing the 'unified self,' Stein suggests the playful dimension of endless multiplication in *Ida*" (74). Meese claims that, in a lifelong meditation on "lesbian : writing" (80), Stein keeps the issue of lesbian identity open and thus interesting, insisting on a personal freedom that reinforced the need for alternatives to the nineteenth-century's sexual/textual legacy (81). She expresses herself in what Meese identifies as a "vertiginous instability of non-sense" that "sheers off, goes blissing across the page in the ecstasy of Stein's life/style" (79). She refused to be the object, the other, the woman associated with nature and excluded from speaking subjectivity, as Margaret Homans has identified the nineteenth-century literary and sexual legacy, and thus she freed herself also from the need to be the subject, the self, the speaker (215).

If bliss and ecstasy have become terms layered with positive political significance by French feminists, they are nonetheless important pointers to an aspect of Stein's writing that such theorists have largely ignored. They indicate both her escape from the subject/object opposition of the patriarchal society in which she lived and, at the same time, the extent to which she acquiesced to the authority of that society. She could only be herself by being funny, excessive, teasing, repetitious. If she were to be the public personage she desired to be, she had to perform. Her bliss and her ecstasy were part of that performance. Behind these feelings and their literary expression, as we have seen, was an extreme sense of guilt, uncertainty, self-hatred, anti-Semitism, expressed frequently and not exactly indirectly in her poetry. That the darker side of her character in these revelations has been largely ignored suggests the success of that performance.

The energy of Stein's creative performance was stoked by her oppositional position. She could boast in "Ada," "And certainly Ada all her living then was happier in living than any one else who ever could, who was, who is, who ever will be living" (SR, 102), because their love was set against the world. Despite her efforts to naturalize it, insisting on its place in an ordinary life, Stein wrote her love in a code that allowed her its most extravagant expression. She and Alice were bound to each other in a remarkable fidelity and in nothing more faithful than in their insistence on living outside the limits of heterosexual society.

Unlike Stein's experimental romp with words or her oppositional attitude toward society, Bishop's poetry, as well as her life, was devoted to good form. Although, like Stein, Bishop too lived in a society of her own making, a long time in exile, such circumstance allowed her a double identity rather than Stein's theatricalized identity. Bishop was both an ordinary woman, in James Merrill's memorable phrase, in touch with various relatives, friends from Vassar, poets such as Marianne Moore and Robert Lowell, even her doctor Anny Bauman, and an extraordinary woman, a poet, lesbian, alcoholic, outsider. She bridged these worlds, playing with words as an accommodation with a culture that would never acknowledge an important part of her life and playing with words also as a way of camouflaging the truths she herself may have been unable to acknowledge. In this position, she could, like Rich, take her place in society and criticize its racism, militarism, sexism, in a way that Stein never did. Living not just with her lesbian lovers but in social groups, however closeted, of gays and lesbians, Bishop did not occupy Stein's oppositional position, and so she was not so impelled to defend herself as uniquely happy. She was free to express the sadness in her attachments, their loss and bitterness, as well.

More than that, as a member of the first generation of poets to achieve a voice distinct from the modernists, Bishop relinquished the experiments of these powerful predecessors in favor of a renewed interest in form, sometimes archaic, often elaborate. When she was asked to talk about poetry, she veered away from Stein's enthusiasm for the theoretical and abstract, insisting rather that "Physique, temperament, religion, politics, and immediate circumstances all play their parts in formulating one's theories on verse. And then they play them again and differently when one is writing it" (Schwartz and Estess, 281). And yet, when she was asked about the source of various poems, she identified none of the list above but rather such details as "a group of words, a phrase" or even "a record of Ralph Kirkpatrick, performing Scarlatti" where the rhythms of the sonata imposed themselves ("An Interview," 296). Elsewhere she admits, sounding like T. S. Eliot on the mystery of creation, that "It takes probably hundreds of things coming together at the right moment to make a poem and no one can ever really separate them out and say this did this, that did that" ("'The Work,'" 318–19).

Her comments here emphasize her enthusiasm for formal structures. Even in chance experiences, Bishop's interest was in form. Writing in the *Vassar Journal of Undergraduate Studies* in 1933, she recounts a fall afternoon of studying when she noticed birds going south: "I saw that some flew a little slower than others, some were trying to get ahead and some flew at an individual rubato; each seemed a variation, and yet altogether my eyes were deceived into thinking them perfectly precise and regular. . . . It was as if there were an invisible thread joining all the outside birds and within this fragile net-work they possessed the sky" (Schwartz and Estess, 271). She concludes: "it came to me that the flying birds were setting up, far over my head, a sort of time-pattern, or rather patterns, all closely related, all minutely varied, and yet all together forming the *migration*, which probably in the date of its flight and its actual flying time was as mathematically regular as the planets" (272).

This early interest in patterns became eventually an awareness of "art" even in the inevitability of loss, in the passage of time and things. It was an understanding hard won, although, as Marilyn May Lombardi argues, the evolution of Bishop's style came from the condition underlying her alcoholism—her radical sense of dislocation (124)—and her sense that somehow she had to "come up with a form that broke the spell of lyric poetry's 'artificial paradise,' giving shape instead to life's energetic discord, its 'untidy activity'" (125).

She developed what she identified early to Frani Blough as a "'proliferal style'" (*OA*, 71) as a way of expressing her commodious imagination. But against the proliferation of life, such a style still set its opposite—the limitation of art. In her whimsical story "In Prison," she plays with the idea of such limitation, acknowledging that she lives "in relationship to society, very much as if I were in prison" (*CPr*, 181). The prison here may be the prison house of art, and so her dreams for herself in this prison, however grandiose, may indicate her creative ambition. First, she intends to "attract to myself one intimate friend, whom I shall influence deeply," like Emily Dickinson's perfect audience of one, and this friend will help her establish herself "as an authority, recognized but unofficial, on the conduct of prison life" (190). In this prison, she claims, she will "have the gift of being able to develop a 'style' of my own, something that is even admired and imitated by others" (190). Thus, even in such fanciful musing, Bishop can reveal her immodest dream for her own success and predict accurately her future reputation. She may also simply be acknowledging what she knew to be true about her career—the importance of influential friends such as Moore and Lowell in establishing her reputation.

Unlike Stein, Bishop was, in part, an establishment poet. She was read seriously by other poets and by prize-awarding committees. These facts made her life both simpler and more difficult than Stein's. She did not need to carry on such extravaganzas of self-presentation as Stein, and yet, of course, she had to keep up appearances as a public figure, especially during her year at the Library of Congress and her stints at teaching at the University of Washington and Harvard University. The stress of these demands also made her life difficult, driving her frequently into the hospital, and although she did not write about these difficulties directly, she did project them onto other situations, onto the misery of "Pink Dog," the loneliness of "Crusoe in England," the sadness of "Sestina," for example. The joys of her life, such as they were, she kept to herself generally. It may have been "marvellous to wake up together," but it was not a marvel that Bishop cared to elaborate in her published poetry. Rather, the range of her emotions there is narrow, deep, and dark. Like the child in "Sestina" drawing "another inscrutable house," Bishop created a poetry that was deliberately closed to all but the most careful scrutiny.

By contrast, Rich has seemed to be generously open to her public, and yet, as we have seen, hers is the saddest voice of all. From the widest range of possibilities, she has chosen to express her pain and anguish, her identity with the victims and the outcasts, her sense of loss in the moments of greatest bliss, her fear of the oppressor. Such choice marks her freedom from both the public and private restraints that impeded Stein and Bishop. She has not felt herself forced to celebrate her hidden passion, nor has she felt constrained to hide it. Although Rich is aware of the legal sanctions still in place against lesbians, she has not allowed them to silence her; rather, she has spoken out against them.

Living more publicly as a lesbian interested in the political ramifications of her sexuality, she has been more willing to confront her private fears and doubts. She does not need to boast of her happiness, celebrate her opposition to society, nor can she any longer blame all the ills on the enemy without. Coming out, she has also had to accept her own inadequacies and limitations, acknowledge her complicity in the silences of her life, and recognize that two against the world are still two who might never quite be made one. Perhaps Rich's greatest achievement is the expression of poignant feeling in such images as the "tear that washes out the eye / the tear that clears the eye" in "Darklight" (*ADW*, 55). Here, she writes of love's pain and sorrow with a directness unavailable to Elizabeth Bishop, whose own tears in "The Man-Moth" had to be rendered surrealistically. At last, a lesbian poet can create a lyric that will accommodate such revelations of feeling as Rich makes here, connecting "Dark summer's outer reaches" to a deeper dark within (55). Partly because she has never been able to write "love" without writing "politics," Rich has learned how to negotiate with the confines of "politics." Writing in the line of women poets from Stein through Bishop who have gone to great extremes to speak their intimate feelings, Rich has expanded the range of a lesbian public lyric voice by returning it to this more modest resonance. She has not only added that voice to twentieth-century poetry; she will perhaps make it prevail.

NOTES

1. Curiously, in this recent essay Rich does not concentrate on the censorship she has endured but rather argues of poetry that "like our past, our collective memory, it remains an unfathomed, a devalued resource. . . . Poetry has been set apart from the practical arts, from civic meaning" (*WIFT*, 19).

2. Yorke, "Constructing a Lesbian Poetic." See also Halliday, "'The Naked Majesty of God'"; Collecott, "What Is Not Said"; Bulkin, "'Kissing / Against the Light.'"

3. Discussions of lesbian poetry tend to emphasize the silence out of which such poetry has arisen. For example, Catharine R. Stimpson writes, "'Lesbian.' For many, heterosexual or homosexual, the word still constricts the throat" ("Adrienne Rich and Lesbian/Feminist Poetry," 12–13); Halliday in "'The Naked Majesty of God'" states, "Contemporary lesbian poetry begins with survival, with anger" (77). Elly Bulkin opens her article, "It was easy, a few years ago, to think that lesbian poetry didn't exist" ("'Kissing / Against the Light,'" 32). Liz Yorke writes: "Growing up during the 1950s and 1960s in a conventional working-class family, I did not have any words to enable me to know about women-loving women—the much censored word *lesbian* had virtually disappeared from the world around me, and certainly did not enter into my consciousness. In poetry, lesbian voices have also been subjected to extensive public and personal censorship" (187). Diana Collecott claims that "Feminist critical attention to women's silences has itself been largely silent concerning the taboo on female homosexuality and its effects on literature" (92).

4. In her important essay, "Upping the Anti [*sic*] in Feminist Theory," Teresa de Lauretis sorts through the feminist debate over essentialism to suggest that feminism is "a developing theory of the female-sexed or female-embodied social subject, whose constitution and whose modes of social and subjective existence include most obviously sex and gender, but also race, class, and any other significant sociocultural divisions and representations; a developing theory of the female-embodied social subject that is based on its specific, emergent, and conflictual history" (89). Some of her insight here might be applied to women's literary history. These particular poets are not the only lyric voices of their respective generations, and often they are in conflict even among themselves; but it is within this conflict that women's poetry has emerged.

5. For a discussion of this difference, see Bok, *Secrets*, 10–14.

6. See Betsy Erkkila's discussion of Bishop's troubled relationship with Moore and the critical rereading and reevaluation of Bishop since *Geography III* that have tended to sharpen her distance, difference, and distinction from Moore (99–151). For an interpretation of Bishop's relationship with Moore using object-relations psychology, see Joanne Feit Diehl's *Elizabeth Bishop and Marianne Moore*.

7. See, for example, Susan Schweik's extremely interesting discussion of Bishop (213–41). Victoria Harrison notes of Bishop's early poems, "Calling forth what is not-war is just as effective in leading us to picture war here as a direct reference to what war might have been" (84).

8. Bishop to Anne Stevenson, quoted in Stevenson's *Elizabeth Bishop*, 66.

9. Gary Fountain's new oral biography of Elizabeth Bishop recounts several versions of a social occasion in which Rich attempted to convince Bishop to be more forthright about her lesbianism. Richard Howard claims that after Rich's visit, Bishop, commenting on her new apartment at Lewis Wharf, said, "'You know what I want, Richard? I want closets, closets, and more closets!'" (329–30).

1. See Gass's entire discussion in *The World within the Word*. Edmund Wilson's comment comes from *The Shores of Light*, 581.

2. DeKoven, "Stein and the Modernist Canon," 9. In *A Different Language*, DeKoven notes the resistance of Stein's poetry to interpretable meaning (179).

3. DeKoven has addressed this insider-outsider nature of Stein's reputation in "Stein and the Modernist Canon," 8–20.

4. Discussing *The Autobiography of Alice B. Toklas* and *Everybody's Autobiography*, Stimpson takes a different interest in this subject, examining what she calls "a sub-genre we insufficiently understand: the lesbian lie" ("Stein and the Lesbian Lie," 152–53). Stimpson is anxious to explore what the lesbian lie does to the lesbian sense of herself and her autobiographical writing. Although DeKoven opens an essay with the statement, "Poetry, for Gertrude Stein, is painfully erotic," she develops that insight only in a brief comparison of Stein to Ezra Pound ("Breaking the Rigid Form of the Noun," 225).

5. In an extremely fruitful reading of *Tender Buttons* that explains how Stein used and displaced the authoritative discourse of domestic guides to living (cookbooks, housekeeping guides, books of etiquette, guides to entertainment, maxims of interior design, fashion advice) in order to explain and justify her own idiosyncratic domestic arrangement with Toklas, Margueritte S. Murphy argues that Stein encoded lesbian intimacies and reconsidered what is "dirt" and what is "tender." For example, she parallels Stein's discussion of "dirt" near the beginning of the "Roastbeef" section of "Foods" with a passage from *The New England Cook Book* on dirty table clothes (397–99).

6. In a discussion of *The Autobiography of Alice B. Toklas*, Leigh Gilmore argues that Stein displaces the function of the autobiographical "I" onto the lesbian couple, revealing her ambivalence about the self as a unified figure, and, I might add, in this respect at last revealing also her agreement with male modernists such as T. S. Eliot ("A Signature of Lesbian Autobiography").

7. Jayne L. Walker notes that portions of the manuscript of "Ada" including nearly half of the final paragraph are in Alice B. Toklas's handwriting, and so the change in style may be attributable to a change in author. Ulla Dydo maintains that Toklas and Stein joined hands by sharing the labor of copying the text from Stein's pocket notebook, but she claims that Stein wrote it (*SR*, 100).

8. Gilbert and Gubar have pointed out that the schematic pattern in "Ada" fits Stein's own life in her effort to extricate herself from her brother Leo Stein (2:241).

9. For example, Walker argues that it starts "a new mode of rendering character, independent of the descriptive apparatus that absorbed individuals into 'kinds' in the novel" (75), and Harriet Chessman identifies its new mode as a movement from "nondialogic to dialogue, from narrative to circular nonnarrative" (68).

10. Pertinent here is Diana Collecott's essay on the silences in lesbian writing. She notes: "The fear of being 'wiped out' is taken into much lesbian writing and may account for many of its self-contradictions and obliquities. But when this fear is counterbalanced by lesbian desire, in works like *Zami* or the poetry of Gertrude Stein, it accounts for the erotics of these texts: their word-play, subversion of grammatical rules, resistance to literal reading or single-minded interpretation" (96).

11. In her study of female homosexuality and modern culture, Terry Castle has claimed that, given the way the lesbian is habitually expelled from the real world, "it is perhaps not surprising how many lesbians in real life have engaged in a sort of self-ghosting, hiding or camouflaging their sexual desires or withdrawing voluntarily from society in order to escape such hostility" (7). Castle is interested in the lives of lesbians, but we might apply her insights to Stein's writing in which, for all her self-vaunting, she engages in a self-ghosting as well.

12. Castle uses the term "worldly," which she extracts from Edward Said, to describe the lesbians she studies, and it seems certainly appropriate for Stein, who always occupied center stage.

13. See DeKoven's discussion of this change in *A Different Language*, 63–84.

14. The opening statement in "Rooms" would appear to identify Stein as a precursor to Derrida and the deconstructionists, and, in her chapter on experimental writing, DeKoven makes such a case for Stein as anticipating not only Derrida but Lacan and Kristeva (*A Different Language*, 3–26). But, as this discussion suggests, Stein is interested in redefining rather than negating the center. Although she argues against certain kinds of conventional authority, she aims to assert her own authority.

15. My reading of "Rooms" as a decentering of traditional authority and then a recentering of Toklas makes the subject, both Toklas and subjectivity itself, a central concern for Stein, and it agrees only partially with Walker's conclusion that "Unseating both the subject and Western logic as privileged centers and guarantors of truth, this text deliberately flaunts the unlimited freeplay of substitution that is possible within the structure of language" (141). Substitution was clearly important to Stein as she toyed with what she wanted to conceal, what to reveal about her relationship with Toklas. But she did not abandon entirely the idea of a center or of truth; rather, it would be her own definition of an "active center" and her "Truth."

DeKoven's Kristevan reading cannot account for the wit of *Tender Buttons*, the word play that is not the same as language-as-play, but much more like the deliberate attempt to release multiple meanings in words that is part of the seriousness of symbolic language. Catharine Stimpson has made the case against a Kristevan reading of Stein ("The Sonograms of Gertrude Stein," 67–80).

Chessman seems to capture the doubled efforts of *Tender Buttons* by admitting that it "entices us with all these potentially erotic objects and foods," but "it turns us around so that we become radically unsure of these metaphors" (97). However, her claims about a female presence in *Tender Buttons* are more abstract than mine; she says, "Indirectly, in this new land we glimpse, not a specific woman or any clear representation, but a circuitously imaged idyll involving a 'wedding' and a 'near[ness]' to 'fairy sea'" (99).

By contrast to these efforts to resist interpretation, Lisa Ruddick's idea that in "Objects" and "Food" Stein "was engaging in a revisionary conversation with the dominant intellectual traditions of Western culture," specifically the sacrificial origins of patriarchal culture, is perhaps too tied to identifiable patterns of thought in interpreting these sections (193). It is interesting that "Rooms" does not have the same status in her discussion because "Rooms" contains few references to sacrifice.

16. In commenting on the opening sections of "Objects," Chessman suggests that Luce Irigaray's theorizing a new form of speculation sheds light on Stein's project here: "Instead of being seen and named as object, the woman may begin to take the 'speculum' in her own hands, to 'press on' into herself, and to find, not the certainty of the named, but the fiery, uncertain, lively, and unlocatable place of the unnamed" (95). In the course of "GLAZED GLITTER," Chessman claims that "Vision has become replaced by a modality of touch" (96). Stein's insistence that the change of style in *Tender Buttons* came from a new way of looking would argue against Chessman's conclusion here.

17. Yet it is Stein's apparent ambivalence toward the text that makes it resistant to theoretical interpretations. Although *Tender Buttons* experiments freely with expressing the erotic, it does not lend itself easily to feminist theories about women's writing. It does not fully respond to a Kristevan reading, as we have seen. Nor does Irigaray's theory of a new form of speculation in women's writing serve to open a text that is so quick to retract or cover up its most daring statements. Even attempting to locate Stein in her period, as Shari Benstock does in describing her as the philosopher-theorist of what she calls "Sap-

phic Modernism," vital in Paris and London at the turn of the century, is not very helpful since Stein was resistant to both other lesbian writers in the Paris community and to Sappho as a model. Nor can Gilbert and Gubar, who note the need in her generation—the first fully self-conscious generation of lesbian writers—for a kind of literary double-talk and the literal doubling of writers as in *The Autobiography*, do justice to this period of her work, finding her writing "tenaciously, even boringly incomprehensible and self-serving" (2:245).

18. Chessman argues: "Stein attempts to present, as immediately as possible, a sense of an ongoing intimacy, yet she carefully refuses to make her representations of this intimacy stable or certain. She achieves this resistance to direct representation partly through the absence of one narrative or lyrical voice speaking throughout the poem from a position of authority, able to describe the figures who speak and make love" (101).

19. Penelope J. Engelbrecht argues that Stein signifies the lesbian sex act with the verb "say," claiming that for Stein, "to speak *is* to act; she conflates text and reality, makes the flesh word/makes the word active flesh. Then she asks if 'you,' the reader can 'read' it, understand it" (99).

20. These words might seem to link Stein to Hemingway's use of such general adjectives, although her use of these terms is not so explicitly ironic as Hemingway's.

21. Discussing "Lifting Belly" in the context of other lesbian writing such as Nicole Brossard's *The Aerial Letter*, Engelbrecht comments, "Back and forth and back, the language of lesbian Desire con/fuses two women, as in Stein's text, each one Desiring to 'tak[e] pleasure in knowledge' and to give knowledge in pleasure." Engelbrecht quotes Brossard's claim that "there is no more plot" in her fiction, acknowledging that the resulting immense calm is not static, but quite the opposite—full of constant movement (103).

22. In her excellent study of women poets and World War II, Susan Schweik notes "a distinct tradition of women's lyrics which use war as metaphor for conflicts in the home or bedroom or psyche (looking backward to Dickinson, forward to Cooper and Plath); but here, as elsewhere in that tradition, the war is also more than metaphor, not only mask" (234). Against this tradition, Stein appears to distinguish love and war, to set love apart from the hazards of war.

23. See Chessman's treatment of "Caesars"; she states that Stein reclaims the name for peaceable purposes (106–8).

24. For a discussion of this tendency, see Castle's *The Apparitional Lesbian*.

CHAPTER TWO

1. Quoted by Edward Burns in his foreword to *Useful Knowledge* (1988), vii.

2. See such readings of "Patriarchal Poetry" in Dydo, "Stein: Composition as Meditation," 56–57; Schmitz, "The Difference of Her Likeness," 126; and Ruddick, *Reading Gertrude Stein*, 197.

3. This is not the only approach to Stein's early novel and to her attitude toward the patriarchy. Clive Bush accords her a much less aggressive attitude, arguing that *The Making of Americans* "is fraught with the melancholy of a very lonely artistic struggle" (366).

4. Quoted in Longenbach, *Wallace Stevens*, 48.

5. Jane Marcus makes the point, however, that "The disorder and disorientation of the body at war are evoked immediately by the narrative voice in the modernist 'continuous present' of Gertrude Stein" (142).

6. Schweik has addressed the issue of the war poetry of men and women, claiming in the

case of Wilfred Owen, for example, that "the pair 'masculine/feminine' wavers and alters, but rarely if ever, 'at pleasure'; there are, for instance, political stakes in emphasizing his sensitivity over his valor, or vice versa" (54). See her entire discussion of "Writing War Poetry 'Like a Woman' Moore (and Jarrell)" (31–58).

7. The editorial "Poems of War" labors over the difficulty of justifying the ways of man to man in "the supreme crisis of the twentieth century" (*Poetry*, 82). It goes on to argue: "The American feeling about the war is a genuine revolt against war, and we have believed that POETRY might help to serve the cause of peace by encouraging the expression of this spirit of protest" (83).

8. For a discussion of Pound's war poetry, see Longenbach, *Stone Cottage*, 105–34.

9. See Brogan's *Part of the Climate* for a definition of Cubist poetry in general (6–7) and for the importance of Stein in the movement (13–14).

10. Diedrich, 92. See this entire article for a cogent discussion of Stein's World War II writing.

CHAPTER THREE

1. Of course, in this construction, Stein, as the South, would represent the conquered territory, not a geographical location in which she generally placed herself. Still, Fifer's discussion of *Useful Knowledge* is extremely interesting. See the entire chapter in *Rescued Readings*, 92–104.

2. In part, Stein's interest in geography might have started in the famous "space-logic" that Joseph Frank identified half a century ago as the central experiment in modern poetry. Like Anderson and Williams, Frank also saw the experiments in modernist poetry as a reorientation in the reader's attitude toward language from the "time-logic" in which meanings accumulate in time to "space-logic" in which the reader must hold in mind the entire poem in order to apprehend the pattern of its references.

3. See Alison Rieke's discussion of Stein's use of negation in *Stanzas in Meditation* (*The Senses of Nonsense*, 60–92).

4. Quoted in Mellow, 420.

CHAPTER FOUR

1. Elizabeth Bishop Papers, box 67, folder 23, Vassar College, Poughkeepsie, N.Y.

2. Moore's comment on "Insomnia" is quoted in Millier, 230. The correspondence over "Roosters" is quoted in MacMahon, 148–49.

3. Lombardi notes that the scene of "The Imaginary Iceberg" was suggested to Bishop by R. H. Dana's description of an iceberg in *Two Years before the Mast*, which she copied into her notebook (88–89).

4. Even David Bromwich, who admits that "Sexuality is the most elusive feature of Bishop's temperament—before writing any of the poems in *North & South*, she had learned to allegorize it subtly," goes on to discuss the poem in terms of the metaphor about the soul (167). Bonnie Costello reads the poem as "Bishop's strongest statement of desire to identify with an antivital ideal," claiming that Bishop "holds the imaginary above the visible, eagerly relinquishing experience to a timeless symbolic vision" (92). Jerome Mazzaro considers the poem as an indication that Bishop prefers the naturally formed iceberg to the man-made ship, but he, too, emphasizes the mind or soul in reading the poem (30). Lorrie Goldensohn sees the poem as "a parable for the untouchable and dangerous wealth of the mind's interior" (108). The emphasis in all these readings on the mind or the soul diminishes the significance of the iceberg itself.

5. Goldensohn notes the echo of Marianne Moore's 1924 version of "A Grave" (108). Even more pertinently Moore's "An Octopus" might have been a source for Bishop, who picks up its interest in seeing, in submerged meanings, and in skewed perspectives.

6. Bonnie Costello names Shelley's "Mont Blanc" as the prototype of Bishop's iceberg, despite the fact that Shelley is looking at a mountain and Bishop at an "imaginary iceberg" shifting in the sea with quite a different range of references (94). She also cites Melville's "The Berg," although the iceberg there is a scene of destruction named "A lumbering lubbard loitering slow" (95). It seems to me that Wallace Stevens's "The Snow Man" might be a more suggestive reference.

7. Robinson, 719–20. See the full discussion of this process in 715–36.

8. Lombardi suggests that the gender reversal in this poem (the presumably female speaker gazing into a mirror only to see herself in the guise of a man) "evokes the myth of the mannish lesbian . . . to which Bishop was exposed in the 1930s" (59).

9. See Bishop's comments in a letter to Moore reprinted in MacMahon, 148–49.

10. Victoria Harrison claims: "Whether or not these poems suggest same-sex lovers, they are nonetheless allusive or underarticulated, as if to protect against a lurking feature of love—its possibility of rejection either by the lover or by the world." She cites Bishop's encouragement of May Swenson and Anne Stevenson to read the poems as "mysterious." "'Any meanings you want to attach are all right, I'm sure—the wilder the better. It should be a sketch for an acute, neurotic, "modern" drama—or "affair," that's all'" (Bishop to Swenson, September 6, 1955, Washington University, quoted in Harrison, 64).

11. Lorrie Goldensohn discovered an unpublished poem, "It is marvellous to wake up together," in Brazil that she finds closely linked to "Rain Towards Morning," although it is more specifically detailed about the erotic relationship that appears to underpin both poems. See her discussion of this poem in the context of Bishop's other poems that share its imagery and its subject (27–52).

12. In an interesting reading of "O Breath," Lombardi calls it one of Bishop's "only published poems about the eroticized female body" and claims that the poem's "gasping, halting rhythms and labored caesuras mimic the wheezing lungs of a restless asthmatic trying to expel the suffocating air" (32–33).

13. Although he does not discuss this particular poem, Thomas Travisano has treated this aspect of Bishop's poetry in "'The Flicker of Impudence,'" 111–25.

14. See MacMahon, 100–102.

15. Both Sandra Gilbert and Susan Gubar in No Man's Land, vol. 1, and Betsy Erkkila in The Wicked Sisters (131–37) stretch their reading of the poem to insist on the ambivalence of Bishop's attitude toward Moore. In proving her thesis that women are less nurturing to each other and more like "wicked sisters," Erkkila must strain to undermine the affection and respect in this poem, claiming: "If Bishop celebrates and invites Moore as a celestial figure whose luminous imagination and 'long nebulous train of words' have inspired her own poetic creation, it is an invitation issued from afar and on Bishop's terms, written in full knowledge of the fact that had she remained under the enchanting spell of Moore's influence she would have been destroyed as a poet" (136). But Erkkila is so anxious to argue her thesis that she never proves that Bishop wrote under Moore's influence. Bishop was encouraged by Moore, helped in her efforts to publish, but her poetry developed along quite different lines.

16. Again, Erkkila must diminish the affection in what she herself calls "Bishop's most moving love poem on her relationship with Lota Soares," admitting that it is "'darkened and tarnished' with the realization that their relationship is at best temporary and passing" (145).

17. My colleague, Anne Williams, reminds me of Eliot's use of "maculate" in "Sweeney among the Nightingales," another poem set in Brazil: "Apeneck Sweeney spreads his

knees / Letting his arm hang down to laugh, / The zebra stripes along his jaw / Swelling to maculate giraffe" (35).

CHAPTER FIVE

1. The military was even closer than the Paris war memorials, she notes, writing from Paris to Frani Blough: "Some of the French Army lives in this house, and I am always squeezing into the elevator with a dashing young thing all spurs, swords, epaulets, and a headdress of red, white and blue feathers (honestly) about 18 inches high" (*OA*, 37–38).

2. See, for example, Ostriker, 54, and Spiegelman in Schwartz and Estess, 156–58.

3. Willard Spiegelman compares Bishop's treatment of Manuelzhino and his mistress to Wordsworth (Schwartz and Estess, 167). Bonnie Costello acknowledges that class differences remain in place in "Manuelzhino," although their stability is shaken. She claims that "the landowner remains within her own world, ambivalently open to new potentialities and freed from cliche" (83).

4. Lorrie Goldensohn comments on the "sinister potential of our bonds to the maternal or surrogate maternal presence" here as she identifies Bishop's acquaintance with this woman who sold lottery tickets in Key West (74–75). In a letter to Robert Lowell, Bishop talks about an early morning visit from Faustina, age eighty-two, who "has to have a small drink of cognac" before she "advises me about what number to buy this week" (Bishop to Lowell, November 18, 1947, Robert Lowell Papers, Houghton Library, Harvard University, Cambridge). Later, she reported that she was still working on "Faustina," "but it is hard to choose among the various versions she gives of her life" (*OA*, 152).

5. Costello cites "Faustina, or Rock Roses" as one of several poems in "which the observer is affronted by the discovery of an alternative culture or will where she had assumed a primitive blank slate on which to impose her own will or imagination" (251 n20).

6. In an interesting discussion of the problems of trust within love in Bishop's work, Goldensohn notes the "historically corrupted" terms of the exchange between a needy white in the care of a powerful black servant (75).

7. For an interesting comparison of Lowell's poem with Bishop's, see McCabe, 187–91.

CHAPTER SIX

1. *New York Herald Tribune*, April 6, 1935, 13. Bishop's letters suggest that she had a keen interest in Stein. She attended the New York production of *Four Saints in Three Acts* (*OA*, 19) and planned to hear Stein lecturing at the New School in 1934.

2. Millier reports that Bishop had gone up to Vassar to hear Stein's lecture, "Portraits I Have Written and What I Think of Repetition, Whether it Exists or No," on November 10, 1934 (74).

3. Two notable exceptions to this critical commonplace are Robert Pinsky's "The Idiom of Self" and Lee Edelman's "The Geography of Gender."

4. Reviewing a spate of books on Elizabeth Bishop in 1994, Langdon Hammer notes that the "old image of Bishop as a geographer reflected readers' ideas of the qualities to be prized in a woman writer. Indeed, Bishop was treated explicitly *as* a woman poet whose achievement, however perfect within the limits she set for herself, could not compete with the major public poems of her male peers." Although Hammer acknowledges that the growing interest in Bishop would be unthinkable without feminism, he seems to identify feminism as a movement bent on revaluing "the minor, the private, and the domestic," so that he is able to reinscribe the old image of Bishop in a new context (138). Edelman's "The Geography of Gender," published almost a decade before Hammer's article, nicely refutes it.

5. Sandra Berry pointed out to me the map of Nova Scotia where its southernmost tip looks as if it were the thumb and finger feeling something.

6. Millier quotes this passage from a 1948 letter: "A sentence in Auden's Airman's Journal has always seemed very profound to me—I haven't the book here so I can't quote it exactly, but something about time and space and how 'geography is a thousand times more important to modern man than history'—I always like to *feel* exactly where I am geographically all the time, on the map,—but maybe that is something else again" (78). In a letter to U. T. and Joseph Summers in 1967, Bishop refers again to Auden's "Journal of an Airman," quoting parts of it as "'If recorded history is—years long and the world is—miles away from the nearest planet (sun?), then geography is—times more important to us than history.'" She claims that she read it after she had begun to publish poems, so she cannot say that it influenced her; but "I just thought, that's a silly notion but I think I agree with it" (*OA*, 477).

7. In her biography, Millier claims that Bishop first began working on the image of the map when she was contemplating the nature of her attachment to Margaret Miller, and the "undefinable emotion is invested in the poem as well" (77).

8. For the influence of Herbert, see Bonnie Costello's discussion of "The Weed" (55–61).

9. Jeredith Merrin mentions "The Weed" briefly in an interesting discussion of what she calls tropes of "thirdness" in Bishop's poetry—"powerful patterns of mind or psychological gestalts that convey her multivalent response to her sexual disposition" (154). Out of the two halves of a severed heart, a third thing, the strange and transformative weed, emerges; but the poem registers elements found in much of Bishop's poetry—"strangeness or monstrosity, the evocation of darkness and dream life, fear and anxiety as prevalent emotions, the teardrop image, the suggestions of emergent artistry" (169).

10. Robert Lowell Papers, February 15, 1960, Houghton Library, Harvard University, Cambridge.

CHAPTER SEVEN

1. Bidart recounts that one of Bishop's students perceived her "schoolmarmish" appearance as a means of hiding her sexuality" (quoted in Fountain and Brazeau, 327).

2. Although Claire Keyes argues for the generativity of Rich's love for women, she acknowledges too that part of the power of "Twenty-One Love Poems" is that Rich brings "the fullness of her powers to these love poems" (169).

3. For a discussion of the polemical issues involved in Rich's coming out as a lesbian, see Werner, 75–121.

4. In a discussion of the gaze of the other woman in Dickinson, Moore, and Rich, Leigh Gilmore reads this eye-to-eye encounter more positively. She finds that this gaze "most completely breaks from the oedipal narrative of desire and transgression, of 'falling' in love, of engendering poetry from an encounter with a muse" and has a "capacity to generate something new, something we do not recognize, a look that does not inspire lack" ("The Gaze of the Other Woman," 101).

5. Throughout her chapter on Rich, Erkkila identifies the structural center of each volume of her poetry, keying it to developments both in her relationship to Emily Dickinson and in the feminist movement from its start in a white female-centered "aesthetic-ethic" to its newest sense of historical complexity and particularity. Certainly Rich's attitude toward the feminist movement has changed, but perhaps not so neatly as Erkkila suggests. Helena Michie notes that the word "dream" in the title of the volume reminds us that this is not simply a book about coming together. She writes: "the poems are filled with spaces: orthographic—Rich often leaves extra room on the page between words—and

psychological—many of the poems, like 'Splittings' and even the lyrical '24 [*sic*] Love Poems,' are about breaking up or the impossibility of coming together in the first place" (124).

CHAPTER EIGHT

1. "Hugh Selwyn Mauberley," in Pound, *Selected Poems*, 63–64.
2. For Rich's comments on how useless the supposed poetic masters of her youth were, see her essay, "Not how to write poetry, but wheretofore," in *What Is Found There*, 190–96.

CHAPTER NINE

1. Betsy Erkkila has traced Rich's involvement with Emily Dickinson and her work from an initial recognition of Dickinson as a problematic figure for a woman poet through an appreciation of her work and finally to a distancing of Dickinson as she begins to separate herself from the New England values and world of Dickinson's poetry (152–84).

CONCLUSION

1. Quoted in Fountain and Brazeau, 329.
2. See Gilbert and Gubar's discussion of Stein and Toklas in their chapter on the dynamic of collaboration that shaped the art of lesbian modernists, " 'She meant what I said': Lesbian Double Talk" (2:238–56).
3. See Kastor's interview with Rich ("Politics and the Poet"), in which Rich comments on the value of coming out. Recent studies of lesbian poetry all repeat the point. See Yorke, "Constructing a Lesbian Poetic"; Collecott, "What Is Not Said"; Bulkin, " 'Kissing / Against the Light' "; Roof, *A Lure of Knowledge*; Halliday, " 'The Naked Majesty of God.' " It is the conclusion, too, of Alicia Ostriker's *Stealing the Language*. Even Joanne Feit Diehl, who acknowledges that sexual truth-telling does not necessarily make powerful poetry, suggests that the development of American women's poetry has been toward the flourishing of imaginative possibilities for women (*Women Poets*, 142–68).

Benstock, Shari. "Expatriate Sapphic Modernism: Entering Literary History." In *Lesbian Texts and Contexts: Radical Revisions*, edited by Karla Jay and Joanne Glasgow, 183–203. New York: New York University Press, 1990.

Bishop, Elizabeth. *The Collected Prose*, edited by Robert Giroux. New York: Farrar, Straus, Giroux, 1984.

———. *The Complete Poems, 1927–1979*. New York: Farrar, Straus, Giroux, 1983.

———. "An Interview with Elizabeth Bishop," by Ashley Brown. In *Elizabeth Bishop and Her Art*, edited by Lloyd Schwartz and Sybil P. Estess, 289–301. Ann Arbor: University of Michigan Press, 1983.

———. *Life World Library: Brazil*. New York: Time, 1963.

———. *One Art*. Letters selected and edited by Robert Giroux. New York: Farrar, Straus, Giroux, 1994.

———. " 'The Work!' A Conversation with Elizabeth Bishop," by George Starbuck. In *Elizabeth Bishop and Her Art*, edited by Lloyd Schwartz and Sybil P. Estess, 312–30. Ann Arbor: University of Michigan Press, 1983.

Blasing, Mutlu Konuk. *American Poetry: The Rhetoric of Its Forms*. New Haven: Yale University Press, 1987.

Bloom, Harold, ed. *Modern Critical Views: Elizabeth Bishop*. New York: Chelsea House Publishers, 1985.

Bok, Sissela. *Secrets: On the Ethics of Concealment and Revelation*. New York: Pantheon Books, 1982.

Brogan, Jacqueline Vaught. *Part of the Climate: American Cubist Poetry*. Berkeley: University of California Press, 1991.

Bromwich, David. "Elizabeth Bishop's Dream-Houses." In *Modern Critical Views: Elizabeth Bishop*, edited by Harold Bloom, 159–74. New York: Chelsea House Publishers, 1985.

Bulkin, Elly. "An Interview with Adrienne Rich." *Conditions* 1 (1977): 50–65.

———. "An Interview with Adrienne Rich." *Conditions* 2 (1977): 53–66.

———. " 'Kissing / Against the Light': A Look at Lesbian Poetry." In *Lesbian Studies: Present and Future*, edited by Margaret Cruikshank, 32–54. New York: Feminist Press, 1992.

Burns, Elizabeth. *Letters to Elizabeth Bishop*. Buffalo, N.Y.: Leave Books, 1991.

Bush, Clive. *Halfway to Revolution: Investigation and Crisis in the Work of Henry Adams, William James, and Gertrude Stein*. New Haven, Conn.: Yale University Press, 1991.

Castle, Terry. *The Apparitional Lesbian: Female Homosexuality and Modern Culture*. New York: Columbia University Press, 1993.

Chessman, Harriet. *The Public Is Invited to Dance: Representation, the Body, and Dialogue in Gertrude Stein*. Stanford, Calif.: Stanford University Press, 1989.

Clark, Suzanne. *Sentimental Modernism: Women Writers and the Revolution of the Word*. Bloomington: Indiana University Press, 1991.

Collecott, Diana. "What Is Not Said: A Study in Textual Inversion." In *Sexual Sameness: Textual Differences in Lesbian and Gay Writing*, edited by Joseph Bristow, 91–110. New York: Routledge, 1992.

Cook, Eleanor. "From Etymology to Paronomasia: Wallace Stevens, Elizabeth Bishop, and Others." *Connotations* 2.1 (1992): 34–51.

Cooke, Miriam. "WoMan, Retelling the War Myth." In *Gendering War Talk*, edited by

Miriam Cooke and Angela Woollacott, 177–204. Princeton: Princeton University Press, 1993.

Corn, Alfred. "Elizabeth Bishop's Narratives." *Shenandoah* 36.3 (1986): 21–46.

Costello, Bonnie. *Elizabeth Bishop: Questions of Mastery*. Cambridge: Harvard University Press, 1991.

DeKoven, Marianne. "Breaking the Rigid Form of the Noun: Stein, Whitman, and Modernist Poetry." In *Critical Essays on American Modernism*, edited by Michael J. Hoffman and Patrick D. Murphy, 225–34. New York: G. K. Hall & Co., 1992.

———. *A Different Language: Gertrude Stein's Experimental Writing*. Madison: University of Wisconsin Press, 1983.

———. "Gertrude Stein and the Modernist Canon." In *Gertrude Stein and the Making of Literature*, edited by Shirley Neuman and Ira B. Nadel, 8–20. Boston: Northeastern University Press, 1988.

de Lauretis, Teresa. "Upping the Anti [*sic*] in Feminist Theory." In *The Cultural Studies Reader*, edited by Simon During, 74–89. London: Routledge, 1993.

Diedrich, Maria. "'A Book in Translation about Eggs and Butter': Gertrude Stein's World War II." In *Women and War: The Changing Status of American Women from the 1930s to the 1950s*, edited by Maria Diedrich and Dorothea Fischer-Hornin, 87–106. New York: Berg, 1990.

Diehl, Joanne Feit. *Elizabeth Bishop and Marianne Moore: The Psychodynamics of Creativity*. Princeton: Princeton University Press, 1993.

———. *Women Poets and the American Sublime*. Bloomington: Indiana University Press, 1990.

Dydo, Ulla E. "Gertrude Stein: Composition as Meditation." In *Gertrude Stein and the Making of Literature*, edited by Shirley Neuman and Ira B. Nadel, 42–61. Boston: Northeastern University Press, 1988.

———. "Reading the Hand Writing: The Manuscripts of Gertrude Stein." In *A Gertrude Stein Companion: Content with the Example*, edited by Bruce Kellner, 84–96. New York: Greenwood Press, 1988.

Edelman, Lee. "The Geography of Gender: Elizabeth Bishop's 'In the Waiting Room.'" In *Elizabeth Bishop: The Geography of Gender*, edited by Marilyn May Lombardi, 91–107. Charlottesville: University Press of Virginia, 1993.

Eliot, T. S. *The Complete Poems and Plays: 1909–1950*. New York: Harcourt Brace and Co., 1952.

Engelbrecht, Penelope J. "'Lifting Belly Is a Language': The Postmodern Lesbian Subject." *Feminist Studies* 16.1 (1990): 85–114.

Erkkila, Betsy. *The Wicked Sisters: Women Poets, Literary History & Discord*. New York: Oxford University Press, 1992.

Estess, Sybil P. "Elizabeth Bishop: The Delicate Art of Map Making." *The Southern Review* 13 (Fall 1977): 705–27.

Fifer, Elizabeth. "Is Flesh Advisable? The Interior Theater of Gertrude Stein." *Signs* 4.3 (1979): 472–83.

———. *Rescued Readings: A Reconstruction of Gertrude Stein's Difficult Texts*. Detroit: Wayne State University Press, 1992.

Fountain, Gary, and Peter Brazeau. *Remembering Elizabeth Bishop: An Oral Biography*. Amherst: University of Massachusetts Press, 1994.

Frank, Joseph. "Spatial Form in Modern Literature." In *The Widening Gyre: Crisis and Mastery in Modern Literature*, 3–62. Bloomington: Indiana University Press, 1963.

Frost, Robert. *The Poetry of Robert Frost*, edited by Edward Connery Lathem. New York: Holt, Rinehart and Winston, 1974.

Frye, Marilyn. *The Politics of Reality: Essays in Feminist Theory*. Trumansburg, N.Y.: Crossing Press, 1983.

Gass, William H. Introduction. *The Geographical History of America or the Relation of Human Nature to the Human Mind*, by Gertrude Stein, 3–42. Baltimore: Johns Hopkins University Press, 1995.

———. *The World within the Word: Essays*. New York: Knopf, 1978.

Gilbert, Sandra, and Susan Gubar. *No Man's Land*. Vol. 1, *The Place of the Woman Writer in the Twentieth Century: The War of the Words*. New Haven, Conn.: Yale University Press, 1988.

———. *No Man's Land*. Vol. 2, *The Place of the Woman Writer in the Twentieth Century: Sexchanges*. New Haven, Conn.: Yale University Press, 1989.

Gilmore, Leigh. "The Gaze of the Other Woman: Beholding and Begetting in Dickinson, Moore, and Rich." In *Engendering the Word: Feminist Essays in Psychosexual Poetics*, edited by Temma F. Berg, 81–102. Urbana: University of Illinois Press, 1989.

———. "A Signature of Lesbian Autobiography: 'Gertrice/Altrude.'" In *Autobiography and Questions of Gender*, edited by Shirley Neuman, 56–75. London: Frank Cass, 1991.

Goldensohn, Lorrie. *Elizabeth Bishop: The Biography of a Poetry*. New York: Columbia University Press, 1992.

Grahn, Judy. *The Highest Apple: Sappho and the Lesbian Poetic Tradition*. San Francisco: Spinsters, Ink., 1985.

H.D. *Collected Poems, 1912–1944*, edited by Louis L. Martz. New York: New Directions, 1983.

Halliday, Caroline. "'The Naked Majesty of God': Contemporary Lesbian Erotic Poetry." In *Lesbian and Gay Writing: An Anthology of Critical Essays*, edited by Mark Lilly, 76–108. Philadelphia: Temple University Press, 1990.

Hammer, Langdon. "The New Elizabeth Bishop." *The Yale Review* 82.1 (January 1994): 135–49.

Harrison, Victoria. *Elizabeth Bishop's Poetics of Intimacy*. Cambridge: Cambridge University Press, 1993.

Hartman, Geoffrey. *Saving the Text: Literature / Derrida / Philosophy*. Baltimore: Johns Hopkins University Press, 1981.

Homans, Margaret. *Women Writers and Poetic Identity: Dorothy Wordsworth, Emily Brontë, and Emily Dickinson*. Princeton: Princeton University Press, 1980.

Jarrell, Randall. *Poetry and the Age*. New York: Knopf, 1953.

Kalstone, David. *Becoming a Poet: Elizabeth Bishop with Marianne Moore and Robert Lowell*. New York: Farrar, Straus, Giroux, 1989.

Kastor, Elizabeth. "Politics and the Poet: Adrienne Rich Adds an Agenda to Her Art, and Makes No Apologies." *Washington Post*, June 8, 1993, C1, 4.

Keyes, Claire. *The Aesthetics of Power: The Poetry of Adrienne Rich*. Athens: University of Georgia Press, 1986.

Lombardi, Marilyn May. *The Body and the Song: Elizabeth Bishop's Poetics*. Carbondale: Southern Illinois University Press, 1995.

Longenbach, James. *Stone Cottage: Pound, Yeats & Modernism*. New York: Oxford University Press, 1988.

———. *Wallace Stevens: The Plain Sense of Things*. New York: Oxford University Press, 1991.

Lorde, Audre. *Zami: A New Spelling of My Name*. Trumansburg, N.Y.: Crossing Press, 1982.

McCabe, Susan. *Elizabeth Bishop: Her Poetics of Loss*. University Park: Pennsylvania State University Press, 1994.

MacMahon, Candace W. *Elizabeth Bishop: A Bibliography, 1927–1979*. Charlottesville: University Press of Virginia, 1980.

Marcus, Jane. "Corpus/Corps/Corpse: Writing the Body in/at War." In *Arms and the Woman: War, Gender, and Literary Representation*, edited by Helen M. Cooper,

Adrienne Auslander Munich, and Susan Merrill Squier, 124–67. Chapel Hill: University of North Carolina Press, 1989.

Mazzaro, Jerome. "The Poetics of Impediment." In *Modern Critical Views: Elizabeth Bishop*, edited by Harold Bloom, 23–51. New York: Chelsea House Publishers, 1985.

Meese, Elizabeth A. *(Sem)erotics: Theorizing Lesbian: Writing*. New York: New York University Press, 1992.

Mellow, James R. *Charmed Circle: Gertrude Stein & Company*. Boston: Houghton Mifflin, 1974.

Merrill, James. "Elizabeth Bishop, 1911–1979." In *Elizabeth Bishop and Her Art*, edited by Lloyd Schwartz and Sybil P. Estess, 259–62. Ann Arbor: University of Michigan Press, 1983.

Merrin, Jeredith. "Elizabeth Bishop: Gaiety, Gayness, and Change." In *Elizabeth Bishop: The Geography of Gender*, edited by Marilyn May Lombardi, 153–72. Charlottesville: University Press of Virginia, 1993.

Michie, Helena. *Sororophobia: Differences among Women in Literature and Culture*. New York: Oxford University Press, 1992.

Millicr, Brctt C. *Elizabeth Bishop: Life and the Memory of It*. Berkeley: University of California Press, 1993.

Montenegro, David. "Adrienne Rich: An Interview by David Montenegro." *American Poetry Review* 20.1 (January–February 1991): 7–14.

Moore, Marianne. "Archaically New." In *The Complete Prose of Marianne Moore*, edited by Patricia C. Willis, 327–29. New York: Viking, 1986.

Murphy, Margueritte S. "'Familiar Strangers': The Household Words of Gertrude Stein's *Tender Buttons*." *Contemporary Literature* 32.3 (1991): 383–402.

Nelson, Cary. *Repression and Recovery: Modern American Poetry and the Politics of Cultural Memory, 1910–1945*. Madison: University of Wisconsin Press, 1989.

Neuman, Shirley, and Ira B. Nadel, eds. *Gertrude Stein and the Making of Literature*. Boston: Northeastern University Press, 1988.

Ostriker, Alicia Suskin. *Stealing the Language: The Emergence of Women's Poetry in America*. Boston: Beacon Press, 1986.

Parker, Robert Dale. *The Unbeliever: The Poetry of Elizabeth Bishop*. Urbana: University of Illinois Press, 1988.

Pinsky, Robert. "The Idiom of Self: Elizabeth Bishop and Wordsworth." In *Elizabeth Bishop and Her Art*, edited by Lloyd Schwartz and Sybil P. Estess, 49–60. Ann Arbor: University of Michigan Press, 1983.

"Poems of War." Editorial. *Poetry: A Magazine of Verse* 5.2 (1914): 49–98.

Pound, Ezra. *The Cantos*. London: Faber and Faber, 1975.

———. *Selected Poems of Ezra Pound*. New York: New Directions, 1957.

Rich, Adrienne. *An Atlas of the Difficult World: Poems, 1988–1991*. New York: Norton, 1991.

———. *Blood, Bread, and Poetry: Selected Prose, 1979–1985*. New York: Norton, 1986.

———. *Collected Early Poems, 1950–1970*. New York: Norton, 1993.

———. *The Fact of a Doorframe: Poems Selected and New, 1950–1984*. New York: Norton, 1984.

———. "An Interview with Adrienne Rich," by Elly Bulkin. *Conditions* 1 (1977): 50–65.

———. "An Interview with Adrienne Rich," by Elly Bulkin. *Conditions* 2 (1977): 53–66.

———. "An Interview with David Montenegro." *American Poetry Review* 20.1 (January–February 1991): 7–14.

———. *On Lies, Secrets, and Silence: Selected Prose, 1966–1978*. New York: Norton, 1979.

———. *Time's Power: Poems, 1985–1988*. New York: Norton, 1989.

———. *What Is Found There: Notebooks on Poetry and Politics*. New York: Norton, 1993.

——. *Your Native Land, Your Life: Poems*. New York: Norton, 1986.

Rieke, Alison. *The Senses of Nonsense*. Iowa City: University of Iowa Press, 1992.

Robinson, Amy. "It Takes One to Know One: Passing and Communities of Common Interest." *Critical Inquiry* 20.4 (Summer 1994): 715–36.

Roof, Judith. *A Lure of Knowledge: Lesbian Sexuality and Theory*. New York: Columbia University Press, 1991.

Ruddick, Lisa. *Reading Gertrude Stein: Body, Text, Gnosis*. Ithaca, N.Y.: Cornell University Press, 1990.

Scarry, Elaine. *The Body in Pain: The Making and Unmaking of the World*. New York: Oxford University Press, 1985.

Schmitz, Neil. "The Difference of Her Likeness: Gertrude Stein's *Stanzas in Meditation*." In *Gertrude Stein and the Making of Literature*, edited by Shirley Neuman and Ira B. Nadel, 124–49. Boston: Northeastern University Press, 1988.

Schwartz, Lloyd, and Sybil P. Estess, eds. *Elizabeth Bishop and Her Art*. Ann Arbor: University of Michigan Press, 1983.

Schweik, Susan. *A Gulf So Deeply Cut: American Women Poets and the Second World War*. Madison: University of Wisconsin Press, 1991.

Scott, Bonnie Kime, ed. *The Gender of Modernism: A Critical Anthology*. Bloomington: Indiana University Press, 1990.

Spiegelman, Willard. *The Didactic Muse: Scenes of Instruction in Contemporary American Poetry*. Princeton: Princeton University Press, 1989.

——. "Elizabeth Bishop's 'Natural Heroism.'" In *Elizabeth Bishop and Her Art*, edited by Lloyd Schwartz and Sybil P. Estess, 154–71. Ann Arbor: University of Michigan Press, 1983.

Stein, Gertrude. "American States and Cities and How They Differ from Each Other." *New York Herald Tribune*, April 6, 1935, 13.

——. *Bee Time Vine and Other Pieces, 1913–1927*. Preface and notes by Virgil Thomson. New Haven, Conn.: Yale University Press, 1953.

——. *Fernhurst, Q.E.D., and Other Early Writings*. New York: Liveright, 1971.

——. *The Geographical History of America, or the Relation of Human Nature to the Human Mind*. New York: Vintage Press, 1973.

——. *Geography and Plays*. Introduction by Cyrena N. Pondrom. Madison: University of Wisconsin Press, 1993.

——. *Lectures in America*. Introduction by Wendy Steiner. Boston: Beacon Press, 1985.

——. *Narration: Four Lectures by Gertrude Stein*. Introduction by Thornton Wilder. New York: Greenwood Press, 1969.

——. *Paris France*. New York: Scribner's, 1940.

——. *Reflection on the Atomic Bomb*. Edited by Robert Bartlett Haas. Los Angeles: Black Sparrow Press, 1973.

——. *Selected Writings of Gertrude Stein*. Edited by Carl Van Vechten. New York: Vintage Books, 1962.

——. *A Stein Reader*. Edited by Ulla E. Dydo. Evanston, Ill.: Northwestern University Press, 1993.

——. "A Transatlantic Interview 1946." In *The Gender of Modernism: A Critical Anthology*, edited by Bonnie Kime Scott, 502–16. Bloomington: Indiana University Press, 1990.

——. *Useful Knowledge*. London: Bodley Head, 1929.

——. *Useful Knowledge*. Foreword by Edward Burns, introduction by Keith Waldrop. Barrington: Station Hill Press, 1988.

——. *Wars I Have Seen*. New York: Random House, 1945.

——. *The Yale Gertrude Stein*. Selections with an introduction by Richard Kostelanetz. New Haven, Conn.: Yale University Press, 1980.

Stevenson, Anne. *Elizabeth Bishop*. New York: Twayne Publishers, 1966.
Stimpson, Catharine R. "Adrienne Rich and Lesbian/Feminist Poetry." *Parnassus: Poetry in Review* 12–13.2–1 (1985): 249–68.
———. "Gertrude Stein and the Lesbian Lie." In *American Women's Autobiography: Fea(s)ts of Memory*, edited by Margo Culley, 152–66. Madison: University of Wisconsin Press, 1992.
———. "The Sonagrams of Gertrude Stein." *Poetics Today* 6.1–2 (1985): 67–80.
Travisano, Thomas. *Elizabeth Bishop: Her Artistic Development*. Charlottesville: University Press of Virginia, 1988.
———. "'The Flicker of Impudence': Delicacy and Indelicacy in the Art of Elizabeth Bishop." In *Elizabeth Bishop: The Geography of Gender*, edited by Marilyn May Lombardi, 111–25. Charlottesville: University Press of Virginia, 1993.
Vendler, Helen. "Adrienne Rich, Jared Carter, Philip Levine." In *The Music of What Happens: Poems, Poets, Critics*, 368–87. Cambridge: Harvard University Press, 1988.
Walker, Jayne L. *The Making of a Modernist: Gertrude Stein from Three Lives to Tender Buttons*. Amherst: University of Massachusetts Press, 1984.
Werner, Craig. "The Lesbian Vision: 'The Meaning of Our Love for Women Is What We Have Constantly to Expand.'" In *Adrienne Rich: The Poet and Her Critics*, 75–121. Chicago: American Library Association, 1988.
Williams, William Carlos. "The Work of Gertrude Stein." In *Selected Essays of William Carlos Williams*, 113–20. New York: New Directions, 1969.
Williamson, Alan. "*A Cold Spring*: The Poet of Feeling." In *Elizabeth Bishop and Her Art*, edited by Lloyd Schwartz and Sybil P. Estess, 96–108. Ann Arbor: University of Michigan Press, 1983.
Wilson, Edmund. *The Shores of Light: A Literary Chronicle of the Twenties and Thirties*. New York: Farrar, Straus and Young, 1952.
Yorke, Liz. "Constructing a Lesbian Poetic for Survival: Broumas, Rukeyser, H.D., Rich, Lorde." In *Sexual Sameness: Textual Differences in Lesbian and Gay Writing*, edited by Joseph Bristow, 187–209. London: Routledge, 1992.